INDIAN BANKING SYSTEM

INDIAN BANKING SYSTEM

Growth, Challenges and Government Initiatives

BY

Dr Rajib Mallik

Dr Suman Kalyan Chaudhury

Dr Sukanta Sarkar

KALPAZ

First Published, 2018

Published by

Kalpaz Publications
C-30, Satyawati Nagar,
Delhi – 110052
E-mail: kalpaz@hotmail.com
Ph.: 9212142040

Printed at: G. Print Process, Delhi

Cataloging in Publication Data—DK
Courtesy: D.K. Agencies (P) Ltd. <docinfo@dkagencies.com>

Mallik, Rajib, author.
Indian banking system : growth, challenges and government initiatives / by Dr. Rajib Mallik, Dr. Suman Kalyan Chaudhury, Dr. Sukanta Sarkar.
pages cm
Includes bibliographical references.
ISBN 9789386397201 (HB)

1. Banks and banking—India. I. Chaudhury, Suman Kalyan, 1972- author. II. Sarkar, Sukanta, author. III. Title.

LCC HG3284.M35 2017 | DDC 332.10954 23

Contents

PART - II

FUNCTIONS AND ACTIVITIES

Preface

Bank is generally understood as an institution. It provides fundamental banking services such as accepting deposits and providing loans. Non-banking institutions provide certain services without meeting the legal definition of a bank. Banks are a subset of the financial services. A banking system is being referred to as a system offering cash management services for customers, reporting the transactions of accounts and portfolios, throughout the day. The history of banking begins with the first prototype banks of merchants of the ancient world, which made grain loans to farmers and traders, who carried goods between cities. The first bank in India, called The General Bank of India was established in the year 1786. After independence, the government of India ventured on to encourage the spread of banking in India.. Fourteen of the major private sector banks were nationalized [1969]. This was an important milestone in the history of Indian banking.

Thanks are due to Dr. K.B. Das, former Professor, P.G. Dept. of Commerce, Utkal University, Bhubaneswar, Dr.D.P. Mishra, Professor, Dept. of MBA, F.M. University, Balasore, Dr.Hitesh Shukla, Professor, Dept. of MBA, Shaurastra University, Dr.R.P.Dash, Vice -Chancellor, Berhampur University, Dr.P.K.Padhy, Professor, Dept. of MBA, Berhampur University, Dr.P.C.Mishra, former Professor, P.G. Dept. of Commerce, Berhampur University, Dr. R.Prasad, Professor, Pt.Ravisankar Shukla University, Raipur, Dr. N.G.Pendse, Professor, Rani Durgabati University, Jabalpur, Dr. D.Pulla. Rao, Professor, Andhra University for constant encouragement, advice and extended help to us. We express our heartily thankfulness to each and every person who directly/indirectly helped us in preparing the work.

It is hoped that this book will be very much useful to bankers and students in particular in the field of banking. The text appear in the most simple and lucid manner. Comments and suggestions are appreciable.

Dr. S.K.Chaudhury
Dr. Rajib Mallik
Dr. Sukanta Sarkar

Abbreviations

AACS : As applicable to Cooperative Societies
AAOIFI : Accounting and Auditing Organization of Islamic Finance Institutions
ACD : Agricultural Credit Department
AFI : Alliance for Financial Inclusion
APRs : Annual Percentage Rates
ARDBs : Agriculture and Rural Development Banks
ARDC : Agricultural Refinance and Development Corporation
ARDC : Agricultural Refinance and Development Corporation
BBL : Bank Bruxelles Lambert
BIS : Bank for International Settlements
BMB : Bharatiya Mahila Bank
CASA : Current and Savings Accounts
CB : Central Bank
CBs : Commercial Banks
CDR : Corporate Debt Restructuring
CFSR : Committee on Financial Sector Reforms
CGTMSE : Credit Guarantee Fund Trust for Micro and Small Enterprises
CIBIL : Credit Information Bureau of India Limited
CPs : Core Purposes
CRAR : Capital to Risk weighted Assets Ratio
CRR : Cash Reserve Ratio
CRR : Cash Reserve Ratio
CWE : Common Written Examination
DCB : District Co-operative Banks

DCCB	: District Central Co-operative Banks
DFI	: Development Finance Institutions
DICGC	: Deposit Insurance and Credit Guarantee Corporation of India
ECOWAS	: Economic Community of West African States
EXIM	: Export-Import
FHA	: Federal Housing Administration
GCIBFI	: General Council for Islamic Banking and Finance Institutions
GDC	: German Development Corporation
GIC	: General Insurance Corporation
GTB	: Global Trust Bank Limited
HDFC	: Housing Development Finance Corporation Limited
HUDCO	: Housing and Urban Development Corporation
IBPS	: Institute of Banking Personnel Selection
ICICI	: Industrial Credit and Investment Corporation of India
ICIF	: Indian Centre for Islamic finance
IDB	: Islamic Development Bank
IFC	; Industrial Finance Corporation
IFD	: Industrial Finance Department
IFSB	: Islamic Financial Service Board
IOB	: Indian Overseas Bank
IPO	: Initial Public Offerings
IRBI	: Industrial Reconstruction Bank of India
KSIDC	: Kerala State Industrial Development Corporation
LAB	: Local Area Banks
LIC	: Life Insurance Corporation
LLP	: Limited Liability Partnership
LOCs	: Lines of Credit
LTCCS	: Long-Term Cooperative Credit Structure
MDGs	: Millennium Development Goals
MoU	: Memorandum of Understanding
MSME	: Micro, Small and Medium-scale Enterprises
NABARD	: National Bank for Agriculture and Rural Development
NBFC	: Non-Banking Financial Corporation
NBFI	: Non-Banking Financial Intermediaries

NGOs : Non-governmental organizations
NHB : National Housing Bank
NIA : New India Assurance Company Limited
NIC : National Insurance Company Limited
NPA : Non-Performing Assets
OIC : Organization of Islamic countries
OIC : Oriental Insurance Company Limited
OMOs : Open Market Operations
PACS : Primary Agricultural Credit Societies
PCARDB : Primary Co-operative Agriculture and Rural Development banks
PDs : Primary Dealers
PLPs : Potential Linked Credit Plans
PNB : Punjab National Bank
PSBs : Public Sector Banks
PSU : Public Sector Undertaking
RBI : Reserve Bank of India
RFIs : Rural Financial Institutions
RHS : Rural Housing Service
RIDF : Rural Infrastructure Development Fund
RMD : Resource Management Discussions
RPCC : Rural Planning and Credit Cell
RRBs : Regional Rural Banks
SBBJ : State Bank of Bikaner and Jaipur
SBH : State Bank of Hyderabad
SBIR : State Bank of Indore
SBP : State Bank of Patiala
SBS : State Bank of Saurashtra
SBT : State Bank of Travancore
SCARDBs : State Co-operative Agriculture and Rural Development Banks
SCB : State Co-operative Banks
SDTT : Sir Dorabji Tata Trust
SEBI : Securities and Exchanges Board of India
SFCs : State Financial Corporations
SHG : Self Help Group

SLR : Statutory Liquidity Ratio
SRI : System of Rice Intensification
STCCS : Short-Term Co-operative Credit Structure
SUUTI : Special Undertaking of Unit Trust of India
TAC : Technical Advisory Committee
TAFCUB : Task Force for Cooperative Urban Banks
TSCB : Tripura State Cooperative Bank Limited
UBI : Union Bank of India
UCBs : Urban Co-operative Banks
UIIC : United India Insurance Company Limited
UPNRM : Umbrella Programme on Natural Resources Management
UTI : Unit Trust of India
VA : Veterans Administration
VCL : Venture Capital Ltd.

PART - I

TYPE OF BANKS

Chapter - 1

An Overview

"A bank is a place where they lend you an umbrella in fair weather and ask for it back when it begins to rain." — ***Robert Frost***

Introduction

Finance is more important on the current global business. The three main sources of funding for a business are revenues from business operations, investor finances such as owner's, partners or venture capital, and loans from individuals or financial institutions. It is impossible to achieve long-term and short-term goals without effectively managing finances. Inefficient management of finances could lead to liquidity shortages. Long-term sources of finance must be available for achievement of long-term goals, such as purchasing new machines. Every business owner has a vision for his company, and that vision is frequently manipulated by managing and prioritizing the use of financial resources.

Business finance is one of the most crucial factors in the success of a company. The ability to secure its options when needed can make or break any business. In an increasingly globalised and competitive world, comparatively few businesses rely solely on using cash reserves to fund business projects. Business loans can be used for a variety of purposes, including everything from growth to exploratory ventures to stemming losses during lean periods. It can help company not only expand, but can also save it during the harsher periods. The financing options could mean the difference between a successful company and a failed venture, for business owners, accessing a range of business.

Finance remains the life blood of any organization. The financial needs of a business vary according to the type and size of the business. For example, processing businesses are usually capital intensive, and require large amounts of capital. Retail businesses usually require less capital. The importance of financial accounting plays a significant role in keeping track of resources. It is critical for personal and business finances. As corporate budgets become tighter due to economic challenges, business managers should understand the financial side of running a business. Any business decision should not depend on mere sales figures. The study of corporate finance focus on the conflicts and tensions that arise from matching the needs of those who want to invest the excess of wealth and those who need it produce goods and services. According to Crowther, modern banking owes to three ancestors: (i) the merchant; (ii) the goldsmith; and (iii) the money-lender.

Bank: Definition

According to Banking Encyclopedia, Bank is a financial institution which receives deposits from the public and lends them for investment purpose i.e., deposits of money and advances of the main function of banks, but in the era of globalization, banks indulges in many activities like Insurance, Mutual Fund Business and Investment in Stock Exchanges. In general terms, it means the business activity of accepting and safeguarding money owned by other individuals and entities, and then put this money for a profit.

In other words, it can be said, an[y] organization, usually a corporation, chartered by a state or federal government, which does most or all of the following: receives demand deposits and time deposits, honors instruments drawn on them, and pays interest on them; discounts notes, makes loans, and invests in securities; collects checks, drafts, and notes; certifies depositors checks; and issues drafts and cashier's checks.[1]

According to Hildreth (2001), a bank is generally understood as an Institution, which provides fundamental banking services such as accepting deposits and providing loans. Non-banking institutions also provide certain banking services without meeting the legal definition of a[such] bank. Banks are a subset of financial services industry. A banking system referred also as a system provided by the bank, extending cash management services for customers, reporting the transactions of accounts and portfolios, round-the-clock. In India, the definition of the business of banking has been given in the Banking Regulation Act, (BR Act), 1949.

According to Section 5(c) of the BR Act, 'a banking company is a company transacting the business of banking in India.' Further, Section 5(b) of the BR Act defines banking as, 'accepting, for the purpose of lending or investment, of deposits of money from the public, repayable on demand or otherwise, and withdraw able, by cheque, draft, order or otherwise.' The definition points to three primary activities of any commercial bank differentiating from other financial institutions. These are: (i) maintaining deposit accounts, include current accounts, (ii) issue and pay cheques, and (iii) collect cheques for the bank's customers.

Prof. Sauers defines the terms back and banking distinctly. He defines a bank as *"an institution whose debts (bank deposits) are widely accepted in settlement of debts other people to each other."Again, accordingly to Sauers, "Ordinary banking business consist cash for bank deposits and bank deposits of cash; transferring bank deposits from one person or the corporation to another; giving bank deposits in exchange for bills of exchange, government bonds, the secured promises of businessmen to repay and so forth."* Banks essentially perform two functions. First, they provide liquidity. Every time, customers withdraw money from an automated teller machine [ATM] or write a check, they rely on them in liquidity provision function.

Still, there is very little difference between a demand deposit that an investor holds and a line of credit extended to any firm. The products require the bank to pay the client money, on demand. It seems natural to infer that bank provides liquidity on either side of the balance sheet to depositors and borrowers alike. A banking system resembles the nervous system of the bank. It has to be highly reliable and reactive to ensure transactions sail through the market and get stored in the very system. It has also a strong risk management function, as an important constraint with regulation rules and risks associated with variety of financial products dealt on the market.

Origin and Development

The history of banking begins with the first prototype bank of merchants of the ancient world. This made grain loans to farmers and traders, who ferried goods between cities. The banking development spread from northern Italy across the Holy Roman Empire, and in the 16th, century the position of Medicis was eventually taken over by the Fuggers and the Welsers, followed by a number of important innovations of Amsterdam during the Dutch Republic in the 17th century and in London in the 18th century.

The first regular institution resembling what we call a bank was established at Venice, nearly seven hundred years ago.

By degree, the Venetian merchants fell into the habit of placing money with the chamber, for safe upkeep; and thus the business of deposit, a second branch of modern banking. The Bank of Venice remained without a rival; but was introduced around the 15 century, similar institutions were established at Genoa and Barcelona, cities, and remain the pride of Europe, second only to Venice, in the extent of trade. The business in which this new corporation principally intended to do by virtue of its charter was the purchase and sale of bills of exchange. The bank of England, chartered in 1694, remained the prototype and grand exemplar of our modern banks. The charter was periodically renewed, always on condition of extending some new loan to the government.

Private bankers established in all the principal cities and towns with the increase of wealth and commerce in Europe. They acknowledged money on deposit; managed the money affairs of states and individuals; lent money to such borrowers against necessary security; and bought and sold bills of exchange, bullion, and coin. Two banks were established in Scotland by charter from the king; the Bank of Scotland [1695] ; and, the Royal Bank of Scotland [1727]. The banks have branches in the principal towns of Scotland; but a multitude of private banks sprang up to dispute their business, and divide on their profits. Banks were among the oldest businesses in American history— for example, the Bank of New York [1784], and as the recently renamed Bank of New York Mellon it had its 225th anniversary [2009].[2]

In India, the premier institution, The General Bank of India was established in the year 1786. The East India Company established three banks, viz., the Bank of Bengal/Calcutta (1809), Bank of Bombay (1840) and Bank of Madras (1843). Subsequently, the Bank of Hindustan was established in 1870. The three individual units (Bank of Calcutta, Bank of Bombay, and Bank of Madras) were called as Presidency Banks. Allahabad Bank , established in 1865 was completely run by Indians for the first time. Punjab National Bank Ltd. headquartered at Lahore was set up in 1894. Bank of India, Central Bank of India, Bank of Baroda, Canara Bank, Indian Bank, and Bank of Mysore were set up between 1906 and 1913. In 1921, the presidency banks found amalgamated into the Imperial Bank of India, run by the European shareholders. In 1860, the concept of limited liability was introduced in Indian banking. It yielded to the establishment of joint-stock banks. Reserve Bank of India [RBI] was established in April 1935.

Reserve Bank of India Act was passed in 1934. It was constituted as an apex body without major government ownership. Banking Regulations Act was passed in 1949. This regulation brought RBI under the government control. The RBI got wide ranging powers for supervision and control of banks. The Act vested with licensing powers and the authority to conduct inspections in RBI. In 1955, the RBI acquired control of the Imperial Bank of India, renamed as the State Bank of India. In 1959, SBI took over the control of eight private banks floated in the erstwhile princely states, making them as its 100 per cent subsidiaries.[3] SBI has acquired local banks in rescue.

The first subsidiary was the Bank of Behar (Est. 1911), which SBI acquired in 1969, along with 28 branches. SBI acquired in the year ahead, National Bank of Lahore (Est. 1942), which had 24 branches. Five years later, in 1975, SBI acquired Krishnaram Baldeo Bank, in Gwalior State [Est. 1916], under the patronage of Maharaja Madhao RaoScindia. The bank had been the Dukan Pichadi, a small moneylender's enterprise, owned by the Maharaja. The new bank's first manager was Jall N. Broacha, a Parsi. In 1985, SBI acquired the Bank of Cochin in Kerala, with 120 branches. SBI acquired its affiliate, the State Bank of Travancore, with an extensive network in Kerala.[4]

The financial activities were handled by money lenders and individuals before their establishment. The interest rates were often very high. Again there was no security of public savings and no uniformity on loan terms. An organized fully regulated banking sector was established to counteract the problem. The general banking scenario remained dynamic those days. The picture of Indian Banking was completely different before pre-liberalization era, as the Government of India initiated measures to play an active role in the economic life of the nation. The Industrial Policy Resolution adopted by the government in 1948 envisaged a mixed economy. This resulted into greater involvement of the state in different segments of economy including banking and finance.[5]

According to Ravi (2011), the term Banking Technology refers to the use of sophisticated information and communication technologies together with computer science to enable them offer better services for its customers in a secure, reliable and affordable manner and sustain competitive advantage over other banks. It subsumes advanced computer algorithms in unraveling the patterns of customer behavior by sifting through his/her demographic, psychographic and transactional data. It is also known as *data mining*, to help banks achieve the business objectives by solving marketing problems, such as customer segmentation, customer scoring, target marketing, market-basket analysis, cross-sell, up-sell, customer retention by modeling churn etc. Successful use of data mining helps them achieve significant increase in profits, thereby retaining sustainable advantage over competitors.

From the functional perspective, Banking Technology has three important dimensions. They are: (i) the use of appropriate hardware for conducting business and servicing customers through delivery channels and payment systems and the associated software constitute one dimension of Banking Technology. The use of computer networks, security algorithms in its transactions, use of ATM and credit cards, Internet banking, tele-banking and mobile banking are being covered by this dimension. The advances made in information and communication technologies take care of this dimension. (ii) On the other hand, the use of advanced computer science algorithms to solve several interesting marketing related problems such as customer segmentation, customer scoring, target marketing, market-basket analysis, cross-sell, up-sell and customer retention etc. faced by the banks to reap profits and outperform their competitors constitutes the second dimension. It covers the implementation of data warehouse for banks and conducting data mining studies on customer data, and (iii) Moreover, banks cannot ignore the risks in conducting business with other counterpart servicing customers, for otherwise, their very existence could be at stake.[6]

The Reserve Bank of India is the central banking and monetary authority of India. It acts as the regulator and supervisor of commercial banks. The scheduled banks comprise those commercial and cooperative banks. The scheduled commercial banks form the bedrock of Indian financial system, currently accounting for more than three-fourth assets of all financial institutions. The RBI acts as a centralized body monitoring any discrepancies and shortcoming in the system. It is the foremost body monitoring in the Indian financial sector.[7]

The nationalized banks continue to dominate the Indian banking arena.The industry estimates that out of 274 commercial banks operating in India, 223 banks are in the public sector and 51 are in the private sector. The private sector bank grid includes 24 functioning foreign banks. Specialized banking institutions come under the ambit of nationalized Banks. These co-operatives, rural banks focus on areas of agriculture, rural development etc.[8]

It was considered necessary to have social control over banks, to better align the system over needs of planning and economic policy,. In 1969, 14 of the major private sector banks were nationalized. It was an important milestone in the history of Indian banking. The nationalization of another six private banks followed in 1980. [9]

The major segment of banking sector came under the Government with the three-phased nationalization drive. It imparted major impetus to branch expansion in un-banked rural and semi-urban areas, resulting in huge deposit mobilization, shaping the overall savings rate of the economy. Lending to agriculture and its allied sectors found pitched in. However, this arrangement had its demerits like reduced bank profitability, weak capital bases, and overburdening of banks with large non-performing assets.[10]

The first phase of nationalization in India [1969] saw the light by Mrs. Indira Gandhi, the then prime minister. She nationalized 14 banks, owned and managed by businessmen. Central Bank of India, Bank of Maharashtra, Dena Bank, Punjab National Bank, Syndicate Bank, Canara Bank, Indian Bank, Indian Overseas Bank, Bank of Baroda, Union Bank, Allahabad Bank, United Bank of India, UCO Bank, and Bank of India fell under the category.[11]

The target of nationalizing banks was to reach clients in rural areas with quality services. In the second phase, 14 more banks were nationalized [1969]. Six more banks [1980] were added to the mainstream. The state bank remained the best commercial bank in India, outperforming among top five banks in the whole world.[12]

According to Ali (2012), nationalized banks in India offer great and quality services to customers, insurance services like health insurance enabling the customer save money for any accidents in life. Banks are the custodians of public money, but were in private hands. Some of their directors used to utilize those funds for personal benefit, through partnership with some business and sanction loans in lieu of profits. Thus public money was used for personal profit. In a welfare state, a government cannot sleep over the matters against public interest. Nationalization was in accordance with national policy of adopting socialistic pattern of society. An objection against nationalization was raised forthwith that the drive made Banks inefficient.[13]

The Times of India (June 20, 2013) quoted what was central to liberalization was the reversal of the post-1969 policy, wherein the banking was made a largely public preserve by the nationalizing major private banks. India's major banks, other than the State Bank of India and its subsidiaries, till then were directly or indirectly controlled by big business mandates, resulting in the capture of a dominant share of the nation's savings by large firms to the exclusion of small borrowers and the agricultural sector.[14] According to Chellasamy and Sumathi (2014), seizing the ownership and bringing them into the public sector established social control. Some private banks remained were small domestic or foreign players with restricted operations. In two decades that followed, India's banking sector, judged by behavior or social performance went through dramatic transformation. The need for nationalization was felt mainly because of the failure of private commercial banks in achieving social and developmental goals, essential for any industrializing country.

The State Bank of India, [1955], the expansion of commercial banking had largely excluded rural areas and small scale borrowers, despite the enactment of Banking Regulation Act in 1949. The developmental goals of financial intermediation were not being achieved other than for some favored large industries and established business houses. Agriculture alone has received two per cent of total credit [1951-68]. Nationalization was essential for various reasons like as: (a) to break the ownership and control of banks by a few business families; (b) to prevent the concentration of wealth and economic power; (c) to mobilize savings from masses across the country; and (d) to cater to the needs of the priority sectors.[15]

According to Singh (2014), The Indian banking has finally worked up to the competitive dynamics of new Indian market, addressing over the relevant issues to take on multifarious challenges of globalization. Banks that employ IT solutions were perceived to be futuristic and proactive players, capable of meeting the multifarious requirements of the large customer's base. Private Banks have been fast on the uptake and were reorienting the strategies using the Internet and Intranet as a medium. The Internet has emerged as the challenging frontier of marketing anew with conventional physical world tenets being just as applicable like in any other marketing medium.

The Indian banking has come from a long way from being a sleepy business institution to somewhat highly proactive and dynamic entity. Larger doses of liberalization and economic reforms allowed banks to explore business opportunities anew rather than generating revenues from conventional streams. The Indian banking saw dramatic changes in the decade gone by, since the advent of liberalization and India's integration with the world economy. The economic reforms and the entry of private players saw nationalized banks revamp services and product portfolio to incorporate new, innovative customer-centric schemes. The banking finally woke up to the surging demands of ever-discerning Indian consumer. The need to become highly customer focused (generated by high competitive levels) forced the slow-moving public sector counterparts adopt a fast track approach.[16]

Pursuant to the provisions of the State Bank of India Act (1955), the Reserve Bank of India, which is India's Central Bank, acquired a controlling interest in the Imperial Bank of India. The Imperial Bank of India became the State Bank of India [April 30, 1955]. The Government of India recently acquired the RBIs stake in SBI, so as to remove any conflict of interest, because the RBI has been the country's banking regulatory authority.[17] SBI has acquired local banks in rescue. Various subsidiaries of SBI are:

1. *State Bank of Saurashtra* (Merged in SBI): State Bank of Saurashtra (SBS) is one of the Associate Banks of State Bank of India (now with State Bank of India). The history of SBS can be traced back to pre-independence period. Prior to 1948, the region of Saurashtra (a part of the present day Gujarat), consisted many small, medium and large princely states. After the formation of a separate state of Gujarat in 1960, SBS started its main area of operation from Saurashtra, which became a part of Gujarat. It was in the same year, when State Bank of India took over State Bank of Saurashtra, under the State Bank of India (Subsidiary Banks) Act, 1959.[18]
2. *State Bank of Indore*: State Bank of Indore, popularly known as Indore Bank in Malwa Region, originally known as the Bank of Indore Ltd. was incorporated under a special charter of His Highness Maharaja Tukojirao Holker-III, the then ruler of the region. In terms of State Bank of India (Subsidiary Banks) Act, 1959, the Bank of Indore Ltd. became a subsidiary of SBI. The State bank of Indore is popularly known as Indore Bank in Malwa Region, is a subsidiary body of the SBI. The economy of Indore is appreciable and the State bank of Indore is an integral part of such growth. In October 2009, the Government of India gave its in-principle approval to a merger between State Bank of India and State Bank of Indore. At the time of merger, the bank had over 470 branches spread in more than 300 cities and towns. In March 2009, the business turnover of State Bank of Indore crossed Rs.50, 000 crore. The State Bank India has set in motion the

process of merging State Bank of Indore with itself by agreeing to give 34 shares of SBI to minority shareho lders for every 100 shares of the associate bank. The SBI central board, in its meeting held on March 26, 2010, approved issuance of maximum 1,16,052 shares, at face value of Rs.10 each to the minority shareholders of State Bank of Indore, as on record date at the agreed swap ratio (34 shares of SBI for every 100 shares of State Bank of Indore). [19]

3. *State Bank of Bikaner and Jaipur*: The genesis of State Bank of Bikaner and Jaipur dates back to the year 1943-44, when the Bank of Jaipur Ltd. and the Bank of Bikaner Ltd. came into existence. In 1960, both banks were incorporated as the subsidiaries of State Bank of India and named as State Bank of Bikaner and State Bank of Jaipur. On January 1, 1963, these were merged into one entity viz., State Bank of Bikaner and Jaipur. The constitution, capital, management and other matters pertaining to the bank are governed by the provisions of SBI (Subsidiary Banks) Act, 1959. 75 percent of the shares of SBBJ are held by SBI and the remaining by institutions and the general public. The number of branches increased to 1049 (862 in Rajasthan) as on 30.09.2013. SBBJ had sponsored three Regional Rural Banks viz. Marwar Gramin Bank (set up in 1976), Sriganganagar Kshetriya Gramin Bank (1984) and Bikaner Kshetriya Gramin bank (1985). These were merged into single RRB viz. MGB Gramin Bank in June 2006. On 25.02.2013 the MGB Gramin Bank (RRB sponsored by SBBJ) and Jaipur Thar Gramin Bank (RRB sponsored by UCO Bank) were amalgamated into a single Regional Rural Bank named 'Marudhara Gramin Bank' sponsored by SBBJ with Head 27 office at Jodhpur. The bank shoulders Lead Bank responsibility in nine districts of the State.[20]

4. *State Bank of Hyderabad*: The bank originated as the central bank of the erstwhile Nizam state under the name, Hyderabad State Bank. It was established in 1942, during the reign of the last Nizam of Hyderabad, Mir Osman Ali Khan. State Bank of Hyderabad was constituted as Hyderabad State Bank on 08.08.1941 under Hyderabad State Bank Act, 1941. The Bank started with the unique distinction of being the central bank of the erstwhile State of Hyderabad, covering present-day Telangana region of Andhra Pradesh, Hyderabad-Karnataka of Karnataka and Marathwada of Maharashtra. Its first branch was opened at Gun foundry,

Hyderabad on April, 05, 1942. In 1953, it took over the assets and liabilities of the Hyderabad Mercantile Bank Ltd. It went on simultaneously conducting Government and Treasury business as the agent of Reserve Bank of India. In 1956, the Reserve Bank of India took it as the first subsidiary when its name was changed from Hyderabad State Bank to the State Bank of Hyderabad. It became a subsidiary of the SBI on the October 01, 1959 and is now the largest Associate Bank of the SBI.

5. *State Bank of Mysore*: State Bank of Mysore was established in the year 1913 as The Bank of Mysore Ltd. under the patronage of then Maharaja Krishna Raja Wadiyar IV of erstwhile Govt. of Mysore, at the instance of the banking committee headed by the pioneer engineer-statesman, Bharat Ratna Sir M.Viswesvarayya. Now it is an Associate Bank under the State Bank Group and the State Bank of India holds 92.33 percent of shares. It has over 745 branches and 10,200 employees (September 2012) and 606 branches alone (80 per cent) in the state of Karnataka. It has regional offices in Bengaluru, Mysore, Mangalore, Mandya, Hassan, Shimoga, Davangere, Bellary, Tumkur, Kolar, Chennai, Coimbatore, Hyderabad, Mumbai and New Delhi. The turnover for the year 2008-2009 stood at US $10 billion accruing profit of about US $65 million.[21]

6. *State bank of Patiala*: The rich heritage of State Bank of Patiala dates back to the year 1917, when it was founded by Late His Highness Bhupinder Singh, Maharaja of erstwhile Patiala state, with one branch by the name of 'Chowk Fort, Patiala' to begin with. The Bank, then known as the 'Patiala State Bank' was state Indian Banking System: An Overview owned and set up for the explicit purpose of fostering growth of agriculture, trade and industry. The constitution, scope and operations of the bank underwent a sea change with the formation of the Patiala and east Punjab States Union (PEPSU) in 1948. The bank was then reorganized and brought under the control of RBI. It was christened as the Bank of Patiala. Another milestone in its history was its becoming a subsidiary of the State Bank of India on April, 01, 1960 when it was named as the State Bank of Patiala and since its growth in terms of size and volume. During those glorious years, the bank played an important role in banking sphere. Its business grew manifold since its establishment. The recent records say it to have networked by some 830 service outlets. There are more than

1,000 branches, spread across the major cities of India, out of which, the majority of whom were in home State, Haryana, Himachal Pradesh, Rajasthan, Jammu and Kashmir, Delhi and Chandigarh. It provides easy access to money for its customers through its ATMs spread over 16 states of India.[22]

7. State Bank of Travancore: State Bank of Travancore (SBT) was originally established as Travancore Bank Ltd. in 1945 sponsored by the erstwhile princely state of Travancore. Under a special statute of the Indian Parliament (SBI subsidiary Banks Act 1959), it has been made an Associate of the State Bank of India and a member of the State Bank Group, the largest banking group in India. The bank is alive to its developmental role and actively participates in meeting the need -based requirements of small and medium enterprises and agriculture. It has consistently met with the benchmarks for priority sector advances stipulated by the government from time to time. It attaches priority to this vital sector and encourages technocrats and women entrepreneurs. The Technical Consultancy Cell assists the small units in evaluation of techno-economic feasibility of projects. Bank has set up exclusive small and medium enterprises branches for this sector. It caters to the needs of farmers through its rural and semi-urban branches. It has introduced scheme to extend assistance to tenant farmers, who are holding only lease hold rights over the land wherein they cultivate.[23]

Types of Banks

Banks can be classified into various types on the basis of their function, ownership, domicile etc. The following types of banks are in operation:

Commercial Bank[24]

It provides services such as accepting deposits, making business loans, and offering basic investment products. It can refer to a bank or its division dealing mostly with deposits and loans from corporations or large businesses, as opposed to individual members of the public. These perform many functions. They satisfy the financial needs of sectors such as agriculture, industry, trade, communication, so they play very significant role in a process of economic social needs. The functions performed by banks, since recently, are becoming customer centred and are widening their functions. Generally, the banks roll through - primary functions and the secondary functions. Along with primary functions, these perform several secondary functions, including many agency or general utility functions. Their secondary functions can be assorted into agency and utility functions.

Credit creation is the most significant part in banking. These provide loans and corporate bonds to the households, new start ups and small medium enterprises to run their businesses. It also obtains money from the households and invests that money into other profitable investments. The money held as customer account then accrues interest, which is being given to the customer in the form of periodic payments. These play an important part of economy when they are being involved in bidding process of government securities. Various services and products provided by commercial banks such as car leasing, mortgage financing, credit cards etc provide easy accessibility of funds to the customers.

The banks are also an important element in implementing the monetary and fiscal policy by the central bank. The commercial banks ought to increase the interest rates to comply with the central bank, when the central bank decides to introduce concretionary policy. The place of banks in the British economy was remarkable. They stood at the very centre of business and could promote prosperity or deflate the economy into unemployment almost at will. For this reason, the banks are being closely controlled in their credit policies by the Bank of England, which was influenced and controlled by the Treasury.

Investment Bank[25]

Investment bank mobilizes economy as a financial institution. It assists the individuals, corporations, and governments in raising capital by underwriting or acting as the client's agent in the issuance of such securities (or both). It may assist companies involved in mergers and/or acquisitions and extend ancillary services such as market making; trading of derivatives and equity securities, and FICC services. It helps the corporations in raising capital. It facilitates with the trading of securities thereby, increasing the liquidity of securities. It provides investment opportunities to the individuals or entities.

Most of the corporations get advisory services from the investment banks on mergers, acquisitions and divestiture. In addition, the banks seldom perform such roles, because of its importance. There are two main lines of business in investment banking. Trading securities for cash or for other securities, or the promotion of securities is the "sell side"; while buy side is a term used to refer to advising institutions concerned with buying investment services. Private equity funds, mutual funds, life insurance companies, unit trusts, and hedge funds are the most common types of buy side entities.

An investment bank can be split into private and public functions separating for the data cross-over. The private areas deal with private insider information that may not be publicly disclosed, while the public areas such as stock analysis deal with public information. Investment banking is split into front office, middle office, and back office activities. Wuer and hile large service investment banks offer all the lines of business, sell-side and buy-side, s maller sell side investment firms such as boutique investment banks and small broker dealers focus on investment banking and sales/ trading/research, respectively.

Industrial Bank[26]

It is a financial institution with a limited scope of services. Industrial banks sell certificates, labeled as investment shares and accept customer deposits. They invest the proceeds in installment loans for consumers and small businesses. These banks are known as Morris banks or industrial loan companies. Investment bank is a financial institution, handling a very important role in the economy. It helps the corporations in raising capital. It facilitates trading of securities thereby, increasing the liquidity of securities. It provides investment opportunities to individuals or entities.

Most of the corporations get advisory services from investment banks regarding mergers, acquisitions and divestiture. In addition, the roles of investment banking, the commercial banks seldom perform such roles. The exact model for an industrial bank will vary somewhat, depending on the sector of consumer market of target audience. It may focus on granting loans to individuals, who work within a given industry, with many of those borrowing simple short-term loans facilitating purchase of a vehicle or make minor repairs at home.

The bank may extend loans for specific purposes related to the owner of the institution. For example, a furniture manufacturer may establish an industrial bank as a means of handling the purchase of products, either by furniture stores or by individuals, who meet with credit requirements set by the institution. It can often simplify the process of such financing, and may even support the customer with slightly better interest rates and other repayment terms than obtained elsewhere. It is important to note that an industrial bank seldom offers similar range of services as other banks. Most will focus on lending activities rather than other types of accounts for customers. Any individual or the company, who does business with lending institution of this kind will also maintain bank accounts at other institutions, including checking and savings accounts.

The main functions of industrial bank are: (i) accept long-term deposits; (ii) help selling debentures and shares of industrial firms; and (iii) help provide information regarding the general economic position of the economy.[27]

Agricultural Bank[28]

Agricultural credit needs are not same as industry and trade. Generally, these are not dealt by industrial and commercial banks. These may be in the mode of short-term and long-term credit for cultivation. Seed, manure and fodder, payment of rent, wages, irrigation of crops; hire charges of pumps, purchase of livestock, repair of agricultural implements, land improvement, for laying of orchard and capital expenditure on agriculture are some of the categories. An agriculturist may require credit for production and consumption. The loans used for such productive purpose are called the productive credit.

Exchange Bank[29]

Exchange bank always deals in foreign exchange, and focus on foreign trade. They assist in international payments through the sale and purchase of bills of exchange facilitating such foreign trade.

Savings Bank[30]

Savings bank is a financial institution, whose primary purpose is to accept deposits and paying interest on them. They originated in Europe during the 18th century providing access to savings products for all levels of population. The early banks were designed to encourage lower income strata, save money and access banking services on good will thereupon.

The original objective was to facilitate easily accessible savings products for all the strata of population. Nowadays, European savings banks focus on retail banking: payments, savings products, credits and insurances for individuals or small and medium-sized enterprises. Internet banking at the end of 20th century through its operation paid higher levels of interest in return for online clients only.

Central Bank[31]

Central bank always manages a state's currency, money supply, and interest rates. These usually oversee the commercial banking system of respective countries. In contrast to a commercial bank, the central bank possesses a monopoly on increasing the amount of money in the nation, and prints the national currency, which usually serves as the nation's legal tender. The primary function of the bank is to manage the nation's money supply, interest rates, setting the reserve, and acting as a lender of last resort to the sector during times of insolvency or financial emergency. They have supervisory powers, preventing bank runs and reduce the risk from commercial banks and other financial institutions engaged in reckless or fraudulent behavior. They implement a country's chosen monetary policy.

A central bank may use another country's currency either directly, or indirectly.[32] Typically, certain types of short-term interest rates are being looked after. These influence the stock and bond markets as well as mortgage and other interest rates. The main monetary policy instruments available to them are open market operation, bank reserve requirement, interest rate policy, re-lending and re-discount and credit policy. The central bank must hold foreign exchange reserves and official gold reserves enabling open market operations. It influences money supply in an economy. Each time it buys securities, its effect creates money on buying binge of securities. The bank exchanges money for the security, increase money supply, while lowering the supply of specific security. Conversely, their selling of securities reduces money supply.

Central bank is a financial institution, set-up by the government of a country. It provides financial and banking services for the government, commercial banks and other financial institutions. A central bank is being set-up with the objectives: (i) to regulate and control money supply of a nation, and (ii) to foster economic growth without inflation. Generally, there is a significant level of government control over the system, though certain systems enjoy varying levels of autonomy. The main functions of a central bank can be broadly classified as: (i) issue of bank notes; (ii) manage public debt and the government's accounts; (iii) manage foreign exchange rate; (iv) act as the nodal banker to commercial banks; (v) control money supply in economy; (vi) organize the interest rate structure; (vii) hold gold reserves and foreign currency of the country; and (viii) manage dealings with other central banks.[33]

The central bank regulating money supply through instruments could be classified as quantitative or qualitative methods. The quantitative methods aim at regulating the quality of credit, bank rate, open market operations, reserves, SLR and moral suasion. The qualitative techniques of credit control refer to the borrower's quality and various restrictions on lending by banks either to a particular industry or for particular activities. The use of one or more or a combination of such instruments depends upon the objectives and the prevailing economy. The regulatory role of RBI assumes paramount importance, since the overall price and credit levels in economy ought to be regulated from time to time, reflected from the international scenario. The RBI ought to safeguard the global value of Indian rupee through healthy banking system. It ought to remove financial market anomalies and ensure accountability in operations from various players. Its regulations are varied and cover different sectors of economy. The regulation and supervision of financial intermediaries however remains dominant.[34]

All banks are required to hold a certain percentage of assets as capital, established by the central bank or the banking supervisor. Some central banks may require the exchange of some or all foreign exchange receipts (generally from exports) for local currency. In some countries, the central banks may have other indirect tools to limit lending practices, else restrict or regulate capital markets. These banks often have requirements for the quality of assets of financial institutions; which may limit the extent of risk and leverage created by the system.

In some countries, the central bank monitors the banking sector through subsidiaries. There has been a trend towards increasing their dependence for improving long-term economic performance. It is argued that an independent central bank can run through a more credible monetary policy, making market expectations more responsive to its signals. The governments generally have some degree of influence over even "independent" central banks; whose aim is to prevent short-term interference. International organizations such as the World Bank, the Bank for International Settlements and the International Monetary Fund are strong supporters of central bank independence.

Cooperative Bank[35]

Cooperative banking is retail and commercial banking is organized on a cooperative basis. The institutions take deposits and lend money in most parts of the world. It owes to the close of 19th century, inspired on those of Britain and Germany. The banks are an important constituent of the Indian financial system. They are the primary financiers of agricultural activities, some small-scale industries and self-employed workers.

The Anyonya Co-operative Bank in India has been the premier cooperative bank in Asia. The more recent phenomena of microcredit and microfinance are often based on a cooperative model. They focus on business lending.[36] In 2006, Dr. Muhammad Yunus, founder of the Grameen Bank in Bangladesh, won the Nobel Peace Prize for his intrinsic idea on the development of microcredit concept.[37] The history of co-operative movement in India is about a century old. The movement commenced at home with a view to encourage and promote thrift and mutual help for development of persons of small means such as agriculturists, artisans and other segments of the society. It was aimed at concentrating the efforts in releasing the exploited classes out of the clutches of money lenders. Credit societies were formed under Co-operative Societies Act of 1904. India's co-operative banking structure finds assorted into agricultural and non-agricultural credit. These are two separate structures in the case of agricultural credit - one for short and medium-term credit and the other for long-term credit.

The co-operative credit structure for short and medium terms is a three-tier one, with primary agricultural credit societies at the base level, the central co-operative bank at the district level and state co-operative bank at the apex level. Primary Agricultural Credit Societies (PACS) are the foundation of the co-operative credit structure and form the largest number of cooperative institutions in India. Most of these societies have been organized mainly to extend credit facilities and inculcate the habit of thrift and economy among the members. The District Co-operative Banks (DCBs) occupy the middle level position in the three-tier co-operative credit structure of the country. The PACSs, could not function effectively without gaining financial support from an outside agency.

The Co-operative Societies Act of 1912 permitted the registration of DCBs. Some DCBs were established to cater to the needs of primary society, even before the enactment of this Act. The DCBs are formed in meeting the credit requirements of member societies. The State Co-operative Banks (SCBs) or the apex banks occupy a crucial position in the three-tier co-operative credit structure. The apex banks or the State Co-operative Banks are being formed by federating DCBs in each state. The apex banks assume a key-position in the co-operative credit structure because the financial assistance from RBI and the NABARD are being invariably routed through them.[38]

Three types of cooperative banks operate in the country. They are (i) primary credit societies; (ii) central cooperative banks, and (iii) state cooperative banks. The primary variety is being formed at the village or town level or town level. It extends (a) credit to farmers, distribute inputs like fertilizers and run outlets under the PDS; (b) short-term and medium-term credit for agriculture and allied activities; (c) the short -term loans are repayable within a period of 12 to 15 months, whereas the medium-term loans are repayable within three to five years, (d) crop loan is being the prominent credit given to farmers by Primary Agricultural Cooperative Credit Societies [PACCS], without collateral security up to ten acre in respect of registered sugar cane growers and up to Rs. one lakh in respect of other crops. (e) the loan amount exceeding this limit is secured with mortgage of property or pledge of jewels. (f) these also issue loans for other agricultural purposes like purchase of farm machineries and for non-agricultural purposes including loans for purchase of consumer durables, housing loans, education loans and professional loans. (g) marketing facilities for the sale of agricultural produce, and (h) associate with economic and social welfare programmes of the village.

The PACCS will act as Paddy Procurement Centres on behalf of Tamil Nadu Civil Supplies Corporation and procure paddy at the minimum support price, announced by the government in the non-delta areas, apart from Direct Purchase Centres operated by Tamil Nadu Civil Supplies Corporation. They will assist the Cooperative Marketing Societies, Tamil Nadu Cooperative Marketing Federation and National Agricultural Cooperative Marketing Federation of India to procure the agricultural produce directly from the farmers. Such societies will expand their produce pledge loan operations, substantially to prevent distress sale by the farmers during peak harvest.[39]

According to Muraleedharan (2009). Central Cooperative Bank operates at the district level. They provide loans to their members and function as a link between the primary credit societies and state cooperative banks. State Cooperative Bank is the apex cooperative bank in the respective state of the country.[40]

The Economic Times (Jan 16, 2013) reports, the parliament to have recently passed the Banking Laws (Amendment) Bill, 2012, which now permits the RBI to assume additional regulatory powers over co-operative banks. It facilitates the regulator the power to withdraw freedom given to primary co-operative credit societies to operate as banks without a licence from the RBI. Section 22 of the BR Act also says that no cooperative society shall carry on banking business unless it is a licencee of the RBI. But this provision is not applicable to the primary credit societies. From a combined reading of the above provisions, it is clear that a primary credit society, with a capital of less than Rs one lakh, can do business without being required to take a licence from the RBI. Such primary credit societies, although functioning as banks, are not within the purview of RBI.

The operation of such credit societies is not restricted to their members. The provisions of the BR Act permit them do banking and use the words e-bank, e-banking or e-banker in their operation. Amendments to the BR Act, 1949, impose licensing requirements for unlicensed primary cooperative credit societies and strengthen regulatory powers in respect of cooperative banks. RBI is empowered to direct the cooperative banks maintain assets not exceeding 40 per cent of demand and time liabilities. Earlier, under the provisions of Section 22, on becoming a co-operative bank, a credit society could continue to carry on its banking until the RBI grants them a licence. The Amendment Act now provides that a primary credit society will have to obtain a licence to continue banking operation.It upholds the primary co-operative credit societies, engaged in banking business, to convert themselves into co-operative banks and obtain a licence from RBI.[41]

Regional Rural Bank[42]

Regional Rural Banks operate in different states. They were being created to serve the rural mass through banking and financial services. However, RRB's may have branches set up for urban operations and the area of operation may include urban areas. The Narsimhan committee conceptualized the creation of RRBs in 1975 as a new set of regionally-oriented rural banks, combining the local feel and familiarity of rural problems, characteristic of cooperatives with the professionalism and large resource base of commercial banks. Their main purpose is to mobilize financial resources from rural/ semi-urban areas and grant loans and advances mostly to small and marginal farmers, agricultural laborers and rural artisans.

The area of operation of RRBs is limited to the area as notified by the government of India covering one or more districts in the state. Regional Rural Banks were established under the provisions of an Ordinance passed on September 26, 1975. The RRB Act 1976 facilitate sufficient banking and credit facility for agriculture and other rural sectors. The development process of RRBs started on October 02, 1975 with the forming of the Prathama Bank. Also on October 02, 1975, five regional rural banks were set up on with a total authorized capital of Rs. 100 crore ($ 10 million) which was later augmented to Rs. 500 crore ($ 50 million) in Punjab National Bank, the State Bank of India, Syndicate Bank, United Bank of India and United Commercial Bank, which sponsored the regional rural banks.[43]

Development Banks

Business needs fund for purchasing equipments. The Development banks are being involved in such cases, besides subscribing to shares and debentures issued by companies. The Industrial Finance Corporation of India and State Financial Corporation are examples of development banks in India. Their number has increased rapidly since the 1950s and were encouraged by the International Bank for Reconstruction and Development and its affiliates. The large regional development banks include the Inter-American Development Bank, [Estd.1959]; the Asian Development Bank [Operations in 1966]; and the African Development Bank [Estd 1964]. They facilitate loans for specific national or regional projects to private or public bodies or may operate in conjunction with other financial institutions.

One of the main activities of development banks has been the recognition and promotion of private investment opportunities. These may be publicly or privately owned and operated although governments frequently make substantial contributions to the capital of private banks. The form (share equity or loans) and cost of financing offered by development banks depend on their cost of obtaining capital and their need to show a profit and pay dividends.[44]

Specialized Banks

The specialized banks are being involved in some specific area or activity. These are otherwise known as the Development Finance Institutions (DFI), to contribute to the development of specific sectors of the economy.[45] They cater to the requirements and provide overall support for selling up business. EXIM bank, SIDBI and NABARD are some examples. Export-Import Bank of India is the premier export finance institution of the country [Estd 1982] under the Export-Import Bank of India Act 1981. The government of India launched the institution with a mandate not to just enhance exports, but to integrate the foreign trade and investment with an overall economic growth. The bank remains catalyst and a key player in the promotion of cross -border trade and the investment. It has been guided by the expertise at the board level, by senior policy makers, expert bankers, leading players in industry and international trade as well as professionals in exports or imports or financing thereof. As per the Exim Bank Act, at a particular point in time, the bank can have a maximum of sixteen directors on its Board.[46]

Small Industries Development Bank of India is an independent financial institution, aimed at facilitating the growth and development of micro, small and medium-scale enterprises (MSME) in India. Set up on April 2, 1990 under an act of parliament, it was incorporated initially as a wholly owned subsidiary of Industrial Development Bank of India. It is the principal financial institution for the promotion, financing and development of the micro, small and medium enterprise sector and co-ordinate with those institutions engaged in similar activities, through refinance options and short-term lending.[47]

The parliament, through Act, 61 of 1981, endorsed the setting up of NABARD. The bank came into existence on July 12, 1982 by transferring the agricultural credit functions of the RBI and refinance functions of the then Agricultural Refinance and Development Corporation. It was dedicated to the service of the nation by the late prime minister Smt. Indira Gandhi on November 05, 1982. It was set up with an initial capital of Rs.100 crore. The paid up capital [as on March 31, 2013] stood at Rs 4,000 crore with the government of India holding Rs.3,980 crore (99.50 per cent) and the Reserve Bank of India with Rs. 20 crore (0.50 per cent), consequent to the revision in the composition of share capital between the government and the RBI. It promotes sustainable and equitable agriculture and rural prosperity through effective credit support, related services, institution development and other innovative initiatives.[48]

Public Sector[49]

Public sector banks find the government of India holding majority stake. These make up together the largest category of the Indian banking system. Currently, there are 27 public sector banks, wherein the SBI and its six associate banks (such as State Bank of Indore, State Bank of Bikaner and Jaipur etc), besides 19 nationalized banks (such as Allahabad Bank, Canara Bank etc) and the IDBI Bank Ltd were in the fray. The government has appreciable stake beyond 50 per cent with Public Sector Banks (PSBs). The shares of banks find listed on the stock exchanges. 29 PSBs find their slots. The central government has entered the business with the nationalization of the Imperial Bank of India in 1955. A 60 per cent stake was taken by the Reserve Bank of India and the new bank was named as the State Bank of India. The seven other state banks became its subsidiaries, when it was nationalized on July 19, 1960.

The share of banking sector held by the public banks continued to grow through the 1980s, and by 1991 the public sector banks accounted for 90 per cent of the banking sector. The combined branches held by the public sector banks was 60,646 across India, with deposits accounted for Rs. 1,10,000 crore. The banks find divided into two groups i.e., Nationalized Banks and the State Bank of India and its associates, with the government harping on appreciable stakes. 19 nationalized banks and eight SBI associates dominate 75 per cent of overall deposits and 71 per cent of advances in the banking industry. The banks dominate commercial banking. These can be further classified into: State Bank of India, Nationalized banks, and Regional Rural Banks.

Banking regulator has openly expressed concern over the state of affairs, through new set of guidelines on asset classification and resolution. Their balance sheets can be expected to reflect a truer picture on their condition. The rise in savings rate of economy from the low levels, at which they were till the '60s has been attributed to two policy actions: (a) bank nationalization and branch expansion; and (b) launching of the Unit Trust of India. It was also recognized that the revolution in customer service at banks were led by the private sector banks, and their adoption of information technology perforce public sector banks to follow suit.

The banks were expected to offer customers some choice of insurance products from different companies as against the products from one company. The Union finance ministry has asked them to become insurance brokers instead of corporate agents. Life Insurance Corporation has been the major beneficiary, since it has the highest brand recall and most banks are likely to include its policies in their insurance package plans.

The banks could now be directly responsible for mis-selling as against earlier role, acting as agents of insurance companies.

The insurance industry was split over the issue of banks distributing products of multiple companies. The bank-promoted company's favoured banks being tied to one company, while the non-bank promoted insurers wanted an open architecture. Although, banks offer customers a choice of multiple mutual funds, they could sell insurance policies of only one such company. The Insurance Regulatory and Development Authority used to license firms as brokerages and banks were eligible only to take up a corporate agency on behalf of one each of life, non-life and health insurance companies.

Private Sector Banks[50]

Private sector banks came to supplement the performance of public sector banks and serve the needs of the economy. These were merely acquired in the hands of government, without any incentive for profits and improve the financial counterpart. The public sector banks follow the RBI interest rates whereas those in the private are being controlled by private lenders with the approval from the RBI. The interest rates are slightly costly when compared to the public sector banks. The private sector banks are being split into two groups by financial regulator in India, old and new. The old private sector banks hung before 1969 nationalization drive. They stayed in the business as independent banks following their smaller size or specialized in terms of operation.

Initially, during 1921, the private banks like bank of Bengal, bank of Bombay and bank of Madras were in service, which formed altogether Imperial Bank of India. The Reserve Bank of India came in picture in 1935 and became the centre of every other bank taking away all the responsibilities and functions of Imperial bank. The old private-sector banks have been operating since a long time and may be referred to those banks in operation before 1991 and those banks after 1969 nationalization drive were called as new private-sector banks. The banks, which were not nationalized in the two-stage drive [1969 and 1980] were referred to the old private sector banks.

These were not nationalized, because of their small size and regional focus. New private sector banks were set up after 1990.

Table 1: Gives the List of Private Sector Banks in India

Old Private Sector Banks	*New Private Sector Banks*
• Bank of Rajasthan Ltd.·	• Bank of Punjab Ltd.
• Bharat Overseas Bank Ltd.·	• Centurian Bank Ltd.
• Catholic Syrian Bank Ltd.·	• HDFC Bank Ltd.
• City Union Bank Ltd.·	• ICICI Bank Ltd.
• Development Credit Bank Ltd.·	• Indusland Bank Ltd.
• Dhanalekshmi Bank Ltd.·	• Kotak Mahindra Lyd
• Federal Bank Ltd.·	• Axis Bank Ltd.
• Ganesh Bank of Kurundwad Ltd.·	• Tes Bank Ltd.
• Jammu and Kashmir Bank Ltd.	
• Karnataka Bank Ltd.	
• Karur Vysys Bank Ltd.	

(*Contd...*)

• Lakshmi Vilas Bank Ltd.	
• Lord Krishna Bank Ltd.	
• Nainital Bank Ltd.	
• Ratnakar Bank Ltd.	
• Sangli Bank Ltd.	
• SBI Cpmm. And International Bank Ltd.	
• South Indian Bank Ltd.	
• Tamil Nadu Mercantile Bank Ltd.	
• United Western Bank Ltd.	
• ING Vysys Bank.	

Source: D. Muraleedharan (2009). Modern Banking: Theory and Practice, p. 58.

Functions of Commercial Bank[51]

According to Ahuja (2010), bankers play very important role in the economic life of the nation. The health of the economy is closely related to the soundness of the system. Although, banks create no new wealth, but borrowing, lending and related similar activities facilitate the process of production, distribution, exchange and consumption of wealth. They have become very effective partners in the process of economic development. Modern banks are very useful for the utilization of resources of the country. The banks are mobilizing the savings of the people for investment purposes. Appreciable capital of the country would remain idle without banks. A bank, as a matter of fact, resemble a heart in the economic structure and the capital provided by it is like blood outflow. Loan facility extended however, works as an incentive to the producer to augment the production.

Many difficulties in the international payments have been overcome with the volume of transactions. Cheques, drafts bills of exchange and letters of credit are very important instruments of the banks. The banks collect them drawn on banks in other cities or countries and proceeds according to the customer's concern. Banking is now an essential part of our economic system. Modern trade and commerce would be impossible without the availability of suitable banking services. Banking promotes savings for ordinary labourers and workers besides the rich land owners and businessmen. Even, the UN has the World Bank. It is like a big deposit cache for member countries. They can borrow, according to needs subject to certain terms and conditons. The functions of commercial banks were assorted as primary, secondary and general utility functions.

The commercial banks can borrow, receive deposits and advance. loans are the two main functions. The borrowal will be in the form of deposits, depending on public deposited funds. If the money is in the current account, s[he] can withdraw it in part, or in full at any time, s[he] likes without notice or payable interest. The current account can be opened by any business enterprise or higher net worth, any time involving third party cheques, drafts etc or need to borrow as overdrafts against some security. Fixed deposits are made for a fixed period of time. These deposits cannot be withdrawn before the expiry of that period. A higher rate of interest is being paid on them.

In savings deposits, the depositor can withdraw money without any restrictions. The deposits carry lower rate of interest than the fixed deposits. It gives a nominal rate of interest and money can be withdrawn as and when the need arises. The position of account is depicted in a small booklet called *Pass book*. The rate of interest in savings account is being fixed by the RBI. The bank extends loans to others including advancing loans. A great care has to be exercised in the matter of lending and keeping resources. Short-term loans are given as personal loans against security.[52] According to Muraleedharan (2009), the loans and advances are given to members of the public and the business community at a higher rate of interest than that allowed on various deposit accounts. The rate of interest charged on loans and advances varies, according to the purpose and the period of loan and the mode of repayment. Bank lends money in various forms and on various bases, for practically every activity.

A very important function of a modern bank is to discount bills or *hundies* of businessmen. Bank discounting is considered a very suitable investment for a bank. The bills are certain to be paid on maturity. They can be rediscounted with the central bank, if necessary. It is a major activity with some smaller banker. Under this type of lending, the bank takes the bill drawn by the borrower on his customer and pays him immediately deducting some amount as discount/commission. The bank then presents the bill to the borrower's customer on the due date of the bill and collects the total amount. If the bill is delayed, the borrower or his customer pays the bank a predetermined interest depending upon the terms of transaction.

Agency services are rendered by commercial banks as agents of customers: The services includes: (i) collection and payments of cheques and bills on behalf of customers; (ii) collection of dividends, interest, rent etc on behalf of customers, if so instructed by them. (iii) purchase and sale of shares and securities on behalf of customers; (iv) payment of rent, interest, insurance premium, subscriptions, on behalf of customers, if so instructed;

(v) acting as the trustee or executor; and (vi) acting as agents or correspondents on behalf of customers for other banks and financial instructions at home and abroad. Apart from transferring money from one place to another place. Banks are also in the business of collecting the client's money from other places.[53] According to Ahuja (2010), bank now-a-days serves customers in various ways. It has lockers or safe deposit vaults. They are meant to keep the valuables of customers in safe custody. It purchases and sells stocks and shares of companies for clients.[54]

Mortgage bank

A mortgage bank specializes in originating and/or servicing mortgage loans. It is a state-licensed banking entity that makes mortgage loans directly to consumers. The difference between a mortgage banker and a mortgage broker is that the mortgage banker funds loans with its own capital. Generally, a mortgage bank originates a loan and places it on a pre-established warehouse line of credit until the loan can be sold to an investor. The banks frequently use the secondary market to sell loans, because the funds received pay down their warehouse lines of credit, which enables them continue to lend.

A mortgage bank is not regulated as a federal or state bank and does not take deposits from consumers or businesses. It raises some equity, to guarantee the warehouse line and the bulk funds are being provided by warehouse lender. It can vary in size. Some mortgage banking companies are nationwide. A few originate with larger volume of loan, exceeding that of a nationwide commercial bank. Many mortgage banks employ specialty servicers for repurchase and fraud discovery. The primary sources of revenue owe to loan origination fees, and loan servicing fees. Many mortgage bankers opt not to service the loans they originate. By selling them shortly after they are closed and funded, they are eligible for earning a service released premium. The secondary market investor that buys the loan will earn revenue for the servicing of the loan for each month the loan is kept by the borrower.[55]

Mortgage banker is a company, individual or institution that originates mortgages. These use own funds, or that borrowed from a warehouse lender, to fund mortgages. After a mortgage is originated, a mortgage banker might retain it in the portfolio, or might sell it to an investor. The primary business is to earn the fees associated with loan origination. Most bankers do not retain the mortgage in their portfolio. Larger service mortgages, while smaller mortgage bankers tend to sell the servicing rights. The distinguishing feature between the banker and the broker is that bankers close mortgages in their own names, using their own funds, while brokers facilitate originations for other financial institutions. The brokers do not close mortgages in their own names.[56]

Mortgage bankers are usually companies or individuals that originate their own mortgages. This is in contrast to mortgage brokers, who don't originate (meaning fund) their own mortgages. Bankers, though have the ability to close home loans in their own name. Brokers find the funding sources and facilitate the loan origination on behalf of those sources. Bankers might not discount but sell those loans off immediately after closing. The function of mortgage banking is to make a profit for the banker and its investors. A variety of methods are being used.[57] Mortgage banks serve often depository banks as well. These banks service the checking and savings needs of the customers. As opposed to brokerage firms and finance companies, mortgage banks often avoid heavy marketing or solicitation to attract new mortgage customers.

Most mortgage originations at mortgage banks are handled entirely in-house. The brokers outsource nearly financial work to competing banks. Most mortgage loans that originate at mortgage banks are serviced there as well. Mortgages originated by mortgage brokers are sold almost immediately to larger financial institution with the infrastructure to service such loan. Small, local mortgage banks are often popular as customers develop relation with their loan officers and banking representatives. In addition, if a mortgage customer runs into financial problems, solutions emerge, if people have personal relationship with a bank.[58]

According to Burks (2014), Mortgage bankers essentially are loan officers, who specialize in financing to buy homes or refinance earlier mortgages. The officers often take on sales roles, so they attend real estate meetings, home-buying seminars and other events to find new borrowers. The federal government regulates some parts of lending process, but banks set their own preliminary standards in determining whether an applicant is qualified for a mortgage.[59]

Niche Bank

These banks cater to and serve the needs of a certain demographic segment of population. They typically target a specific market or type of customer, and tailor some advertising, product mix and operations to this target market's preferences. A good example of a niche bank is the Golf Savings Bank, which sponsors tournaments and offers up to $10,000 for

PGA members, who score a hole in one and have a specific account at the bank. Other good examples of Niche banks include Reid Temple AME Church Federal Credit Union, which has convenient hours before and after church worship on Sundays, and BowieBanc, which offered an ATM card with a picture of singer David Bowie, the singer, before it shut.[60]

The Daily Telegraph (Nov 16, 2013), reports former Union finance minister P. Chidambaram to have suggested preferring banking licence needs for entities proposing innovative models over those replicating lenders. The RBI has received as many as 26 proposals for new bank licences. Besides, big industrial groups owned by the Tatas and billionaires Anil Ambani and Kumar Mangalam Birla, India Post and micro-finance institutions, such as Bandhan Financial Services and Janalakshmi Financial Services are in the fray. At present, a panel led by former RBI governor Bimal Jalan has been examining the applications. Chidambaram believes some need to look at different models as many people live without access to banking services.[61]

Types of Banking

Various types of banking are being discussed as below:

Branch Banking

According to *Investopedia* (2014), the branch banking is engaged in banking activities such as accepting deposits or making loans at facilities away from a bank's home office. Branch banking has gone through significant changes since the 1980s, in response to a more competitive nationwide financial services market. Financial innovation such as Internet banking will greatly influence the future of branch banking by potentially reducing the need to maintain extensive branch networks to service consumers. Branch banking networks are gradually evolving into multistate financial services networks, where depositors can access their accounts from any banking office.[62]

According to Sinha (2013), the rapid growth and wide popularity of branch banking system in the 20 century owe to various advantages. Under the system, the bank with a number of branches possesses huge financial resources and enjoys the benefits of large-scale operation. Another advantage of the system is the lesser risk and greater capacity to meet risks. Under the system, a particular branch can operate without keeping large amounts of idle reserves. In terms of the need, resources can be transferred from one branch to another. There is greater diversification of deposits and assets under the system, because of wider geographical coverage. Since the branches are spread over the whole country, it is easier and cheaper to transfer funds from one place to another. Inter-branch indebtedness is more easily adjusted than inter-bank indebtedness.

Under branch banking system, the mobility of capital increases, which in turn, brings about equality in interest rates. Funds are being transferred from areas with excessive demand for money to areas with deficit demand. As a result, the uniform rate of interest prevails in the whole area; it is prevented from rising in the excessive demand area and from falling in the deficit demand area. The customers' get better and greater facilities under the branch banking system.[63]

Unit Banking

Unit banking refers to a system, where the operations of the bank are confined generally to a single office. The United States of America is a typical country, which follows the unit banking system. The united banks are generally linked together by the correspondent bank system. Unit banking have the benefits like as: (i) each bank is small scale unit without any management and supervision. (ii) every bank is an independent unit. (iii) the system being a small scale independent unit; it can maintain good personal relation with the customer, (iv) the overhead cost will be lower than that incurred in case of branch making system, (v) it is free from the diseconomies and problems of large scale operation, (vi) weak, inefficient and non-profitable branches will be removed, (vii) the managers were given more discretionary powers, (viii) the managers are fully acquainted with local problem, (ix) there won't be any transfer of resources from rural to backward areas to behemoth industrial and commercial centers, and (x) it is possible to create socialistic pattern of society.[64]

According to Singha (2013), Unit banking is localized banking. The banks have full knowledge of and greater involvement in local problems. These are generally of small size. There is no possibility of generating monopolistic tendencies under unit banking system.[65] The following are the disadvantages of the system: (i) under unit banking, the bank operations are highly localized. (ii) limited resources restrict their ability to face financial crisis. (iii) the banks cannot afford to open uneconomic business in smaller towns and rural area. (iv) It has no branches at other places. As a result, it ought to depend upon the correspondent banks for some expensive transfer of funds, (v) since the banks are highly localized in business, local pressures and interferences generally disrupt their normal functioning.[66]

Group Banking

Group Banking is the system, wherein two or more independently incorporated banks are being brought under the control of some holding company. The latter may [may not] be a banking company. Under group banking, the individual banks may be unit banks, or banks operating branches or combination of the two. Participating banks retain their boards of directors, responsible to the supervising and regulatory authority and depositors for the proper operation of the bank, i.e. each bank in the group has got a separate entity. Group banking in the sense of holding companies in control of banks consists of a holding company with a majority share in two or more banks. The banks have their own boards and are run as independent entities, but the holding company controls their activities and has the power to outvote other shareholders.[67]

According to Singh (2013), the Group Banking System have the following advantages: the participating banks enjoy the benefits of centralized administration. (ii) the operational efficiency of participant banks is enhanced through shared knowledge and experience. (iii) group banking offers broader market to the small banks for their excess resources, and (iv) group banking paves the way for large scale operation. The member banks can get the economies of large scale operation. The disadvantages of the system are: (i) the control and management is ineffective for the control is indirect and more flexible. It cannot offer specialized management. (ii) the inefficiency of one partaking bank affects another. (iii) The system cannot provide facilities offered by branch banking, and (iv) it does not have the capacity to mobilize funds as that of branch banking.[68]

Mixed Banking[69]

Certain banks undertake commercial and industrial banking. This system is known as mixed banking. It attracts deposits and raises the capital and loans from the public and make them available to industries over short and long periods. The traditional view of banking was that commercial bank should strictly confine them to short term lending and maintain a high degree of liquidity, as they are traders in other's deposit. Such banks in Germany are known as universal bank. The need for mixed banking are (i) the industrial revival realized by the government and the banks. Many industrial units to which the banks had supplied short-term loans were not in a position to repay, (ii) The deposits of commercial banks were fast increasing, it was advisable for them advance loans for longer periods, (iii) The growth of big industries led to a decrease in the dependence of bank finance, as they have built up their own surplus funds to supplement the working capital, (iv) The government policy was for quick industrialization in countries like Germany and Japan. The bank undertook the responsibility of supplying long-term finance to industries for speedy industrialization, and (v) stock exchanges were increased for the marketability of securities of joint stock companies. The bank companies could sell them in the stock exchange at any time and convert them into cash.

The advantages of mixed banking are: (i) it grants short-term loans for purchase of raw materials and the payment of wages and salaries besides granting long-term loans for purchase of plant, machinery and other assets. (ii) a commercial bank raises large funds from the public by way of deposits. Many people do not like to subscribe shares and debentures of the industrial banks, because they prefer to keep money in various deposits, (iii)aA mixed bank appoints experts to access the soundness of industrial unit and evaluate its securities. It can provide various services to industrial undertaking like management of capital issues. It does so by short and long-term financial accommodation. The disadvantages of mixed banking are (i) it reduces bank liquidity, (ii) when a bank grants long-term loans, its funds find locked up for which it couldn't pay depositors when they demand it back, (iii) banks suffer heavy losses during depression, when the securities lose their value on fall in demand for sale of securities. The system of mixed banking has serious evils despite the fact that it has several advantages.

Chain Banking

Chain banking is a situation, where three or more independent chartered banks were found controlled by a small group of people. The mechanisms of such arrangement normally involves securing enough stock between the individuals to have a controlling interest in each of the involved bank corporations.. The arrangement can be managed with the establishment of interlocking directorates or boards of directors that effectively create a network between banks without the need for some central holding. The concept of chain banking is different from group banking, wherein the involved entities remain autonomous and are not owned by a single holding company. By contrast, the group banking model requires a holding company to own the involved banks, effectively creating an umbrella under which they operate. Chain banking is different from branch banking. It is a situation where its local branches are being owned by a single banking institution.[70]

Conceptually, it is a form of bank governance from a small group of people controlling at least three independently chartered banks. Usually, the controlling parties are majority shareholders or the heads of interlocking directorates. Chain banking as an entity has declined with the surge in interstate banking.[71] It has afforded several benefits for investors.

Such strategy has facilitated to earn steady returns from several banks in the same community, without any fear of a great deal of competition from other area banks.

The network approach facilitated investors use cumulative influence for services and their attendant fees similar from an enterprise to another, ensuring consistent returns. The chain banking process enables investors create a network, where each bank in the chain served a different part of the market within the area. Over time, the chain banking approach has become less popular in a number of nations. This is due to changes in banking laws therein that helped redefine the process of interstate as well as the international banking. This redefinition has made it possible for somewhat restricted banks in what they could offer customers a range of services.[72]

Correspondent Banking

An equal or unequal a financial institution on behalf of another conducting transactions, or accept deposits and gather documents. The correspondent banks are more likely to conduct oversea business as domestic bank's agent. Domestic banks use them for such transactions on their limited access failing to handle client accounts without opening up any branch in another country.[73]

Scotiabank is one of North America's leading financial institutions. It has distinguished since 1832 as the most international body of Canada's banks. The bank's commitment still holds global team of relationship. The product managers provide correspondence with expert, innovative and customized solutions.[74]

Narrow Banking

Narrow banking restrict the banks to hold liquid and safe government bonds. Loans would be made by another financial intermediaries, i.e., the deposit taking and payment activities would be separated from financial intermediation activities.[75] A *'Narrow Bank'* in its narrow sense, can be defined as that system under which it places funds in risk-free assets with maturity match period profile. The quality of assets remains intact without leading to emergence of sub-standard assets.

Indian banking system endorses the system partly, as banks mobilize appreciable deposits in government securities. It will serve as the safe avenue with low return for investment. The levels of NPA and capital adequacy ratio hung low. The risk weight factor for such securities is only 2.5 per cent compared to 100 percent on loan assets.[76]

Rural Banking

Rural banking is done in distant towns or cities, making it difficult for the aspirants. Often an agent of the bank offer services in the concerned area. The system won't have any impact in the US as it has in the rural belt of India, in India, Africa and elsewhere.[77]

Agriculture and rural development play an important role at home. The government has promoted the Regional Rural Banks [RRBs] through RRBs Act of 1976, to bridge the gap in the credit flow to the rural poor. The RRBs have a special place in the multi-agency approach in extending agricultural and rural credit. These banks are state-sponsored, regionally-based and rural -oriented. Besides, commercial and co-operative banks have been catering to the credit requirements from time to time.

Universal Banking

A universal bank partakes in many activities. It is a commercial entity and an investment bank extending insurance services. The concept is most relevant in the UK and the US, where a distinction between pure investment and commercial banks yielded variety of commercial and investment services. The system is common in some European countries, including Switzerland. However, in the US, these were required to separate commercial and investment services.

The advocates and opponents, as such, were divided over the extent of risk involved in the system.

The banks may offer credit, loans, deposits, asset management, investment advisory, payment processing, securities transactions, underwriting and financial analysis. Such banking system allows banks to offer a multitude of services; it does not require them to do so. Banks in a universal system may still choose to specialize in a subset of banking services.[78]

The benefits of universal banking are: (i) can hold stakes of many companies. (ii) results in economic efficiency, reduces cost, increase output and quality, (iii) uses the client's resources as per the client's ability on risk, (iv) diversify their activities, (v) can easily market financial products and services through many branches, and (vi) offers financial products and services under one roof.[79]

Banks were allowed to provide a variety of services. In universal banking, these were not limited to just loans, checking and savings accounts, and other similar activities, but were allowed to offer investment services as well. The system is less common in the US than in Europe.[80]

Former Union Finance Minister P.Chidambaram addressed at the Bharatiya Mahila Bank, New Delhi eulogizing it as the universal bank, establishing branches across India offering regular commercial products It would design and offer special products tailor -made towards the needs of women. It is expected to cater everybody from SHGs to lower middle class women on to high net worth individuals. He expected some 26 per cent of women to have bank accounts and whose per capita credit is currently 80 per cent, lower than that for men. He said, "there is deep seated bias, at the institutional and individual levels against women. Since fewer women have bank accounts, fewer women get bank loans. Hence, the need for a bank that caters predominantly to women's needs."

The minister added that "the seed we have sown today, when it branches out and flowers, it will bring enormous benefits to half the population of the country." Apart from the Nariman Point branch in Mumbai, Bharatiya Mahila Bank has six other branches at Kolkata, Chennai, Bangalore, Ahmedabad, Lucknow and Guwahati. Two other branches, in Delhi and Indore, were on the pipe line. The bank expects to open at least 25 branches eyeing a presence in every state capital. The bank network would be expanded in subsequent years to reach 770 branches by 2020, covering Tier- II and -III cities, rural areas and the unbanked area. An ambitious business plan to touch Rs. 60,000 crore total businesses (deposits plus advances) by 2020. BMB, headquartered in New Delhi, is being headed by Usha Ananthasubramanian, a public sector banker with 31 years of experience. The minister announced an eight ember all-women board of directors of the bank. The minister in his Union Budget 2013-14 announced about the setting up of all-women bank with an initial capital of Rs. 1,000 crore.[81]

Historically India's financial institutions have played a very significant role in meeting with the financing needs of long-term investments in economy, as an alternative source of long-term funds. Universal banking seeks to address over the issues of harmonizing the roles of DFIs and banks. Its definition differs from the globally accepted, more technical definition. In that context, universal banking carries somewhat larger and different connotation: it refers to the combination of commercial banking and investment. The issue that is of immediate concern in India's financial sector is harmonization of the roles of banks and DFIs.

The assets and liabilities of commercial banks are different from that of DFIs. The portfolios of universal banks consist largely of short-term assets and liabilities, but that of DFIs relatively on longer term ones. Banking sector reform process will pose challenges for banks and FIs, as they would then have to deal with risks galore anew, i.e., credit risk, interest rate risk, foreign exchange risk, etc.[82]

Social Banking

Social Banking describes the provision of banking and financial services that consequently pursue, as their main objective, a positive contribution to the potential of beings to develop. The focus remains on satisfying existing needs in the real economy and the society whilst simultaneously taking into account their social, cultural, ecological and economic sustainability, in anticipation of multiple returns.

Generating the monetary profit is not an end, but a frequent prerequisite to guarantee about the necessary flexibility in a continuously changing environment. The concept is ever conscious of its responsibility in dealing with money as a formative medium. It understands money, banking and finance as conceived means for meeting its objective. It describes a process, but not a steady state, about jointly identifying and testing creative new ways to come closer to the above-described objective. It involves multiple aspects and demands, which are sometimes conflicting and often necessitate compromise.[83]

Historically, social banks were founded in Italy in the 15th Century. The primary responsibility was to be an intermediary between those with money to save and those who needed for business. The variety, as such, was not a new concept, but an idea prevalent at home and abroad for longer period. Human beings seldom encourage business harming the very eco-system other than that sustainable in nature. It would understand the requirements of customers and develop such products best suited for their basic needs.

Social banking can contribute to poverty alleviation. Low cost products customized to the needs of the poor, affordable credit for entrepreneurial and emergency purposes, financial literacy initiatives, and awareness among the underprivileged about financial products and their utility are some of the services. Banks can also contribute towards making the poor creditworthy through training and counseling programmes. Though its initiatives were introduced through measures such as the cooperative banking movement, bank nationalization, creation of Regional Rural Banks, etc, their success was withheld by the size and population of the country and non-availability of banking services. The emergence of appropriate technology could enhance the scenario. The concept of social banking, despite inherent merits, faces several significant challenges in the scale-up process. An efficient business/delivery model capable of delivering services to the masses in a cost-effective manner is yet to be implemented by them.[84]

Online Banking

Online or Internet or E-banking allows customers of a financial institution to conduct transactions on a secured website operated by the institution. It can be a retail or virtual or credit union or building society, to access online facility, a customer having personal Internet access must register with its service, with Kapcha code and password (under various names) for customer verification. The password for online banking is normally not the same as for [telephone banking]. Institutions now routinely allocate numbers, whether or not, the customers intend to access such facility. The customer would go to the blog, and enter online facility using the customer number and password.

Some institutions have set up additional security steps for access, but there is no consistency to the adopted approach. The precursor for the modern home online banking services were the distance banking services over electronic media from the early 1980s. The term online became popular in the late '80s. It is being referred for the use of a terminal, keyboard and t.v. (or monitor), or access the banking system using a phone line. Security of a customer's information is very confidential. The institutions have set up various security processes to reduce the risk of unauthorized online access to a customer's records, but in vain.[85]

Mobile Banking

Mobile banking allows customers proceed with a number of financial transactions through a mobile phone or personal digital assistant. The earliest services were offered over SMS, a service known as SMS banking. Smart phones with WAP support enable the use of the mobile web in 1999. The first European banks started to offer mobile banking on this platform to customers.

Mobile banking is used in many parts of the world with or without infrastructure, especially in remote and rural areas. This is popular in countries, where appreciable population is unbanked. Banks can only be found in big cities, and customers have to travel hundreds of miles to the nearest bank.[86]

Some twelve million people used mobile banking services in 2009, according to a research firm, Frost & Sullivan. It went up to 45 million by 2014.

It has many advantages, such as good security, easy access and wider applications for smart phones.

Offshore Banking

An offshore bank is a bank located afar the country of the depositor, typically in a low tax jurisdiction that provides financial and legal advantages. The advantages include: greater privacy, low or no taxation, easy access to deposits and protection against local, political, or financial instability. Countries/territories conducting such business are called offshore financial centres. Some people endorse it as banking operation by non-resident persons in a jurisdiction.[87]. Offshore Banking Units is a shell branch located in an international financial center.

Offshore banking units (OBUs) make loans in the Eurocurrency market, when they accept deposits from foreign banks and other OBUs. The latter are not restricted by local monetary authorities or governments, but are being prohibited from accepting domestic deposits. These have proliferated across the continents since the 1970s and throughout Europe, as well as in the Middle East, Asia and the Caribbean. U.S. OBUs are concentrated in the Bahamas, the Cayman Islands, Hong Kong, Panama and Singapore.[88]

Offshore banking, has various advantages like as (i) providing access to politically and economically stable jurisdictions; (ii) may operate with a lower cost base and provide higher interest rates than the legal rate in the home country due to lower overhead costs and a lack of government intervention; (iii) help developing countries enhancing economies, and redistribute world finance from the developed to the developing world; (iv) Interest is generally paid without tax deduction; (v) offer banking services unavailable from domestic banks such as anonymous bank accounts, higher or lower rate loans based on risk and investment opportunities unavailable elsewhere.

The disadvantages are (i) less financially secure source. It swept the world in 2008, when some savers in those countries lost uninsured deposited funds. Those who had deposited onshore received their money back; (ii) offshore banking has been associated with the underground economy and organized crime, through money laundering; (iii) offshore jurisdictions were often remote and expensive making personal visit and data access quite difficult.

Offshore banking constitutes a sizeable portion of the international financial system. Experts believe that as much as half the world's capital inflows enter through these centers. Assuming even just the lower estimate of £13 trillion on deposit in offshore accounts, if these assets are being earned an average three per cent every year in income for their owners taxable at 30 per cent, then the offshore funds would generate £121 billion in tax revenues. The regulation of offshore banking is allegedly increasing, although critics maintain it remains largely insufficient. The quality of regulation is being monitored by supra-national bodies, such as the International Monetary Fund. Banks are generally required to maintain capital adequacy in accordance with international standards. They must report at least quarterly to the regulator on the current state of their business.viz., in terms of offshore banking centres, total deposits, as the global market is dominated by two key jurisdictions: Switzerland and the Cayman Islands.[89]

Core Banking

Core banking is group networked bank services. The customers may access funds and other simple transactions from any of the member branch offices. It is normally defined as the business conducted by a banking institution amongst retail and small business customers. Many banks treat the retail customers as their core banking customers, and have a separate line of business to manage small businesses. Larger businesses are being managed via the corporate banking division of the institution. Core banking basically is depositing and lending of money. Normal core banking functions include the deposit accounts, loans, mortgages and payments. Banks make these services available across multiple channels like ATMs, Internet banking, and branches.[90]

Core Banking Solution (CBS) is networking of branches. It enables customers operate their accounts, avail banking services from any of its branch on CBS network, regardless of where he maintains his account. S[He] won't be any more the customer, but become its customer. Thus CBS is a step towards enhancing customer convenience anywhere and anytime banking.[91]

Retail Banking

Retail banking is when a bank executes transactions directly with consumers, rather than corporations or other banks. Services offered include savings and transactional accounts, mortgages, personal loans, debit cards, and credit cards. The term is generally used to distinguish the banking services from investment banking, commercial banking or wholesale banking. It may also be used to refer to a division of a bank dealing with retail customers and can be termed as Personal Banking services.[92]

A retail bank is a bank that works with consumers, otherwise known as 'retail customers'. These banks provide basic services to the general public, including checking and savings accounts, CDs, safe deposit boxes, mortgages and second mortgages, auto loans, and unsecured and revolving loans such as credit cards.[93]

Wholesale Banking

Wholesale banking is the provision of services by banks to organizations such as mortgage brokers, large corporate clients, mid-sized companies, real estate developers and investors, international trade finance businesses, institutional customers, and services offered to other banks or other financial institutions. Modern wholesale banks are being engaged in: wholesaling financing, underwriting, market making, consultancy, mergers and acquisitions, fund management.[94]

It is a banking service between merchant banks and other financial institutions. Wholesale banking deals with larger institutions, whereas the retail banking would focus more on the individual or smaller business. Some services might include currency conversion, working capital financing and large trade transactions. This type of banking will provide services to other banks or large corporations. Some retail banking covers the business transactions, but not in the same scale as wholesale banking.[95]

The Differences:

[a] Branch Banking and Unit Banking[96]

Unit banking refers to a single bank. It renders services and operates without any branches elsewhere. This system is common in the US. Unit banking operate one full banking service. Branch banking center or financial center refers to a single bank, which operates through various branches in a city or in different locations or outside the cities. This system is common in India, i.e., State Bank of India.

Financial institutions reduce their costs by having no branches and present sometimes known as virtual banks. [See the chart]:

Area	Branch Banking	Unit Banking
Operational freedom	Less Operational freedom	More Operational freedom
Financial resources	Larger financial resources in each branch	Larger financial resources in one branch
Decision-making	Delay in Decision-making as they have to depend on the head office	Time is saved as Decision-making is in the same branch.
Cost of supervision	High	Less
Concentration of power in the hand of few people	Yes	No
Competition	High competition with the branches	Less competition within the bank
Profits	Shared by the bank with its branches	Used for the development of the bank
Distribution of Capital and power.	Proper distribution of capital capital and power.	No proper distribution of

[b] Commercial Bank and Private Bank[97]

According to Ingram (2014), a commercial bank is a type of bank that provides services such as accepting deposits, making business loans, and offering basic investment products. Private Banks are being owned by either an individual or a general partner(s) with limited partner(s), but are not incorporated. The creditors in any such case, can look into the "entirety of the bank's assets" as well as that of the sole-proprietor's/ general-partners' assets.

[c] Retail Banking and Corporate Banking[98]

According to Investopedia (2014), retail banking refers to the division of a bank dealing directly with retail customers. It is known as consumer banking or personal banking. Retail banking is the visible face of banking to the general public, with many branches in major cities. These focus purely on relatively few clientele through separate divisions – large and small. Corporate banking, also known as business banking, refers to the aspect of banking that deals with corporate customers.

Retail banking encompasses a wide variety of products and services. Customers are generally charged a monthly fee for checking - accounts; savings accounts offer slightly higher interest rates than checking accounts but generally cannot have cheques written on them. The level of personalized retail banking services offered to a client depends on his or her income level and the extent of the individual dealings with the bank. The corporate banking segment of banks typically serves a diverse range of clients, ranging from small to mid-sized local businesses with a few million in revenues to large conglomerates with billion in sales and offices across the country.

[d] Scheduled bank and Non-Scheduled Bank[99]

According to Willis (2013), scheduled banks at home are being in the RBI-II Schedule Act, 1934. The latter includes those banks in this schedule, which satisfy the criteria laid down vide section 42 (6) (a) of the Act. Nonscheduled banks also function in the banking space at home, in the form of Local Area Banks (LABs). There were only four LABs operating in India [March 31,2009]. LABs were set up under the government of India 1996 scheme for the establishment of new private banks of a local nature; with jurisdiction over a maximum of three contiguous districts.[100]

Scheduled banks comply with the classifications defined in the Second Schedule of the 1934 act. The criteria include paid-up capital, reserves, total value and certification by the RBI ensuring their fiduciary responsibilities to depositors. They include several nationalized banks, the State Bank of India, Regional Rural Banks and scheduled cooperative banks. Non-scheduled banks are depository or lending institutions away from of Reserve Bank of India Act - Schedule II. These banks may be legal entities, but won't have procedural endorsement.

[e] Public Bank and Private Bank[101]

A public sector bank operates through institutions owned by the people through their representative governments. The government controls the bank. A well-run public sector bank can help the state and local governments in sailing through cash crunch. The private banks are being managed and controlled by private promoters, who are free to operate under the market control. Their interest rates are generally costlier as compared to the public sector banks. The process has been expensive in the form of private banking. Generally, the private banks are being looked as a large organization with global operation.

The government holds a major share in public sector banks. Important decisions are being made by the government in the public interest . Their main aim is to carry out banking activities catering to all the sections of the society. On the other hand, a private bank mainly focuses on short-term interest. The objective is to carry out the banking activities connecting all the sections of the society. On the other hand, the private bank mainly focus on short-term interest. These seldom interfere with the government but the lack administrative support. The private sector banks have been using the advanced software to stay on in the business.

Private ownership brings competition, professionalism and operational efficiency. Public ownership makes it easier to pursue social objectives such as mass banking, financial inclusion etc. Private Banks have comparatively greater freedom in terms of recruitment, salary and compensation. PSBs on the other hand, are being perceived to offer more job security, with least employee turnover.

The job security comes as a part of the package. An employee is given several chances to improve one's performance, if there is any gap between the optimum and that output produced. Private sector banking is the right arena for ambitious people where the salary packages are better opportunities are more. The promotion is irrevocably tied to seniority, [public sector] whereas the go-getters willing to invest extra time and energy [private sector].[102]

References

1. <http://www.gkworld.org/2013/06/what-is-banking-and-features-of-banking.html>
2. Richard Hildreth (2001). The History of Banks, <http:// www.efm.bris.ac.uk/het/hildreth/bank.pdf>
3. An Overview of the Banking Sector (2014), Chapter 1, <http:// shodhganga.inflibnet.ac.in/bitstream/10603/2031/10/10_chapter%201.pdf>
4. State Bank of India (2014), <http://en.wikipedia.org/wiki/State_Bank_of_India>
5. An Overview of the Banking Sector, Chapter 1, <http:// shodhganga.inflibnet.ac.in/bitstream/10603/2031/10/10_chapter%201.pdf>
6. Vadlamani Ravi (2011), Introduction to modern banking technology and Management, <http://www.igi-global.com/chapter/introductionmodern-banking-technology-management/46233>

7. Commercial banks in India: A beginners module, <http:// www.nseindia.com/ content/ncfm/ncfm_CBBM_workbook.pdf>
8. Indian Banking-Introduction, <http://www.asiatradehub.com/india/banks.asp>
9. Commercial Banks in India: A beginners module, <http:// www.nseindia.com/ content/ncfm/ncfm_CBBM_workbook.pdf>
10. Public sector Banks in India (2014), <http:// www.bankpoexamsindia.com/ index.php/banking-awareness/public-sector-banksin-india>
11. Indian Financial System, <http://finance.indiamart.com/ investment_in_india/ nationalisation_banks.html>
12. Nationalized Banks in India, <http://dpprsystems.in/products/27/manual.pdf?>
13. Safina Ali, Short essay on Nationalization of Banks in India, <http:// www.preservearticles.com/201105136580/short-essay-on-nationalizationof-banks-in-india.html>
14. The Hindu (June 20, 2013), How private are public banks, <http:// www.thehindu.com/opinion/columns/Chandrasekhar/how-private-are-publicbanks/article4832977.ece>
15. P.Chellasamy and N.Sumathi, Role Of Banking System In India, <http:// www.rcssindia.org/main/online/files/journals/1/articles/199/submission/ original/ 199-350-1-SM.pdf>
16. Dr. Pallavi Singh, Banking in India: An Analytical Study on Trends and Progress, <http://mba.rkgit.edu.in/Final%20Book———RKGIT.pdf>
17. Public Sector Banks, <http://shodhganga.inflibnet.ac.in:8080/jspui/ bitstream/ 10603/3974/14/14_chapter%204.pdf>
18. State Bank of Saurashtra (2014), <http://en.wikipedia.org/wiki/State_Bank_of_Saurashtra>
19. State Bank of Indore (2014), <http://en.wikipedia.org/wiki/State_Bank_of_Indore>
20. State Bank of Bikaner and Jaipur (2014), <https://www.sbbjbank.com/About-Us/history.htm>
21. State Bank of Mysore (2014), <http://www.statebankofmysore.co.in/our-profile.html>
22. State Bank of Patiala (2014), <https://www.sbp.co.in/AboutUs.aspx>
23. State Bank of Travancore(2014),<http://www.statebankoftravancore.com/about-us.pdf>
24. Commercial Bank (2014), <http://en.wikipedia.org/wiki/Commercial_bank>
25. Investment Banking (2014), <http://en.wikipedia.org/wiki/Investment_banking>
26. Industrial Banks(2014), <http://www.investopedia.com/terms/i/industrial-bank.asp>
27. Banking awareness, <http://fi.ge.pgstatic.net/attachments/ aa482ddf26164c758f87f654400e28ae.pdf>
28. Agricultural Bank (2014), <http://en.wikipedia.org/wiki/Agricultural_Bank>
29. Exchange Bank (2014), <https://www.exchangebank.com/>
30. Savings Bank (2014), <http://en.wikipedia.org/wiki/Savings_bank>

31. Central Bank (2014), <http://en.wikipedia.org/wiki/Central_bank>
32. *Ibid.*
33. An Overview of the Banking Sector, Chapter 1, <http://shodhganga.inflibnet.ac.in/bitstream/10603/2031/10/10_chapter%201.pdf>
34. Central Banking (2006), Icfai university press, pp. 70-120.
35. Cooperative Banking (2014), <http://en.wikipedia.org/wiki/Cooperative_banking>
36. Cooperative Bank (2014), <http://shelf3d.com/i/cooperative%20bank>
37. Cooperative Banking (2013), <http://en.wikipedia.org/wiki/Cooperative_banking>
38. NABARD, <https://www.nabard.org/english/scbs.aspx>
39. Primary Agricultural Cooperative Credit Societies (2013), <http://www.agritech.tnau.ac.in/banking/crbank_cooperative_pacb.html>
40. D. Muraleedharan (2009). Modern Banking: Theory and Practice, p.42.
41. The Economic Times (Jan 16, 2013). Primary credit societies needs RBI nod to be a bank, <http://articles.economictimes.indiatimes.com/2013-01-16/news/36374087_1_credit-societies-cooperative-banks-bank-rate>
42. Regional Rural Bank (2014), <http://en.wikipedia.org/wiki/Regional_Rural_Bank>
43. Regional Rural Bank (2013), <http://oldsite.nabard.org/pdf/craficard/Chapter_07.pdf>
44. Development Bank (2013). <http://www.britannica.com/EBchecked/topic/160098/development-bank>
45. <http://www.nigeriasite.com/finance/banks2.html>
46. Export-Import Bank of India (2013), <http://www.eximbankindia.in/?q=organization>
47. Small Industries Development Bank of India (2013), <http://en.wikipedia.org/wiki/Small_Industries_Development_Bank_of_India>
48. NABARD (2013), <https://www.nabard.org/english/mission.aspx>
49. <http://en.wikipedia.org/wiki/Public_sector>
50. Private Sector Banks in India (2014), <http://en.wikipedia.org/wiki/Private-sector_banks_in_India>
51. Commercial bank (2014), <http://en.wikipedia.org/wiki/Commercial_bank>
52. H.L.Ahuja (2010), Macro Economics: Theory and Practice, pp. 270-73.
53. D. Muraleedharan (2009). Modern Banking: Theory and Practice, p.62.
54. H.L.Ahuja (2010), Macro Economics: Theory and Practice, p.277.
55. Mortgage Bank (2013). <http://en.wikipedia.org/wiki/Mortgage_bank>
56. Mortgage Banker, <http://www.investopedia.com/terms/m/mortgagebanker.asp>
57. About Mortgage Bankers, <http://homeguides.sfgate.com/mortgage-bankers-7426.html>
58. List the Functions of a Mortgage Bank, <http://www.ehow.com/list_5973462_list-functions-mortgage-bank.html>

59. Frances Burks, What Are the Responsibilities of a Mortgage Banker? Retrieved from <http://smallbusiness.chron.com/responsibilities-mortgage-banker-34830.html>
60. Niche Banks, <http://www.investopedia.com/terms/n/niche_banks.as>
61. The Telegraph (Nov 16, 2013), FM roots for niche banking, <http://www.telegraphindia.com/1131116/jsp/business/story_17575591.jsp#.UtK2zDtQHFw>
62. Branch Banking (2013), <http://www.investopedia.com/terms/b/branch-banking.asp>
63. Aparjita Sinha (2013), What are the various advantages of Branch Banking?, <http://www.preservearticles.com/201012281859/advantages-ofbranch-banking.html>
64. Unit Banking: Its Merits and Demerits, <http://www.gr8ambitionz.com/>
65. Aparajita Singha, What are the advantages of unit banking? <http://www.preservearticles.com/201012281861/advantages-of-unit-banking.html>
66. Aparajita Sinha (2013). What are the disadvantages of unit banking?, <http://www.preservearticles.com/201012281862/disadvantages-of-unitbanking.html>
67. What is group banking?, <http://www.wisegeek.com/what-isgroup-banking.htm>
68. Nupur Singh (2013). What are the advantages of group banking?, <http://www.preservearticles.com/2012033129386/what-are-the-advantagesof-group-banking.html>
69. Mixed banking-Its merits and demerits, <http://www.managementhub.com/cm-mixed-banking.html>
70. What is chain banking?, <http://www.wisegeek.com/what-is-chainbanking.htm>
71. Chain banking, <http://www.investopedia.com/terms/c/chainbanking.asp>
72. What is chain banking? <http://www.wisegeek.com/what-is-chainbanking.htm>
73. Correspondent Banking (2013) <http://www.investopedia.com/ terms/c/correspondent-bank.asp>
74. Correspondent Banking Services,<http://www.scotiabank.com/ ca/en/0,,3153,00.html>
75. Narrow Banking (2013). <http://en.wikipedia.org/wiki/Narrow_banking>
76. Narrow Banking (2013). <http://bankingindiaupdate.com/narrowbanking.htm>
77. What is Rural Banking?, <http://www.ask.com/question/ruralbanking>
78. Universal Banking (2013), <http://www.investopedia.com/terms/u/universalbanking.asp>
79. <http://kalyan-city.blogspot.com/2011/10/universal-banking-meaningadvantages.html>
80. Universal Banking (2013), <http://www.investorwords.com/6953/universal_banking.html>
81. The Hindu (November 20, 2013). Mahila bank to offer universal banking services, <http://www.thehindu.com/business/Industry/mahila-bank-tooffer-universal-banking-services/article5368575.ece>

82. Universal Banking in India (2012), <http://articles.economic times.indiatimes.com/2002-08-24/news/27339241_1_ universal-banking-dfisterm-funds>

83. Our definition of social banking, <http://www.social-banking.org/ the-institute/ what-is-social-banking/?

84. Social Banking and Finance – Opportunities in Inclusion, <http://www.rbi.org.in/ scripts/BS_SpeechesView.aspx?id=743>

85. Online banking (2013), <http://en.wikipedia.org/wiki/Online_banking>

86. Mobile banking (2013), <http://en.wikipedia.org/wiki/Mobile_banking>

87. What is offshore banking business? <http://www.centralbankbahamas.com/ faqs.php?cmd=view&id=10266>

88. Offshore banking units, <http://www.investopedia.com/terms/o/offshore-banking-unit.asp>

89. Offshore bank (2013), <http://en.wikipedia.org/wiki/Offshore_bank>

90. Core Banking (2013), <http://en.wikipedia.org/wiki/Core_banking>

91. Bank of Baroda (2013), <http://www.bankofbaroda.co.in/cbs.asp>

92. Retail Banking (2013). <http://en.wikipedia.org/wiki/Retail_banking>

93. Justin Pritchard (2013). Retail banking, <http://banking.about.com/ od/ businessbanking/a/retailbank.htm>

94. Wholesale banking (2013). <http://en.wikipedia.org/wiki/Wholesale_banking>

95. <http://www.investopedia.com/terms/w/wholesalebanking.asp>

96. <http://www.diffen.com/difference/Branch_Banking_vs_Unit_Banking>

97. David Ingram, Investment Bank Vs. Commercial Bank, <http:// smallbusiness. chron.com/investment-bank-vs-commercial-bank-3450.html>

98. Investopedia Staff on July 12, 2013, Retail banking vs corporate banking, <http:/ /www.investopedia.com/articles/general/071213/retailbanking-vs-commercial-banking.asp>

99. John Willis (2013). What Are the Functions of Scheduled & Non-Scheduled Banks?, <http://www.ehow.com/info_8693100_functionsscheduled-nonscheduled-banks.html>

100. Evolution of the Indian Banking Industry, <http:// www.dnb.co.in/ bfsisectorinindia/BankC2.asp>

101. <http://www.differencebetween.info/difference-between-public-sector-bank-andprivate-sector-bank>

102. Public Sector Banks vs. Private Sector Banks, <http:// www.tcyonline.com/bank-exam-preparation/private-public-sector-bank.php>

Chapter - 2

Reserve Bank of India

"The principle that a central bank, charged with controlling inflation, should be independent from the government is unassailable. It may also be true that it's easier for the central bank to guard its independence from political pressure when it mainly holds government securities." — ***Janet Yellen***

Introduction

According to Debelle and Fischer (2014), a central bank is the term used to describe the responsible authority for policies that affect a country's supply of money and credit. The case for an independent central bank is being increasingly accepted. The central banks of Chile, France, Mexico, New Zealand, and Venezuela have had their enhanced independence; the Maastricht treaty requires national central banks participating in the European System of Central Banks to meet a prescribed standard of independence; and a lively discussion is under way in Britain of the desirability of making the Bank of England, now explicitly subservient to the Treasury, independent.[1]

During the last two decades, many countries have reformed their central bank legislation with the objective of defeating inflation. One of the pillars of this reform was restricting the central bank financing of government, as this was a chronic source of inflation. Limiting such financing was considered critical for building central bank credibility, a key ingredient for achieving monetary policy effectiveness.[2] According to Bindseil et. al (2004), in the last two decades, the issue of commercial banks capital adequacy became one of the most analysed topics in banking and finance.

Banks, regulators and academics have devoted substantial resources to developing capital adequacy regulations that could be applied to banks everywhere in the world.[3]

History

According to Bordo (2007), the story of central banking goes back at least to the seventeenth century, to the founding of the first institution recognized as a central bank, the Swedish Riksbank. Established in 1668 as a joint-stock bank, it was chartered to lend the government funds and to act as a clearing house for commerce. A few decades later (1694), the most famous central bank of the era, the Bank of England, was founded also as a joint stock company to purchase government debt. Other central banks were similarly set up later in Europe , though some were established to deal with monetary disarray.[4]

The origins of the RBI can be traced to 1926, when the Royal Commission on Indian Currency and Finance, also known as the Hilton-Young Commission. It recommended the creation of a central bank for India to separate the control of currency and credit from the government and to augment banking facilities throughout the country. The Reserve Bank of India Act of 1934 established the Reserve Bank and set in motion a series of actions culminating in the start of operations in 1935. Starting as a private shareholders' bank, the Reserve Bank was nationalized in 1949. It then assumed the responsibility to meet with the aspirations of a newly independent country and its people. The Preamble to the Reserve Bank of India Act, 1934 (the Act), under which it was constituted, specifies its objective as "to regulate the issue of Bank notes and the keeping of reserves with a view to securing monetary stability in India and generally to operate the currency and credit system of the country to its advantage"[5]

Importance of Central Bank

According to Singha (2010), in the developing countries, the central bank has to play a much wider role. Besides performing the traditional functions, the central bank has to undertake responsibility of economic growth with stability in these economies.[6] According to Heakal (2010), RBI plays an important part in the development strategy of the Government of India. It is a member bank of the Asian Clearing Union. The bank is also active in promoting financial inclusion policy and is a leading member of the *Alliance for Financial Inclusion*. The central bank has been described as "the lender of last resort", it is responsible for providing its economy with funds when commercial banks seldom compensate a supply shortage. In other words, the central bank prevents the country's banking system from failing. However, the primary goal of central banks is to provide their countries' currencies with price stability by controlling inflation.[7]

The Structure

The structure of Reserve Bank of India is:

1. *Central Board of Directors*: The Central Board of Directors is at the top of the Reserve Bank's organizational structure. The Central Government nominates fourteen Directors on the Central Board, including one Director each from the four Local Boards. The other ten Directors represent different sectors of the economy, such as, agriculture, industry, trade, and professions. All these appointments are being made for a period of four years[8]
2. *Governors*: The current Governor of RBI is Raghuram Rajan. There are 4 Deputy Governors. Two of the Deputy Governors are traditionally from RBI ranks, and are selected from the Bank's Executive Directors. As for the rest, one is nominated from among the Chairpersons of Public Sector Bank, and the other is an economist of repute.[9]
3. *Local Boards*: The Reserve Bank also has four Local Boards, constituted by the Central Government under the RBI Act, one each for the Western, Eastern, Northern and Southern areas of the country, which are located in Mumbai, Kolkata, New Delhi and Chennai. Each of these Boards has five members appointed by the Central Government for a term of four years.
4. *Offices and Branches*:The Reserve Bank has a network of offices and branches through which it discharges its responsibilities. The units operating in the four metros — Mumbai, Kolkata, Delhi and Chennai are known as offices, while the units located at other cities and towns are called branches. Currently, the Reserve Bank has its offices, including branches, at 27 locations in India.[10]

The Subsidiaries

The Reserve Bank has the following fully - owned subsidiaries:

1. *Deposit Insurance and Credit Guarantee Corporation*: It is a subsidiary of Reserve Bank of India. It was established on 1961 under Deposit Insurance and Credit Guarantee Corporation Act,

Reserve Bank of India 1961 for the purpose of providing insurance of deposits and guaranteeing of credit facilities. It insures all bank deposits, such as saving, fixed current, recurring deposits for up to the limit of Rs. 100,000 of each deposit in a bank. The preamble of the Deposit Insurance and Credit Guarantee Corporation Act, 1961 states that it is an Act to provide for the establishment of a Corporation for the purpose of insurance of deposits and guaranteeing of credit facilities and for other matters connected therewith or incidental thereto.[11]

2. *National Housing Bank*: It was set up on July 9, 1988 under the National Housing Bank Act, 1987 as a wholly-owned subsidiary of the Reserve Bank to act as an apex level institution for housing. The Hon'ble Prime Minister of India, while presenting the Union Budget for 1987-88 on February 28, 1987 announced the decision to establish the National Housing Bank (NHB) as an apex level institution for housing finance. Following that, the National Housing Bank Bill (91 of 1987) providing the legislative framework for the establishment of NHB was passed by Parliament in the winter session of 1987 and with the assent of the Hon'ble President of India on December 23, 1987, became an Act of Parliament. The Head Office of NHB is at New Delhi.[12]
3. *Bharatiya Reserve Bank Note Mudran Private Limited*: It is the RBI one of the subsidiaries of the RBI, which prints bank notes (Indian rupees) for the apex bank. It was established in 1995 to address the demand for bank notes. It has two presses one in Mysore and Salboni.[13]
4. *National Bank for Agriculture and Rural Development* [NABARD]: It is an apex development bank in India having headquartered at Mumbai (Maharashtra) with branches are all over the country. It has been accredited with matters concerning policy, planning and operations in the field of credit for agriculture and other economic activities in rural areas in India. It is active in developing financial inclusion policy and is a member of the *Alliance for Financial Inclusion.* It is the apex institution in the country, which looks after the development of cottage industry, small industry and village industry, and other rural industries. Its refinance finds to State Co-operative Agriculture and Rural Development Banks, State Co-operative Banks, Regional Rural Banks, Commercial Banks and other financial institutions approved by RBI.[14]

Its Functions

According to Heakal (2010), a central bank can be said to have two main kinds of functions: macroeconomic when regulating inflation and price stability and microeconomic functioning as a lender of last resort. As it is responsible for price stability, the central bank must regulate the level of inflation by controlling money supplies by means of monetary policy. the central bank can buy government bonds, bills, or other government-issued notes. to increase the amount of money in circulation and decrease the interest rate for borrowing, The establishment of central banks as lender of last resort has pushed the need for freedom from commercial banking. A commercial bank offers funds to clients on a first come, first serve basis. If the commercial bank does not have enough liquidity to meet its clients' demands, the commercial bank can embrace to the central bank to borrow additional fund.[15]

A central bank is an entity responsible for the monetary policy of its country, or group of member states. The central bank's main responsibility is the management of monetary policy to ensure a stable economy, including a stable currency. It aims to manage inflation as well as deflation. Furthermore, it will hold foreign exchange reserves such as Dollar, Yen and Euro currencies and official gold reserves. The banks' role as the largest buyers of physical gold on the planet makes the decisions to buy or sell that gold one of the single most influential aspects of the market.[16]

The central bank now-a-days is primarily an agency for monetary policy. It has important financial stability functions, which became more prominent during times of financial turmoil. Appreciable majority of central banks operate under the presumption that they have a policy responsibility for financial stability. Monetary policy decision-making and implementation are the defining characteristics of central bank. Operations to support policy are prominent among the functions of central banks. The nature of such operations changed as central banks came to rely more heavily on transactions in open financial markets, dispensing with often distorting regulatory and administrative interventions in the process.[17]

Most countries have some form of Central Bank serving as the principle authority for nation's financial matters. A primary role for them is to supply operational capital to the country's commercial banks. Its primary duties include: (a) implement a monetary policy for that provides consistent growth and employment; (b) Promote the stability of the financial system; (c) Manage the production and distribution of the nation's currency; and

(d) Inform the public on the overall state of the economy by through economic statistics.[18]

Central Bank is viewed as one of the primary mechanisms of macroeconomic stabilization. A number of arguments about its areas of operation may vary on different legislations and the presence of various stakeholders.[19] Interest rates play the most important role in moving the prices of currencies in the foreign exchange market. As the institutions that set interest rates, central banks are the most influential actors. An increase in interest rates encourages traders invest within that market and causes the demand for currency to rise. As demand rises, the currency becomes scarcer and consequently more valuable.[20]

According to Mishkin (2011), increased transparency of monetary Policy-making is another important way to increase central bank accountability. Central banks need to communicate clearly on their monetary policy strategy in order to explain the objectives and how they plan to achieve them. Each time they change their policy instruments, such as the interbank interest rate, they need to clear state the decision and the rationale. Transparency through publication of its forecast and the minutes of discussion of monetary policy. In addition, they need to pursue many outreach vehicles to communicate with the public. These include the continual making of speeches to all elements of society, more openness with the press and media, and the development of brochures and accessible reports to the public.[21]

Management of currency is one of the core central banking functions of the Reserve Bank, for which it derives the necessary statutory powers from Section 22 of the RBI Act, 1934. The Reserve Bank carries out the currency management function through its Department of Currency Management located at its Central Office in Mumbai, 19 Issue Offices located across the country and a currency chest at its Kochi branch. The Government of India on the advice of the Reserve Bank decides on the various denominations of the notes to be printed. The RBI coordinates with the government in designing banknotes, including their security features. As a banker to the government, the RBI receives and pays money on behalf of the various government departments. As it has offices in only 27 locations, the Reserve Bank appoints other banks to act as nodal agents for undertaking banking business on behalf of the governments.

The RBI undertakes to float loans and manage them on behalf of the governments. It manages with the public debt and issues new loans on behalf of the Central and State Governments. It involves with the issue and retirement of rupee loans, interest payment on the loan and operational matters about debt certificates and their registration. The bank continuously monitors operations of the accounts to end up defaults. Among other provisions, the bank stipulates minimum balances to be maintained by banks in these accounts. The bank's regulatory and supervisory domain extends not only to the Indian banking system, but also to the development financial institutions, non-banking financial companies, primary dealers, credit information companies and select segments of the financial markets. In 1995, the bank introduced the system of primary dealers in the government securities market, which comprised independent entities undertaking Primary Dealer activity.[22]

Monetary Policy

One of the most important functions of central banks is the formulation and execution of monetary policy. In the Indian context, the basic functions of the RBI as enunciated in the Preamble to the RBI Act, 1934 are: "to regulate the issue of bank notes and keeping of reserves with a view to secure monetary stability and operate generally the currency and credit system of the country to its advantage." Over time, the objectives of monetary policy in India have evolved to include maintaining price stability, ensuring adequate flow of credit to productive sectors of the economy for supporting economic growth, and achieving financial stability. The Governor of the Reserve Bank announces the Monetary Policy in every April for the financial year that ends in the following March, followed by three quarterly reviews in July, October and January.

The bank traditionally relied on direct instruments of monetary control such as Cash Reserve Ratio and Statutory Liquidity Ratio. Cash Reserve Ratio indicates the quantum of cash that banks are required to keep with the Reserve Bank as a proportion of their net demand and time liabilities. It prescribes the amount of money that they must invest in securities issued by the government. In the late 1990s, the RBI restructured operating framework for monetary policy to rely more on indirect instruments such as Open Market Operations. The RBI had constituted a Technical Advisory Committee on Monetary Policy in July 2005 with a view to strengthen the consultative process in the conduct of monetary policy. The committee is chaired by the Governor, with the Deputy Governor in charge of monetary policy as the vice-chairman. The RBI holds resource management discussions meetings with select banks about one 45 days prior to the announcement of the Monetary Policy and the Second Quarter Review.[23]

References

1. Guy Debelle and Stanley Fischer (2014), Haw Independent Should a Central Bank be? <https://www.bostonfed.org/economic/conf/conf38/ conf38f.pdf>
2. Central Bank Credit to the Government: What Can We Learn from International Practices? <https://www.imf.org/external/pubs/ft/wp/2012/ wp1216.pdf>
3. Ulrich Bindseil, Andres Manzanares and Benedict Weller (2004), The role of central bank capital revisited, <https://www.ecb.europa.eu/pub/ pdf/scpwps/ ecbwp392.pdf>
4. Michael D. Bordo (2007), A brief history of central banks, <http:/ / www.clevelandfed.org/research/commentary/2007/1207.pdf>
5. Reserve Bank of India: Functions and Working, <http:// rbidocs.rbi.org.in/rdocs/ Content/PDFs/FUNCWWE080910.pdf>
6. Aparajita Singha, What are the important roles played by central bank in developing countries? <http://www.preservearticles.com/201012291869/role-of-central-bank-in-developing-countries.html>
7. Reem Heakal (2010), what are central banks? <http:// www.investopedia.com/ articles/03/050703.asp>
8. Reserve Bank of India, <http://en.wikipedia.org/wiki/Reserve_Bank_of_India>
9. Reserve Bank of India: Functions and Working, <http:// rbidocs.rbi.org.in/rdocs/ Content/PDFs/FUNCWWE080910.pdf>
10. Reserve Bank of India: Functions and Working, <http:// rbidocs.rbi.org.in/rdocs/ Content/PDFs/FUNCWWE080910.pdf>
11. Deposit Insurance and Credit Guarantee Corporation, <http:// en.wikipedia.org/ wiki/Deposit_Insurance_and_Credit_Guarantee_Corporation>
12. National Housing Bank, <http://www.nhb.org.in/AboutUs/ about_us.php# Preamble>
13. Bharatiya Reserve Bank Note Mudran Private Limited, <http:// en.wikipedia.org/ wiki/Bharatiya_Reserve_Bank_Note_Mudran_Private_Limited>
14. National Bank for Agriculture and Rural Development, <http:// en.wikipedia.org/ wiki/National_Bank_for_Agriculture_and_Rural_Development>
15. Reem Heakal (2010), what are central banks? <http:// www.investopedia.com/ articles/03/050703.asp>
16. Why are Central Banks Important? <http://www.blanchardonline. com/ investment_news/vol9_why.php>
17. Roles and objectives of modern central banks, <http://www.bis.org/ publ/ othp04_2.pdf>
18. The role of central bank, <http://fxtrade.oanda.com/learn/introto-currency-trading/fundamental-analysis/central-bank>
19. The role of central bank, <http://www.ivoryresearch.com/samples/ economics-essay-example-the-role-of-central-bank/>
20. Central bank and rate of Interest, <http://www.cmsfx.com/en/ forex-education/ online-forex-course/chapter-2-fundamental-factors/centralbank-interest-rates/>

21. Frederic S. Mishkin, What Should Central Banks Do? <http:// research. stlouisfed.org/publications/review/00/11/0011fm.pdf>
22. Reserve Bank of India: Functions and Working, <http:// rbidocs.rbi.org.in/rdocs/ Content/PDFs/FUNCWWE080910.pdf>
23. Reserve Bank of India: Functions and Working, <http:// rbidocs.rbi.org.in/rdocs/ Content/PDFs/FUNCWWE080910.pdf>
24. C.A.E. Goodhart, Central Banks' Function to Maintain Financial Stability: An Uncompleted Task, <http://graduateinstitute.ch/files/live/sites/iheid/files/sites/ international_economics/shared/international_economics/events/Swoboda/ Goodhart.pdf>
25. Challenges for central banks: wider powers, greater restraints: The financial crisis and its aftermath, <http://www.ey.com/Publication/vwLUAssets/Challenges_ for_central_banks_wider_powers_greater_restraints/$FILE/Challenges_for_ central_banks_wider_powers_greater_restraints.pdf Reserve Bank of India>

Chapter - 3

Commercial Bank

"It is not by augmenting the capital of the country, but by rendering a greater part of that capital active and productive than would otherwise be so, that the most judicious operations of banking can increase the industry of the country."

—***Adam Smith***

Introduction

Banks have played a critical role in the economic development of some developed countries such as Japan and Germany and some of the emerging economies including India. Banks today are important not just from the point of view of economic growth, but also financial stability. Forms of banking have changed over the years and evolved with the needs of economy. The transformation of banking system has been brought about by deregulation, technological innovation and globalization.[1]

A commercial bank is a type of bank that provides services such as accepting deposits, making business loans, and offering basic investment products. It can also refer to a bank or the division dealing with deposits and loans from corporations or large businesses, as opposed to individual members of the public.[2]

Commercial banking activities are different from those of investment banking, which include underwriting, acting as an intermediary between an issuer of securities and the investing public, facilitating mergers and other corporate reorganizations, and also acting as a broker for institutional clients.[3]

Commercial banks form a significant part of the country's Financial Institution System. They are profit seeking institutions accepting deposits from general public and advance money to individuals like household, entrepreneurs, businessmen etc. with the objective of earning profit in the form of interest, commission etc. Their operations find regulated by the RBI, which is the central nodal bank and supreme financial authority in India.[4] Broadly speaking, banks can be classified into commercial banks and central bank. Commercial banks provide banking services for prot. The central bank has the function of controlling commercial banks and various economic activities. There are many types of commercial banks such as deposit banks, industrial banks, savings banks, agricultural banks, exchange banks, and miscellaneous banks.[5]

The type

Commercial Banks refer to both scheduled and non-scheduled commercial banks, regulated under Banking Regulation Act, 1949. (a) Scheduled Commercial Banks find grouped under: SBI and its Associates; Nationalized Banks; Foreign Banks; Regional Rural Banks; Other Scheduled Commercial Banks. (b) NonScheduled Commercial Banks.[6] The commercial banking comprises Scheduled Commercial Banks and Unscheduled Banks. Scheduled commercial Banks have been included in the Second Schedule of RBI Act, 1934.

RBI in turn includes those banks in this schedule, which satisfy the criteria laid down vide section 42 of the Act. Some co-operative banks are scheduled commercial banks albeit not all co-operative banks. Being a part of the second schedule confers some benefits in terms of access to accommodation by RBI during the times of liquidity constraints. At the same time, however, this status subjects the bank certain conditions and obligation towards the reserve regulations of RBI.[7]

Evolution

The commercial banking industry in India started in 1786 with the establishment of the Bank of Bengal in Calcutta. The Indian government often established three Presidency banks, viz., the Bank of Bengal (Estd. 1809), the Bank of Bombay (Estd. 1840) and the Bank of Madras (Estd.1843). In 1921, the three Presidency banks were amalgamated to form the Imperial Bank of India, which took up the role of a commercial bank, a bankers' bank and a banker to the government.

The Imperial Bank of India was established with mainly European shareholders. After independence, the Government of India started taking steps to encourage the spread of banking in India. 14 of the major private sector banks were nationalized [1969] during the preliminary phase. This was an important milestone in the history of Indian banking. This was followed by the nationalisation of another six private banks in 1980. The major segment of the banking sector came under the control of the Government, following nationalisation.[8]

Functions

According to Saini and Sindhu (2014), these banks perform many functions. They satisfy the financial needs of sectors such as agriculture, industry, trade, communication, and play significant role in the process of economic social needs. These become customer-centered and are widening their functions. Generally, the functions are being divided into two categories: primary functions and the secondary functions. The banks perform various primary functions. They accept various types of deposits from public, especially from its clients, including saving account deposits, recurring account deposits, and fixed deposits.[9] Being a short-term credit dealer, they accept the savings of public in the form of Fixed-term deposits; Current A/c deposits; recurring deposits Savings A/c deposits; Tax saving deposits; Deposits for NRIs.[10]

The contributors above emphasized, the bank provides services such as accepting deposits, making business loans, and offering basic investment products. They become the conduits to function or remain general utility centres. Their secondary functions can be divided into agency functions and utility functions. The agency functions are: (a) to collect and clear cheque, dividends and interest warrant, make payments of rent, insurance premium, etc. and deal in foreign exchange transaction, purchase and sell securities; and act as trustee, attorney, correspondent and executor and accept tax proceeds and tax returns; besides (b) provide safety locker facility to customers, provide money transfer facility, issue travellers' cheque, act as referees, accept various bills for payment-phone bills, gas bills, water bills, etc., provide merchant banking facility and various cards: credit cards, debit cards, smart cards, etc.[11]

Any commercial bank accepts deposits from the public, for the purpose of lending. Deposits are the principal sources of funds. A depositor would ensure his/ her money as safe with the bank. The establishment of the Deposit Insurance Corporation in 1962 offered protection to bank depositors, particularly small account holders. The bank deposits can be classified into (i) demand deposits and (b) time deposits. Demand deposits are payable on demand through cheque or otherwise, without fixed term to mature. Time deposits are not payable on demand without drawing cheques cannot be drawn on a fixed term to mature.

The banks attempt to mobilize savings at the lowest possible cost, to maximize their profits. They devise various strategies to expand customer base and reduce the cost of raising deposits, customer-identifying target markets, designing the products as per requirements, taking measures for marketing and promoting the deposit products. As per the RBI guidelines, they are required to extend some services to depositors and recognise their rights. The ultimate objective of the banking industry should be to provide different customer services, rightfully entitled to receive without demand.[12]

In recent years, the banks, particularly in developing countries, have been called upon to help achieve certain socio-economic objectives laid down by the state. Under the Differential Interest Scheme, the nationalized banks in India advance loans to persons belonging to scheduled tribes, tailors, rickshaw-pullers/drivers, shoe-makers at the concessional rate of four per cent per annum. This avoids the cost of funds made available to priority sectors. The banks deal in foreign exchange, sell demand drafts, issue letters of credit and help remittance of funds abroad. They act as brokers in foreign exchange. They earn income out of such operations. The financial position of the bank finds reported in its balance sheet. The balance sheet is a statement of assets and liabilities. The assets of the bank are distributed in accordance with certain guiding principles.[13]

Types of Loan

Commercial bank generally gives two types of loans:

1. Secured loan: A secured loan is a loan, where the borrower pledges some asset as collateral, which becomes a secured debt owed to the creditor, who extend it. The debt is thus secured against the collateral. A mortgage loan is a very common type of debt instrument, used to purchase real estate. Under this arrangement, the money is being used to purchase the property. Changes in banking laws now allow the banks make home mortgage loans on a more liberal basis than ever before. In acquiring mortgages on real estate, these institutions follow two main practices.

2. Unsecured loans: Unsecured loans are not secured against the borrower's assets (no collateral is involved). There are small unsecured business loans, such as credit cards and credit lines to large corporate credit lines.

Its nationalization

It is a fact that 14 private banks were nationalized by the then Central Government headed by Prime Minister Indira Gandhi [July 19, 1969]. The history of nationalization of Indian banks dates back to the year 1955, when the Imperial Bank of India was nationalized and re-christened as State Bank of India (under the SBI Act, 1955). Later on July 19, 1960, the seven subsidiaries of SBI viz., State Bank of Hyderabad, State Bank of Indore, State Bank of Saurashtra, State Bank of Mysore, State Bank of Bikaner and Jaipur, State Bank of Patiala, and State Bank of Travancore found nationalized with deposits exceeding Rs. 200 crore.[14]

The private sector banks nationalized were: Central Bank of India, Bank of Baroda, Union Bank, Allahabad Bank, United Bank of India, UCO Bank, Bank of India, Indian Overseas bank, Bank of Maharashtra, Dena Bank, Punjab National Bank, Syndicate Bank, Canara Bank, and Indian Bank. Their drive was part of the focus on public sector growth.[15] In 1980, in order to provide government more power and command over credit delivery, six more commercial banks in India were nationalized. In 1993, New Bank of India merged with Punjab National Bank, which brought the number of nationalized banks in India to 19. It was the only merger between two Indian nationalized banks.

The nationalized banks in India saw a growth rate of around four per cent, close to average growth rate of country's economy in the subsequent period.[16]

Deposit Insurance and Credit Guarantee Corporation of India

In India, bank deposits are being covered under the insurance scheme offered by Deposit Insurance and Credit Guarantee Corporation of India. It was established with the RBI funding. The scheme is being subject to certain limits and conditions. It is a wholly-owned subsidiary of the RBI. All commercial banks, including branches of functioning foreign banks, local area banks and regional rural banks finds insured. Primary cooperative societies were not insured by the DICGC. In the event of its failure, DICGC protects bank deposits that are payable in India.[17] The functions of the DICGC are being governed by the provisions of 'The Deposit Insurance and Credit Guarantee Corporation Act, 1961' (DICGC Act) and 'The Deposit Insurance and Credit Guarantee Corporation General Regulations, 1961' framed by the RBI, in exercise of powers conferred by sub-section (3) of Section 50 of the said Act. The preamble of the Deposit Insurance and Credit Guarantee Corporation Act, 1961 states that it as an Act to provide for the establishment of a Corporation for the purpose of insurance of deposits and guaranteeing of credit facilities and for matters connected therewith or incidental thereto.[18]

Role of the Bank in the Economic Development

The banks form an important part of Indian financial landscape in terms of the role in channeling credit to the commercial sector and facilitating the process of financial inclusion. The banking sector, has retained its predominantly public character, with the onset of economic reforms. There were changes galore in terms of size, efficiency of operation and financial soundness.[19]

According to Thakur and Bhadauria (2013), the bank is a business organization, dealing in money, i.e., borrowing and lending, makes profit. The lending role of interest is higher than it pays to depositors. It is like any other business enterprise. It has performed the difficult task of maintaining equilibrium between liquidity and profitability. It is the custodian of depositor's money. The banks provide these days variety of services. They provide short-term credit and long-term credit. Their customers come from all walks of life from small business to a multinational corporation having its business activities around the world.[20]

Non-Performing Assets (NPA)

According to Rajeev and Mahesh (2010), the issue of non-performing assets, the root cause of the recent global financial crisis, has been drawing the attention of the policy makers and academicians alike. The problem, was ignored till recently, was given considerable attention after liberalisation of the financial sector in India. Broadly speaking, NPA is being defined as an advance payment of interest or repayment of installment of principal (in case of term loans) or both remains unpaid for a certain period. In India, the definition of NPAs has changed over time. According to the Narasimham Committee Report (1991), those assets (advances, bills discounted, overdrafts, cash credit etc.) for which the interest remains due for a period of four quarters (180 days) should be considered as NPAs. Subsequently, this period was reduced, and from March 1995 onwards the assets for which the interest remain unpaid for 90 days were considered as NPAs.[21]

According to Singh (2013), NPA have been classified into following four types: (a) Standard Assets: A standard asset is a performing asset. These generate income and repayments as and when they fall due. Such assets carry a normal risk and are not NPA in the real sense; (b) Sub-Standard Assets: The assets (loans and advances) are considered as non-performing ones for a period of twelve months; (c) Doubtful Assets: The assets were considered so for period exceeding twelve months; and (d) Loss Assets: The assets cannot be recovered at all.[22]

The Indian banking system is loaded with stressed assets. Gross NPAs of 40 listed banks that have announced earnings for the December 2013 quarter rose 36 per cent to Rs.2.43 trln from Rs.1.79 trln in the previous year. About Rs.4 trln of loans was recast by the banks through the RBI corporate debt restructuring mechanism, involving lenders writing off debt and rolling over some more, on a bilateral basis between individual banks and borrowers. Much of this hung on slowing economic growth, rash expansion by companies in the boom years between [2004-11] and delays in large projects from fuel shortages and problems related to land acquisition and environmental clearances.[23]

According to Singh (2013), the banking sector faced serious problems over hike in NPAs. In fact, public sector banks finds exposed to problems more than the private sector counterparts. The NPAs in public sector grew on external as well as internal factors. Under Directed loans system, the banks were required to supply 40 per cent of the credit to priority sectors. Significant sources of NPAs are direct loans, supplied to the micro sector whose recovery was in jeopardy, when some of their units went sick or weak. Most of the bankers believe genuine viability problem of the borrowing units, weakness in the credit appraisal system, absence of effective monitoring and supervision of loan account, absence of credit information sharing among the banks etc. were some of the causative factors of higher level of NPAs internal to the banks.[24]

The Times of India (May 26, 2014) reported, quoting the banking division of the Union finance ministry 'likely to pitch in for stricter measures to deal with non-performing loans and suggest consolidation of public sector banks to create stronger lenders. The ministry was about to make a case for early release of Rs. 8,000 crore, as part of its plans to infuse additional capital in the state- owned lenders. The 26 state-run banks together needed about Rs. 4.15 lakh crore in capital infusion for lending growth under the

Basel guidelines. The government was unable to meet this demand due to its own weak fiscal position and has allocated just Rs. 11,200 crore towards bank capitalisation in the current fiscal year, substantially lower than the amount infused in previous years. The banks presented various options to mobilize capital. The ministry has directed the banks improve their current and savings accounts ratio up to 40 per cent and focus on recoveries.[25]

Conclusion

Commercial bank provides preliminary services such as accepting deposits, making business loans, and offering basic investment products. They satisfy the financial needs of the sectors such as agriculture, industry, trade, communication in the process of economic social needs. The functions performed by banks, since recently, became customer-centred and have been widening their functions. These perform several secondary functions, including many agency related functions or general utility functions.

References

1. Commercial banking in India: A Beginners Module, <http://www.nse-india.com/content/ncfm/ncfm_CBBM_workbook.pdf>
2. Commercial Bank (2014), <http://en.wikipedia.org/wiki/Commercial_bank>
3. Commercial Bank (2014), <http://www.investopedia.com/terms/c/commercial bank.asp>
4. Commercial banks in India, <http://business.mapsofindia.com/finance-commission/institutions/commercial-banks.html>
5. Commercial banking, <http://www.newagepublishers.com/ samplechapter/001636.pdf>
6. Reserve Bank of India, Directory of Bank Offices, <http:// www.rbi.org.in/scripts/certainconcepts.aspx>
7. Commercial banks, <http://www.banknetindia.com/banking/ combank.htm>
8. Commercial banking in India: A Beginners Module, <http:// www.nse-india.com/content/ncfm/ncfm_CBBM_workbook.pdf>
9. Priyanka Saini & Jyoti Sindhu, Role of Commercial Bank in the Economic Development of India, International Journal of Engineering and Management Research, Volume-4, Issue-1, February-2014, <http://www.ijemr.net/Feb2014 Issue/RoleOfCommercialBankInTheEconomicDevelopmentOfIndia(27-31).pdf>
10. Commercial banks in India, <http://business.mapsofindia.com/ finance-commission/institutions/commercial-banks.html>
11. Priyanka Saini and Jyoti Sindhu, Role of Commercial Bank in the Economic Development of India, International Journal of Engineering and Management Research, Volume-4, Issue-1, February-2014, <http://www.ijemr.net/Feb2014 Issue/RoleOfCommercialBankInTheEconomicDevelopmentOfIndia(27-31).pdf>

12. Commercial banking in India: A Beginners Module, <http:// www.nse-india.com/ content/ncfm/ncfm_CBBM_workbook.pdf>
13. Commercial banking, <http://www.newagepublishers.com/ samplechapter/ 001636.pdf>
14. Nationalised Banks in India, <http://business.mapsofindia.com/ banks-in-india/ nationalised-banks-in-india.html>
15. Nationalization of private banks 1969, <http://vannamboodiri.com/2013/07/19/ nationalisation-of-private-banks-in-1969/>
16. Nationalised Banks in India, <http://business.mapsofindia.com/ banks-in-india/ nationalised-banks-in-india.html>
17. Commercial banking in India: A Beginners Module, <http:// www.nse-india.com/ content/ncfm/ncfm_CBBM_workbook.pdf>
18. Deposit Insurance and Credit Guarantee Corporation of India, <http:// en.wikipedia.org/wiki/ Deposit_Insurance_and_Credit_Guarantee_Cor poration>
19. Operation and Performance of Commercial Banks, Chapter IV, <http:// rbidocs.rbi.org.in/rdocs/Publications/PDFs/04CPT081110.pdf
20. Dr. K. S. Thakur & Dr. Anuja Bhadauria, A comparative studies of commercial banks of India (With Special Reference to State Bank of India and Central Bank of India), <http://www.jmveindia.com/Jan-Mar.pdf>
21. Meenakshi Rajeev & H P Mahesh (2010), Banking Sector Reforms and NPA: A study of Indian Commercial Banks, <http://www.isec.ac.in/WP%20252%20-%20Meenakshi%20Rajeev%20and%20H%20P% 20 Mahesh. Pdf>
22. Asha Singh (2013), Performance of Non-Performing Assets in Indian Commercial Banks, International Journal of Marketing, Financial Services & Management Research, Vol.2, No. 9, <http://indianresearchjournals.com/pdf/IJMFSMR/2013/ September/9.pdf>
23. Why United Bank of India is in trouble, <http://www.livemint.com/Industry/ VnlzhCFna00JkvqP5XtUoK/Why-United-Bank-of-India-is-introuble.html>
24. Asha Singh (2013), Performance of Non-Performing Assets in Indian Commercial Banks, International Journal of Marketing, Financial Services & Management Research, Vol.2, No. 9, <http://indianresearchjournals.com/pdf/IJMFSMR/2013/ September/9.pdf>
25. The Times of India (May 26, 2014). Finance ministry may pitch for stricter norms for non-performing assets, <http://timesofindia.indiatimes.com/business/ india-business/Finance-ministry-may-pitch-for-stricter-norms-fornon-performing-assets/articleshow/35617869.cms>

Chapter - 4

Regional Rural Bank

Introduction

According to Ahmad et. al. (2013), Profitability is the basic objective of every business as well as motivating force behind the running of a firm. Opinions differ sharply with regard to the definition of profit, but in general, it is the difference between total revenue and total cost over a period of time. Social profit is the difference between social benefit and social cost. It is yet difficult to find out social profit due to absence of an accurate measuring concept. It is the ability of a given investment to earn return from use. The profitability is a significant index of operational efficiency of banks. The higher degree of profit earning will entail prosperity of the organization. The banks are highly responsive organizations, open to public security and must continuously ensure their profitability, essential for growth and viability as also for infusing public confidence.[1]

According to Ibrahim (2012), activities of modern economy are significantly influenced by the functions and services of banks. Banking sector constitutes the core part of economic system. Indian economy is agricultural economy and real India lies in villages. Village economy is the backbone of Indian economy. Rural people belonging to small and marginal farmers, landless agricultural laborers, artisans and socially and economically backward castes and classes, have been exploited in the name of credit facility by informal sectors.

Regional Rural Banks are being constituted to meet the financial and banking needs of weaker sections of rural areas with a special attention on small and marginal farmers, agricultural labourers, artisans, landless farmers, small traders, tint [?] enterprises etc. In general, RRBs are commercial banks, but adopt some principles of cooperatives, such as location in areas, work for rural population in a limited area etc. Introducing priority sector lending is the most successful and advantageous decision of the government of India. Majority of domestic industries are agro based.[2]

History

According to Shashikumar (2013), the RRBs were introduced to meet the excess demand for institutional credit in rural areas, particularly among the economically and socially marginalized sections. Although, the cooperative banks and the commercial banks had reasonable records in terms of geographical coverage and disbursement of credit, population groups, the cooperative Banks were dominated by the rural rich, while the commercial counterparts had a clear urban bias. In this connection, the government of India conducted a survey on Rural Banks, under the chairmanship of Narasimham in 1975.

The committee recommended for an urgent need of experimentation, especially to improve the rural credit. In this context, the government set up RRBs on October 2, 1975.[3] The development process of RRBs started on October 02, 1975 with the forming the first RRB, the Prathama Bank. Five regional rural banks were set up on October 02, 1976, with a total authorised capital of Rs. 100 crore ($ 10 Million) which was later augmented to 500 crore ($ 50 Million).[4]

Needs

Regional Rural Banks are the banking organizations in different states of India. They have been created to serve the rural areas with banking and financial services. Its main purpose is to mobilize financial resources from rural /semi-urban areas and grant loans and advances mostly to small and marginal farmers, agricultural laborers and rural artisans. The area of operation of RRBs is limited to the area as notified by the government of India covering one or more districts in the State. RRB's also perform a variety of functions.[5]

According to Shashikumar et. al (2013), the major objectives of the RRBs are to develop the rural economy by providing credit facilities for agriculture, trade, commerce, industries and other productive activities in rural areas, particularly to the small and marginal farmers. Further, these were instrumental in extending credit for poverty alleviation schemes. It is felt them being instrumental in recognizing the diversified economic activities in rural areas. These are the third important financial institutions in the Indian Banking system.[6] The idea behind their establishment is to develop a comparatively backward area, where the density of commercial bank and co-operative is relatively poor. The main difference from the commercial bank is that the area of operation finds confined to a region comprising one or two contiguous districts. One of the tasks envisaged was to maintain their cost of operation at a lower level than that of the commercial banks. So, the salary structures of the staff were comparable to that of the state government employees.[7]

At Home

According to Ibrahim (2012), RRBs occupy an important position in the rural credit market. Loans extended to the needy people have been categorized into two. One is priority sector and the other being the non-priority sector. The priority sector bank lending is an active instrument of Indian financial policy with an aim to restore sectoral balance within disbursement and channel credit to the weaker sections of the society. Priority sector is a sector, which is given priority in offering financial services by banks. The concept of priority sector was brought into the financial system following the imposition of social control in 1968. These were directed to lend some percentage of loans to the sectors shortlisted in the priority sector. Agriculture is the mainstay of Indian economy. More than 70 per cent of the population depends on agriculture and its allied activities.

The RRBs take care of this sector by providing short-term and term-loans. The disbursement of term-loans for agriculture and allied activities by them are not quite encouraging. It has been increased to Rs. 3,648 crore [2008-09) from Rs.1, 045 crore [2002-03]. There was 3.49 time increase over the period. RRBs provide loan to various groups have been increasing year after year. The loans to rural artisans showed an increase of 2.3 times, from Rs.238 crore [2002-03] to Rs.552 crore [2008-09]. Likewise, all the groups have been provided loans by the RRBs in an increasing amount.[8]

According to Mishra (2006), RRBs have been in existence for around three decades in the domestic financial scene. Their inception can be seen as a unique experiment as well as experience in improving the efficacy of rural credit delivery mechanism in India. Their genesis can be traced to the need for a stronger institutional arrangement for providing rural credit. The Narsimham committee conceptualized their creation in 1975 as a new set of regionally-oriented rural banks, which would combine the local feel and familiarity of rural problems, characteristic of cooperatives with the professionalism and large resource base of commercial banks.

It is common to expect that their financial health could be a matter of concern with built-in restrictions.

There were 163 RRBs [2003-04] earning profits amounting to Rs 953 crore, while 33 RRBs incurred losses to the extent of Rs.184 crore. Ninety RRBs had accumulated losses as on March 31, 2004. Aggregate accumulated loss of RRBs amounted to Rs. 2,725 crore [2003-04]. Of the loss making 90 RRBs, 53 had eroded funds owned as part of deposits. Furthermore, non-performing assets (NPAs) of the RRBs in absolute terms stood at Rs.3,299 crore [As on March 31, 2004]. The percentage of gross NPAs was 12.6 [March 31, 2004]. 103 RRBs had gross NPAs less than the national average, while 93 had NPAs more than it.[9]

According to Shashikumar et. al. (2013), by 1991, there were 196 RRBs with over 14,000 predominantly rural branches in 476 districts with an average coverage of three villages per branch. These banks had disbursed over Rs. 3,500 crore in credit and mobilized over Rs. 4,100 crore in deposits. Perhaps, their most significant achievement was enabling weaker sections of the rural community access to institutional credit.

Table 1: Regional Rural Banks

Sl No.	*Name of the RRB*	*H.O.*	*State*
1.	Allahabad UP Gramin Bank	Banda	Uttar Pradesh
2.	Andhra Pradesh Grameena Vikas Bank	Warangal	Andhra Pradesh
3.	Andhra Pragathi Grameena Bank	Kadapa	Andhra Pradesh
4.	Arunachal Pradesh Rural Bank	Naharlagun	Arunachal Pradesh
5.	Aryavart Gramin Bank	Lucknow	Uttar Pradesh
6.	Assam Gramin Vikash Bank	Guwahati	Assam
7.	Baitarni Gramya Bank	Baripada	Orissa
8.	Ballia Etawah Gramin Bank	Ballia	Uttar Pradesh
9.	Bangiya Gramin Vikash Bank	Murshidabad	West Bengal
10.	Baroda Gujarat Gramin Bank	Bharuch	Gujarat
11.	Baroda Rajasthan Gramin Bank	Ajmer	Rajasthan
12.	Baroda UP Gramin Bank	Raebareilly	Uttar Pradesh
13.	Bihar Kshetriya Gramin Bank	Munger	Bihar
14.	Cauvery Kalpatharu Grameena Bank	Mysore	Karnataka
15.	Chaitanya Godavari Grameena Bank	Guntoor	Andhra Pradesh
16.	Chhatisgarh Gramin Bank	Raipur	Chhattisgarh
17.	Chikmagalur Kodagu Grameena Bank	Chikmagalur	Karnataka

(Contd...)

18.	Deccan Grameena Bank	Hyderabad	Andhra Pradesh
19.	Dena Gujarat Gramin Bank	Gandhinagar	Gujarat
20.	Durg Rajnandgaon Gramin Bank	Rajnandgaon	Chhattisgarh
21.	Ellaquai Dehati Bank	Srinagar	Jammu and Kashmir
22.	Gurgaon Gramin Bank	Gurgaon	Haryana
23.	Hadoti Kshetriya Gramin Bank	Kota	Rajasthan
24.	Haryana Gramin Bank	Rohtak	Haryana
25.	Himachal Gramin Bank	Mandi	Himachal Pradesh
26.	J &K Grameen Bank	Jammu	Jammu & Kashmir
27.	Jaipur Thar Gramin Bank	Jaipur	Rajasthan
28.	Jhabua Dhar Kshetriya Gramin Bank	Jhabua	Madhya Pradesh
29.	Jharkhand Gramin Bank	Ranchi	Jharkhand
30.	Kalinga Gramya Bank	Cuttack	Orissa
31.	Karnataka Vikas Grameen Bank	Dharwad	Karnataka
32.	Kashi Gomti Samyut Gramin Bank	Varanasi	Uttar Pradesh
33.	Krishna Grameena Bank	Gulbarga	Karnataka
34.	Kshetriya Kisan Gramin Bank	Mainpuri	Uttar Pradesh
35.	Langpi Dehangi Rural Bank	Diphu	Assam
36.	Madhya Bharath Gramin Bank	Sagar	Madhya Pradesh
37.	Madhya Bihar Gramin Bank	Patna	Bihar
38.	Mahakaushal Kshetriya Gramin Bank	Jabalpur	Madhya Pradesh
39.	Maharashtra Gramin Bank	Nanded	Maharashtra
40.	Malwa Gramin Bank	Sangrur	Punjab
41.	Manipur Rural Bank	Imphal	Manipur
42.	Meghalaya Rural Bank	Shillong	Meghalaya
43.	Mewar Anchalik Gramin Bank	Udaipur	Rajasthan
44.	MGB Gramin Bank	Marwar	Rajasthan
45.	Mizoram Rural Bank	Aizwal	Mizoram
46.	Nagaland Rural Bank	Kohima	Nagaland
47.	Nainital Almora Kshetrsaiya Bank	Haldwani	Uttarakhand
48.	Narmada Malwa Gramin Bank	Malwa	Madhya Pradesh
49.	Neelachal Gramya Bank	Bhubaneswar	Orissa
50.	North Malabar GraminBank	Kannur	Kerala
51.	Pallavan Grama Bank	Salem	Tamil Nadu
52.	Pandyan Grama Bank	Virudhnagar	Tamil Nadu
53.	Parvatiya Gramin Bank	Chamba	Himachal Pradesh
54.	Paschim Banga Gramin Bank	Howrah	West Bengal
55.	Pragathi Gramin Bank	Bellary	Karnataka
56.	Prathma Bank	Moradabad	Uttar Pradesh
57.	Puduvai Bharthiar Grama Bank	Puducherry	Puducherry
58.	Punjab Gramin Bank	Kapurthala	Punjab
59.	Purvanchal Gramin Bank	Gorakhpur	Uttar Pradesh
60.	Rajasthan Gramin Bank	Alwar	Rajasthan
61.	Rewa Sidhi Gramin Bank	Rewa	Madhya Pradesh

(Contd...)

62.	Rushikulya Gramya Bank	Berhampur	Orissa
63.	Samastipur Kshetriya Gramin Bank	Samastipur	Bihar
64.	Saptagiri Grameena Bank	Chittoor	Andhra Pradesh
65.	Sarva UP Gramin Bank	Meerut	Uttar Pradesh
66.	Satpura Narmada Kshetriya Gramin Bank	Chhindwara	Madhya Pradesh
67.	Saurashtra Gramin Bank	Rajkot	Gujarat
68.	Sharda Gramin Bank	Satna	Madhya Pradesh
69.	Shreyas Gramin Bank	Aligarh	Uttar Pradesh
70.	South Malabar Gramin Bank	Mallapuram	Kerala
71.	Surguja Kshetriya Gramin Bank	Ambikapur	Chhatisgarh
72.	Sutlej Gramin Bank	Bhatinda	Punjab
73.	Tripura Gramin Bank	Agartala	Tripura
74.	Utkal Gramya Bank	Bolangir	Orissa
75.	Uttar Banga Kshetriya Gramin Bank	Coochbehar	West Bengal
76.	Uttar Bihar Gramin Bank	Muzzafarpur	Bihar
77.	Uttaranchal Gramin Bank	Dehradun	Uttarakhand
78.	Vananchal Gramin Bank	Dumka	Jharkhand
79.	Vidharbha Kshetriya Gramin Bank	Akola	Maharashtra
80.	Vidisha Bhopal Kshetriya Gramin Bank	Vidisha	Madhya Pradesh
81.	Visveshvaraya Grameena Bank	Mandya	Karnataka
82.	Wainganga Krishna Gramin Bank	Solapur	Maharashtra

Source: http://www.ibps.in/career_pdf/CWE_RRB_Advertisement.pdf

Agriculture and rural sector play an important role in India's overall development. RRBs were formed through RBI Act of 1976 to provide the credit to the rural poor. These were expected to evolve as specialized rural financial institutions for developing the rural economy by extending credit to small and marginal farmers, agricultural labourers, artisans and small entrepreneurs.[10]

Procedure for Appointment

The Institute of Banking Personnel Selection is an autonomous body. It is being registered under the Societies Registration Act 1860 and a Public Trust under Bombay Public Trust Act 1950.

Written Examination

As per the procedure for recruitment, aspirant individual to join as the Regional Rural Bank, either as an Officer (Scale-I, II & III), or as an Office Assistant (Multipurpose) will necessarily be required to qualify through the Common Written Examination (CWE). Successful candidates in the CWE who have been issued scorecards and who meet with the stipulated eligibility criteria will then be required to apply to any RRB they wish to, quoting their registration no., roll no. etc. Each Regional Rural Bank will individually shortlist their candidates and carry out their own selection processes such as Interviews etc. for final selection. The candidate may also be required to possess proficiency in the Official Language of the State/UT for which vacancies, s/he wishes to apply to be eligible as per the notifications of the participating RRB.

Prospective candidates should ensure they shall fulfill the specified eligibility criteria, before applying for the CWE. However it should be noted that the eligibility criteria specified is the basic criteria for applying to various RRBs.

However merely applying for and qualifying in CWE does not imply that the candidate will necessarily be eligible for employment in all [any particular] RRB, as each bank will stipulate its own eligibility/qualifying criteri, followed by Interviews etc.

i.e., (a) Nationality/Citizenship:

A candidate must be either a citizen of India or a subject of Nepal or a subject of Bhutan or a Tibetan refugee, who came over to India before January 01, 1962 with the intention of permanently settling in India; or a person of Indian origin who has migrated from Pakistan, Burma, Sri Lanka, East African countries of Kenya, Uganda, the United Republic of Tanzania (formerly Tanganyika and Zanzibar), Zambia, Malawi, Zaire, Ethiopia and Vietnam with the intention of permanently settling in India, provided that a candidate belonging to categories above shall be a person in whose favour a certificate of eligibility has been issued by the Government of India.

(b) Age:

For Officer Scale- III- below 40 years; For Officer Scale- II- above 21 years -Below 32 years; and For Officer Scale- I- Above 18 years - Below 28 years.[11]

Amalgamation of RRBs

According to Bose (2012), for the first time in the year 1989, the conceptualization of the entire structure of RRB was challenged by the Agricultural Credit Review Committee (Khusro Committee), which argued that these banks have no justifiable cause for continuance and recommended their mergers with sponsor banks. At the time such a policy move was politically unthinkable, so the RBI and the government of India quite prudently pushed the Khusro Committee report under the carpet without a public debate.[12]

According to Soni and Kapre (2012), the Committee on Financial Systems, 1991 (Narasimham Committee) stressed over the exclusion of every other performance indicator on poor financial health of the RRBs. 172 of the 196 RRBs were recorded unprofitable with an aggregate loan recovery performance of 40.8 percent. (June 1993). performance of 40.8 percent. (June 1993). The low equity base of these banks (paid up capital of Rs. 25 lakh) didn't cover for their loan losses. A few RRBs, there had also been eroded of public deposits, besides capital. In order to impart viability to the operations of RRBs, the Narasimham Committee suggested these be permitted to engage in all types of banking business, ignoring of restricting to target groups. The acceptance of the proposal served as a major turning point in the functioning of RRBs.[13]

The RBI in 2001 constituted a committee under the chairmanship of Dr V S Vyas on "Flow of Credit to Agriculture and Related Activities from the Banking System" which examined their relevance in the rural credit system for some viable alternatives. The consolidation process was initiated in the year 2005 as an off-shoot of Dr Vyas Committee recommendations. The first phase of amalgamation was initiated sponsor bankwise within a State in 2005 and the second phase was across those sponsor banks within a State in 2012. The process was initiated for better customer service by better infrastructure, computerization, experienced work force, common publicity and marketing efforts etc. The amalgamated RRBs also benefit from larger area of operation, enhanced credit exposure limits for high value and diverse banking activities. As a result of amalgamation, the number of the RRBs has been reduced from 196 to 64 [As on 31 March 2013]. The number of branches of RRBs increased to 17, 856 [As on 31 March 2013] covering 635 districts throughout the country.[14]

Subsequent to review of their financial status by the Union Finance Minister in August, 2009, it was felt that a large number of RRBs had a low Capital to Risk weighted Assets Ratio (CRAR). A committee was constituted in September, 2009 under the chairmanship of or K C Chakrabarty, Deputy Governor, RBI to analyse their financial outcome, to suggest measures including re-capitalisation to bring their CRAR to at least nine percent in a sustainable manner by 2012. The committee submitted its report in May, 2010.[15]

RRB Act 1976

It is an Act to provide for the incorporation, regulation and winding up of Regional Rural Banks with a view to developing the rural economy by providing, for the purpose of development of agriculture, trade, commerce, industry and other productive activities in the rural areas, credit and other facilities, particularly to the small and marginal farmers, agricultural laborers, artisans and small entrepreneurs, and for matters connected therewith and incidental thereto. It extends to the whole of India. It shall be deemed to have come into force on the September 26, 1975. The central government may, if requested so to do by a sponsor bank, by notification in the Official Gazette, establish in a State or Union territory, one or more RRBs with such name as may be specified in the notification and may, by the said or subsequent notification, specify the local limits within which each RRB shall operate. Every RRB shall be a body corporate with perpetual succession and a common seal with power, subject to the provisions of this Act, to acquire, hold and dispose of property and to contract and may sue and be sued in its name. It shall be the duty of the sponsor bank to aid and assist the RRB. Subject to the provisions of this Act, the general superintendence, direction and management of the affairs and business of an RRB shall vest in a board of directors, who may exercise all the powers and discharge all the functions, which may be exercised or discharged by the RRB. The Board shall often act on business principles and shall have due regards to public interest. A director (other than the chairman) shall hold office for such period not exceeding two years, from the date of his assuming office, as the authority nominating him[her] may specify at the time when the nomination is made, and may, on the expiry of the said period, continue to hold office, until his successor has been nominated and shall also be eligible for re-nomination. The Board of directors of any RRB shall meet at such time and place and shall observe such rules of procedure in regard to the transaction of business at its meetings as may be prescribed. The chairman of the RRB shall preside over every board meeting, and, in his absence, such director as the chairman may generally, or in relation to any particular meeting, authorise in his/her behalf shall preside; and, in the absence of both the chairman and the director so authorised, the directors present at the meeting shall elect one from among themselves to preside over the meeting.

Every RRB shall carry on and transact the business of banking as defined in clause (b) of section 5 of the Banking Regulation Act, 1949 (10 of 1949), and may engage in one or more forms of business specified in sub-section (1) of Section 6 of that Act. Notwithstanding anything contained in this Act, if the Central Government, after consultation with the National Bank, the concerned State Government and the Sponsor bank is of the opinion that it is necessary in the public interest or in the interest of the development of the area served by any RRB or in the interest of the RRBs themselves, that two or more RRBs should be amalgamated, that government may, by notification in the Official Gazette, provide for the amalgamation of such RRB into a single RRB with such constitution, property, powers, rights, interests, authorities and privileges; and with such liabilities, duties and obligations, as may be specified in the notification. An RRB shall, in the discharge of its functions, be guided by such directions in regard to matters of policy involving public interest as the central government may, after consultation with the RBI. Any question arising, whether any such direction relates to a matter of policy involving public interest, the decision of the central government thereon shall be final.[16]

Challenges Ahead!

According to Chand (2014), major problems faced by regional rural banks are as follows: (a) haste and lack of co-ordination in branch expansion; (b) difficulties in deposit mobilisation; (c) constraints in deposit mobilisation; (d) slow progress in lending activity; (e) urban oriented staff; and (f) procedural rigidities. The RRBs, in most cases, seemingly have a mixed record of 'successes' on some fronts and 'failures' on some others in their business and attainment of goals.[17]

According to Singh (2012), the recovery performance of the RRBs is not up to the mark. Lack of training facility concerning these areas also affects the growth of RRBs. Lack of co-ordination between the RRBs and sports or banks regarding branch expansion, policy making, etc., are also the important causes for the slow progress of RRBs. Out of 196 RRBs [1997-98], 70 RRBs incurred losses amounting to Rs. 230.76 crore in total. The accumulated losses of RRBs [Up to the end of March 1998] amounted to Rs. 3,116.00 crore. This may be due to heavy overhead costs, reduction in lending rates, lower profit margins, heavy increase in salaries and allowances of staff, etc.[18]

Conclusion

According to Bose (2012), RRBs play a vital role in the domestic agriculture and rural development. The institution was created to meet the excess demand for institutional credit in the rural areas, particularly among the economically and socially marginalised sections. Although, the cooperative banks and the commercial banks had reasonable records in terms of geographical coverage and disbursement of credit, in terms of population groups, the cooperative banks were dominated by the rural rich, while the commercial banks had a clear urban bias.[19]

The RRBs were allowed to lend outside [w.e.f. March 22, 1997] the target group by classifying their advances into 'Priority Sector' and 'others'. Similarly, the interest rates on term deposits they offer been freed. Subsequently, it has been decided to permit them, at their discretion, to offer differential rate of interest on term deposits of maturity subject to certain conditions.

References

1. J. U. Ahmed, G.P. Bhandari, Rohima Ahmed, Profitability of Regional Rural bank in India: An empirical analysis in Meghalaya Rural Bank, Journal of Rural and Industrial Development, Volume 1 Issue 1 April 2013, <http://www.publishingindia.com/Uploads/SampleArticles/JRID-Sample-Article.pdf>
2. Dr. M.S.Ibrahim, Role of Indian Regional Rural Banks in the Priority Sector Lending: An Analysis, International Management Journal, Vol. 1 No. 1-2 (January-December, 2012), <http://journalshub.com/mrp-admin/ journal/pdf/3—imj2012.pdf>
3. T.P. Shashikumar; K. Rangaswamy; S.P. Kiran, Regional rural bank in India and Karnataka: A time series analysis, International Journal of Marketing, Financial Services & Management Research, Vol.2, No. 2, February 2013, <http://indianresearchjournals.com/pdf/IJMFSMR/2013/February/13.pdf
4. Regional Rural Bank, <http://en.wikipedia.org/wiki/Regional_Rural_Bank>
5. *Ibid.*
6. T.P. Shashikumar; K. Rangaswamy; S.P. Kiran, Regional rural bank in India and Karnataka: A time series analysis, International Journal of Marketing, Financial Services & Management Research, Vol.2, No. 2, February (2013), <http://indianresearchjournals.com/pdf/IJMFSMR/2013/February/13.pdf
7. Regional rural Bank, Retrieved from http://tnau.ac.in/eagri/eagri50/AECO241/pdf/lec07.pdf
8. Dr. M.S.Ibrahim, Role of Indian Regional Rural Banks in the Priority Sector Lending: An Analysis, International Management Journal, Vol. 1 No. 1-2 (January-December, 2012), <http://journalshub.com/mrp-admin/ journal/pdf/3—imj2012.pdf>
9. Biswa Swarup Misra, The Performance of Regional Rural Banks (RRBs) in India: Has Past Anything to Suggest for Future? Reserve Bank of India Occasional Papers, Vol. 27, No. 1 and 2, Summer and Monsoon 2006, <http://rbidocs.rbi.org.in/rdocs/Publications/PDFs/73534.pdf>
10. T.P. Shashikumar; K. Rangaswamy; S.P. Kiran, Regional rural bank in India and Karnataka: A time series analysis, International Journal of Marketing, Financial

Services & Management Research, Vol.2, No. 2, February (2013), <http://indianresearchjournals.com/pdf/IJMFSMR/2013/February/13.pdf>

11. Common Written Examination, <http://www.ibps.in/career_pdf/CWE_RRB_Advertisement.pdf>
12. Sukanya Bose, Regional Rural Banks: The Past and the Present Debate, <http://www.macroscan.net/pdfs/rrb_debate.pdf>
13. Anil Kumar Soni and Abhay Kapre, Performance evaluation of Regional Rural Banks in India, ABHINAV Journal, Volume 1, Issue 11, <http://www.abhinavjournal.com/images/Commerce_&_Management/Nov12/12.pdf>
14. Regional rural banks-NABARD, <https://www.nabard.org/English/ rrbs.aspx>
15. Regional Rural Banks: Conceptions and present scenario, <http://aaptgyan.com/regional-rural-banks-conception-present-scenario>
16. Regional Rural Bank Act 1976, <http://mahagramin.in/downloads/ rrb_act_1976.pdf>
17. Smriti Chand, Major Problems faced by Regional Rural Banks of India, <http://www.yourarticlelibrary.com/banking/6-major-problems-faced-byregional-rural-banks-of-india/26344/>
18. Nupur Singh, Difficulties Faced By Regional Rural Banks, Retrieved from, <http://www.preservearticles.com/2012033129454/9-difficultiesfaced-by-regional-rural-banks.html>
19. Sukanya Bose, Regional Rural Banks: The Past and the Present Debate, <http://www.macroscan.net/pdfs/rrb_debate.pdf>

Chapter - 5

Cooperative Bank

"Investment banking has, in recent years, resembled a casino and the massive scale of gambling losses has dragged down traditional business and retail lending activities as banks try to rebuild their balance sheets. This was one aspect of modern financial liberalization that had dire consequences."

— ***Vince Cable***

Introduction

According to Singh and Pundir (2014), India, since time immemorial, has been, and still continues to be, will remain in the foreseeable future, a land of village communities. Rural development is being influenced by a multitude of factors, such as natural resources, human resources, capital, technology, public policies, and institutions and organisations. Organisations affect rural development in many different ways, including the provision of production inputs and services, reduction of transaction costs, enhancement of bargaining power of rural producers vis-à-vis, those to whom they sell their produce, and from whom they buy production inputs and services, facilitating investments and savings and bringing the two together and so on. Gandhiji saw a great virtue in co-operation as an instrument of rural development. He assigned specific roles to co-operatives in the field of agriculture, commending the promotion of co-operative farming and thereby preventing further fragmentation of land holdings. Pt. Jawahar Lal Nehru, the first Prime Minister of India, also had a strong faith in the co- operatives.[1]

According to Mitra (2012), banks in India can be broadly classified under two heads- commercial banks and co-operative banks. While commercial banks (nationalized banks, State Bank group, private sector banks, foreign banks and regional rural banks) account for an overwhelming share of the banking business, co-operative banks also play an important role. Co-operative banks are a group of financial institutions, organized under the provisions of the cooperative society's act of the states. These banks are essentially co-operative credit societies, organized by members to meet their short-term and medium-term financial requirements. A cooperative is an autonomous association of persons united voluntarily to meet their common economic, social and cultural needs and aspirations through a jointly owned and democratically enterprise. Mutual co-operation leads to co-operatives.[2]

History [Cooperative Movement]

It is concerned with the origins and history of cooperatives. Although, cooperative arrangements, such as mutual insurance, and principles of cooperation existed long before, the cooperative movement began with the application of cooperative principles to business organization. The history of such movement in India is about a century old. It was started in India with a view to encourage and promote thrift and mutual help for the development of persons of small means such as agriculturists, artisans and other segments of the society. The 1904 Act was largely based on the English Friendly Societies Act, 1896. Under this Act, only primary credit societies were permitted to register and non-credit and federal organisations of primary co-operative credit societies were left out. This lacuna was bridged by the Co-operative Societies Act, 1912.[3]

The movement in India had its origin elsewhere and was introduced to this region by foreign rule. But even after independence, the movement continued in the planned economy. The movement has been recognized as an effective instrument for the economic development of the rural masses and for improvement in the socioeconomic conditions of the neglected. It was basically organized against the moneylenders to rescue farmers from the clutches of their poverty and indebtedness. The need for agricultural credit through co-operatives was felt because of rural indebtedness. The Indian co-operative movement was initiated by the government; it spread and diversified with the encouragement and support of the government.[4]

The co-operative movement completed its 50 years dump, the first plan. The Golden Jubilee was celebrated throughout the country with much fanfare and euphoria. This made the people feel the importance of such movement. Attention was given to utilise the credit in productive activities.[5]

What is Cooperative Bank?

A co-operative bank is a financial entity, which belongs to its members, who are at the same time, the owners and the customers of their bank. Cooperative banks are often created by persons belonging to the same local or professional community or sharing a common interest. Co-operative banks generally provide the members with a wide range of banking and financial services (loans, deposits, banking accounts...).

Co-operative banks differ from stockholder banks by their organization, goals, values and governance. In most countries, they are supervised and controlled by banking authorities and have to respect prudential banking regulations, which put them at a level playing field with stockholder banks. Depending on countries, this control and supervision can be implemented directly by state entities or delegated to a co-operative federation or central body.[6]

Basic Needs

The co-operative bank provides personal banking services, including credit cards, current accounts, free online banking, personal loans, savings and more. It is retail and commercial banking organized on co-operative basis. The banking institutions take deposits and lend money in most parts of the world. Co-operative banking, includes retail banking, as carried out by credit unions, mutual savings and loan associations, building societies and co-operatives, as well as commercial banking services from manual organizations (such as co-operative federations) to co-operative businesses.[7] Rural Cooperative Banking and Credit Institutions play an important role in meeting the growing credit needs of rural India. The volume of credit flowing through these institutions as increased.

Characteristics

According to Agrawal and Solanke (2012), in rural parts of India even today the required capital or funds for agricultural activities were raised through unorganized money market agencies i.e. money lenders who were providing moneys act higher rate of interest. The co-operative banks has been moved towards rural areas for overcoming such problems and providing the capital required through short term and long terms borrowings at a reasonable rate of interest. The characteristics of the co-operative bank are (1) The main theme is serving i.e. no profit or no loss; (2) They are based on the principles of cooperation, self help and mutual help; (3) The banks are the first government sponsored, supported and subsidized financial agency in India; (4) The banks have had a three-tier linkage structure and straight line integration; (5) These belong to small scale banking and the average size of whom is quite small; (6) They are subject to monetary policy control and their regulations were earlier controlled by the RBI. They have been deregulated; (7) The borrowings are made by them through RBI, NABARD and other APEX Institutions; and (8) They are featured by functional organizations.[8]

Bank Structure

The co-operative banking structure comprises two main components,—urban co-operative banks and rural co-operative credit institutions. Rural cooperatives have complex structure, in comparison Rural cooperative credit institutions have two distinct structures, viz., the short-term co-operative credit structure (STCCS) and the long-term cooperative credit structure (LTCCS). Primary agricultural credit societies (PACS) within the STCCS, at the village level form the base level, while the district central co-operative banks (DCCBs) are placed at the intermediate level, and the State cooperative banks (SCBs) at the apex level. The STCCS mostly provide crop and other working capital loans primarily for a short period to farmers and rural artisans. The long-term structure of rural co-operatives comprises State co-operative agriculture and rural development banks (SCARDBs) at the State level, and primary co-operative agriculture and rural development banks (PCARDBs) at the decentralized district or block level.[9]

According to the Economic Times (May 13, 2002), India's co-operative banking structure consists of two main segments, viz., agricultural and non-agricultural credit. The co-operative credit structure for short and medium terms is a three-tier one with primary agricultural credit societies at the base level, the central co-operative bank at the district level and state cooperative bank at the apex level.

1. *Primary Agricultural Credit Societies*: Primary Agricultural Credit Societies (PACS) are the foundation of the co-operative credit structure and form the largest number of co-operative institutions in India. Most of these societies have been organised mainly to extend credit facilities and inculcate the habit of thrift and economy among their members. The share capital of a society is divided into units, called shares, contributed by the members. The most important source of finance of PACS is members' deposits. Primary (urban) credit societies that meet certain specified criteria can apply to RBI for a banking license to operate as urban

cooperative banks. Primary (urban) co-operative banks are registered and governed by state governments under the respective cooperative societies acts of the concerned states.[10]

2. *District Co-operative Bank*: District Co-operative Banks (DCBs) occupy the middle level position in the three -tier co-operative credit structure of the country. The Co-operative Societies Act of 1912 permitted the registration of DCBs. Some DCBs were established to cater to the needs of primary societies, even before the enactment of this Act. The funds of the bank consist of share capital, deposits, loans and overdrafts from state co-operative banks and joint stocks. These banks provide finance to member societies within the limits of the borrowing capacity of societies. They also conduct all the business of a joint stock bank.
3. *State Co-operative Banks*: The State Co-operative Banks (SCBs) or the apex banks occupy a crucial position in the three-tier cooperative credit structure in India. These apex banks or State Cooperative Banks are formed by federating DCBs in each state. The apex banks assume a key-position in the co-operative credit structure, because the financial assistance from RBI and the National Bank for Agriculture and Rural Development are invariably routed through them.[11]

Cooperative Banks in India

According to Gupta and Jain (2012), co-operative banks are small-sized units organized in the cooperative sector for urban and non-urban regions. These banks are traditionally-centered on communities, localities and work place groups and they essentially lending small borrowers and businesses. The term Urban Co-operative Banks (UCBs), though not formally defined, refers to primary cooperative banks located in urban and semi-urban areas. These banks provide most services such as savings and current accounts, safe deposit lockers, loan or mortgages to private and business customers. For middle class users, for whom a bank is where they can save their money, facilities like Internet banking or phone banking is not very important.[12]

According to Babu, and Selkhar (2012), the cooperative bank is also regulated by the RBI. They are governed by the Banking Regulations Act 1949 and Banking Laws (Co-operative Societies) Act, 1965. A co-operative bank is defined as "a financial entity which belongs to its members, who are at the same time the owners and the customers of their bank. The term

Urban Cooperative Banks (UCBs), although not formally defined, refers to the primary cooperative banks located in urban and semi-urban areas. These banks, until 1996, were allowed to lend money only to non-agricultural purposes."[13]

The cooperative banks/credit institutions constitute the second segment of Indian banking system, comprising about 14 per cent of the total banking sector asset. The bulk of these banks operates in the rural regions with rural banks accounting for 67 per cent of the total asset and 67 per cent of the total number of branches of these banks.[14] The cooperative credit structure in our country has two separate structures- the short-term and the long-term credit structures. The short-term credit structure consists of the primary agricultural credit societies at the base level, affiliated at the district level into the district central cooperative bank and further into the state cooperative bank at the state level. The DCCB being the middle-tier of the cooperative credit structure, it is functionally positioned to deal with the concerns of both the upper and lower tiers.

The DCCBs are banking entities recognised by the RBI under the Banking Regulations Act. The cooperatives also offer term loans to farmers. These can be delivered either through the PACs or directly to the farmers by the DCCBs. For such financing, the DCCBs can obtain refinance from higher lending agencies like NABARD, who channelize these funds through the state cooperative banks. As per Section 18 of the Banking Regulation Act-1949 [As applicable to Cooperative Societies (AACS)], every cooperative society is required to maintain cash reserve ratio equivalent to three percent of its demand and time liability.[15]

According to the daily Business Standard (May 28, 2014), RBI has advised the urban co-operative banks (UCBs) to refrain from giving large loans to public sector or government entities, saying these transactions go against the core functions of these lenders. It has defined UCBs as loan providers to lower and middle income groups, as well as agriculture and small businesses, instead of government-owned companies. Grant of higher value loans to PSUs is not consistent with the co-operative principles and dilutes the cooperative character of UCBs. UCBs, in view of the above, are advised, as a matter of principle, generally not to grant large value loans to Public Sector/Government Undertakings.[16]

According to Mitra (2012), the Urban Co-operative Bank refers to the primary co-operative banks meeting the banking and credit requirements of urban and semi urban people and protect them from exploitation. One of the vital problems, which vitiate the cooperative banking is the inability of borrower to repay their contractual obligations of interest and principal, leading to Non-Performing Assets. The presence of NPA has had an adverse impact on the productivity and efficiency of UCB.[17]

The Economic Times (Oct 23, 2013) reported about nearly 96,000 co-operative banks to have spread over thousands of villages and post offices located in 2.38 lakh panchayats. The co-operative banks have catered to more people than private ones have, which for the first time came into vogue more than 100 years ago influenced by the co-operative movement in the West. In India, they came into existence mostly through local community initiatives. These banks have come to grief, because of poor governance, poor lending practices, and the bad loans they are saddled with, and not because of providing a very important deposit facility to the poor people. The co-operative banks could be converted with some tight regulations that would help mobilise savings, and at the same time, make them safe.[18]

The Economic Times reported (May 8, 2014), about many smaller and co-operative banks offering around 1.5-2 per cent additional interest on fixed deposits than nationalised banks and private sector banks. For example, Punjab and Maharashtra Co-operative Bank offers 10.5 per cent for an 18-month deposit, Abhinav Sahakari Bank offers 10 per cent for 37 months, Nasik Merchants Co-operative Bank offers 10 per cent for 15-18 months, and Municipal Co-operative Bank offers 10 per cent for 30 months.[19] The Economic Times (Mar 19, 2014)reported, about the RBI to have penalised the Andhra Pradesh-based District Co-operative Bank with Rs 5 lakh fine for non-adherance of KYC and anti-money laundering norms. Earlier, the central bank had issued a show cause notice to the bank in response to which the bank had submitted a written reply. However, after considering the facts, RBI penalised the bank with the monetary fine.[20]

The Economic Times (April 24, 2014) reported, all cooperative banks to have agreed to participate in National Rural Livelihood Mission, where women self-help groups will get subsidised loan on the pattern of commercial banks, said the government of Himachal Pradesh. The banks in the state were performing well and surpassed the targeted budget by disbursing a fresh credit of Rs. 9,265 crore for various activities [Up to December, 2013]. As many as 54 new bank branches were opened [quarter ending December, 2013] raising the total number of branches to 1,760 in the state.[21]

The Economic Times (Mar 13, 2012) reported, West Bengal State Cooperative Bank to have criticised the stance taken by the chief minister Mamata Banerjee when mortgaged properties of defaulters could not be attached by lenders. This is a very serious issue and if the mortgaged properties of willful defaulters are not attached, then the entire cooperative structure in the state will collapse. The chief minister had said that properties of defaulters, who had taken loan from the cooperative system could not be attached and necessary amendments would be made to the West Bengal Co-operative Societies Act of 2006. During the current financial year, loans disbursements by the cooperative banks to agriculture and allied sectors would be around Rs 5,500 crore.[22]

The Tripura State Cooperative Bank Limited was established on 21-01-1957 with its headquarters at Agartala. It has proved to be the flag-bearer among the Cooperative Credit Institutions in the country since inception. It is channeling cooperative credit through its member district cooperative central banks and primary agricultural cooperative. The loan portfolio of TSCB covers crop loans, medium-term loans and long -term loans for agricultural purposes. TSCB is also extending finance to many apex cooperative institutions in the state.[23]

LDB

According to Singh (2012), Land Development Banks have developed a special technique for conducting their business. They obtain funds, not in the shape of short-term deposits like commercial banks, but by the issue of long-dated debentures, sometimes carrying state government guarantee with regard to payment of interest and repayment of principal. They could lend money for longer periods to agriculturists. On account of their importance to the nation, they have enjoyed special powers for the recovery of defaulted loans, exemption from taxes and in some cases, the state guarantee for these bonds. Land Development Banks in India are of quasi-commercial type.

The Land Development Banks derive their funds from share capital reserves, deposits and debentures. They are subscribed for by the public or the government in some cases, the principal and interest of these debentures are guaranteed by the government. The loans granted by land development banks are repayable within 20 to 30 years. The LDBs are now called (state co-operative) Agriculture and Rural Development Banks (ARDBs), since they are providing long-term funds for various agriculture related projects besides development of land.[24]

The first LDB was started at Jhang in Punjab in 1920. Even though the first LDB was started in Punjab, the real progress began when the LDB was established in Chennai in 1929. Without it, land banks, land mortgage banks, agriculture banks, agriculture development banks are now called land development banks in modern world.[25]

UCB

The term Urban Co-operative Banks[UCBs], though not formally defined, refers to primary co-operative banks located in urban and semi-urban areas. These banks, till 1996, were allowed to lend money only for non-agricultural purposes. The origins of the UCB movement in India can be traced to the close of nineteenth century. They mainly rely upon deposits from members and non-members and in case of need, they get finance from either the district central co-operative bank to which they are affiliated or from the apex co-operative bank, if they work in big cities, where the apex bank is headquartered.

The RBI appointed a high power committee in May 1999 under the chairmanship of Shri. K. Madhava Rao, Ex-Chief Secretary, Government of Andhra Pradesh to review the performance of Urban Co-operative Banks and to suggest necessary measures to strengthen this sector.[26] According to Gnanasekaran et. al. (2012), UCBs have to play an important role in meeting with the requirements of small traders, weavers, agriculturists and other lower and middle income group of people. Recently, these have been directed to concentrate their efforts towards the industrial development and other priority sectors of the economy. The progress of the UCBs consists a detailed and systematic assessment of selective variables like share capital, deposits, loans and advances etc.[27]

Restructuring Cooperative Bank

The government of India, is committed to reviving and revitalizing the rural cooperative credit structure and attributes high priority besides commissioning the review afresh. The Union Government constituted a task force to formulate practical and implementable plan of action to rejuvenate the rural cooperative credit structure. Its terms of reference are:(a) to recommend an implementable action plan for reviving the rural cooperative banking institutions, taking into consideration, inter alia, main recommendations made by various committees in this regard; (b) to suggest an appropriate regulatory framework and the amendments, which may be necessary for the purpose in the relevant laws; (c) to make an assessment of the financial assistance that the cooperative banking institutions will require for revival, the mode of such assistance, its sharing pattern and phasing; and (d) to suggest any other measures required for improving the efficiency and viability of rural cooperative credit institutions.[28]

The RBI under MoU, is committed to constitute state level task force for Cooperative Urban Banks (TAFCUB) comprising representatives of the Reserve Bank, State Government and the UCB sector. Accordingly, TAFCUBs have been constituted in all States with which MoUs have been signed. A Central TAFCUB has been constituted for the Multi-State UCBs. The TAFCUBs identify potentially viable and non-viable UCBs in the State and suggest revival path for the viable and non disruptive exit route for the non-viable ones. Urban co-operative banks were prohibited from granting fresh loans in excess of Rs.20 lakh against NRE and FCNR (B) deposits, either to depositors or to third parties. Banks were also advised not to undertake slicing of the loan amount to circumvent the ceiling. Further, arising out of the comfort of coordinated supervision/regulation in States that have signed MoU with the Reserve Bank, certain additional business opportunities have been extended to the eligible banks in such States as also to the MultiState UCBs.

The process of mergers among UCBs was provided a fresh impetus with the issue of transparent guidelines for grant of 'no objection'to merger proposals by the Reserve Bank. UCBs were advised that the bills purchased/ discounted/negotiated under LC (where the payment to the beneficiary is not made 'under reserve') should be treated as an exposure on the LC issuing bank and not on the borrower. Based on directions of Delhi High Court, UCBs were advised to ensure that housing loans are sanctioned only for authorised structures and the banks have to obtain an undertaking on an affidavit from the loan applicants that the building/s will be constructed as per sanctioned plans, which are to be attached with the undertaking.

UCBs were advised to implement the recommendations of the Working Group on *'Formulating a Scheme for Ensuring Reasonableness of Bank Charges'* as accepted by the Reserve Bank. Scheduled UCBs have also been advised to display and update on the homepage of their websites the details of certain service charges and fees at a prominent place under the title of 'Service Charges and Fees'so as to facilitate easy access to the bank customers. In view of the complaints received by the Reserve Bank/Banking Ombudsmen, UCBs were advised not to compel their customers to drop cheques in drop boxes and to invariably display on the cheque drop box itself that: Customers can also tender the cheques at the counter and obtain acknowledgement on the pay-in-slip. UCBs were advised to invariably offer passbook facility to all their savings bank account holders (individuals), as it is more convenient than statement of account for small customers.[29]

Challenges Ahead!

Agrawal and Solanke (2012), justify about the poor vital link in cooperative finance system. They claim them to be too small to operate property. Some exist only on the documents. Their NPAs are higher than those of commercial banks w.r.t NPAs-to-asset ratios. They cash in on the government capital than shareholders contributions. Infrastructural weakness and structural laws have blown them off. They do not have potentials in members, deposits and borrowers. They are being conditioned by political and official intervention in transaction.[30]

Conclusion

The bank was initially set up to supplant indigenous sources of rural credit, particularly money lenders. They now serve the needs of agriculture and allied activities, rural-based industries and to a lesser extent, trade and industry in urban centers. The three-tier structure — primary (agriculture or urban) credit societies, district central co-operative banks and at the apex level, state co-operative banks. serve the rural and urban societies. The institutions serve as the power base for local politicians, supporting sugar crushing units, dairy marketing and para-banking.

Reference

1. Katar Singh and RS Pundir, Co-operatives and Rural Development in India, <https://www.irma.ac.in/pdf/randp/979_76324.pdf>
2. Anupam Mitra, NPA management of urban cooperative banks-A study of Hooghly district of West Bengal, Voice of Research Vol. 1, <http:// www.voiceofresearch.org/doc/V1_I2/V1_I2_11.pdf>
3. Co-operative Banking in India - An Overview, <http:// shodhganga.inflibnet.ac.in/bitstream/10603/1106/9/09_chapter%203.pdf>
4. Cooperative movement in India, Chapter IV, <http:// shodhganga.inflibnet.ac.in/bitstream/10603/2502/10/10_chapter%204.pdf>
5. Essay on the History of Cooperative Movement in India, <http://www.preservearticles.com/201105076374/essay-on-the-history-of-cooperativemovement-in-india.html>
6. What is cooperative bank? <http://www.icba.coop/co-operativebank/what-is-a-co- operative-bank.html>
7. Cooperative banking in India, Section II, <http://ietd.inflibnet.ac.in/ bitstream/10603/2031/11/11_chapter%202.pdf>

8. Sachin R. Agrawal & Dr. S.S.Solanke, Problems faced by co-operative banks and perspectives in the Indian Economy, International Journal of Commerce, Business and Management (IJCBM), Vol. 1, No.2, October 2012, <http://www.iracst.org/ijcbm/papers/vol1no22012/4vol1no2.pdf>
9. Developments in Co-operative Banking, <http://rbidocs.rbi.org.in/ rdocs/Publications/PDFs/81457.pdf>
10. The Economic Times (May 13, 2002),What is a cooperative bank? <http://articles.economictimes.indiatimes.com/2002-05-13/news/27357297_1_cooperative-bank-ucbs-banking-regulation-act>
11. Co-operative Banking in India - An Overview, <http:// shodhganga.inflibnet.ac.in/bitstream/10603/1106/9/09_chapter%203.pdf>
12. Jyoti Gupta & Suman Jain, A study on Cooperative Banks in India with special reference to Lending Practices, International Journal of Scientific and Research Publications, Volume 2, Issue 10, October 2012, <http:// www.ijsrp.org/research-paper-1012/ijsrp-p1039.pdf>
13. Dr.K.V.S.N Jawahar Babu, & B.Muniraja Selkhar, The Emerging Urban CoOperative Banks (Ucbs) In India: Problems and Prospects, Journal of Business and Management (IOSRJBM), Volume 2, Issue 5 (July-Aug. 2012), <http://iosrjournals.org/iosr-jbm/papers/vol2-issue5/A0250105.pdf>
14. See <>http://www.icrier.org/pdf/Mandira%20Sarma.pdf>
15. Managing District Central Cooperative Banks, <http://cab.org.in/Lists/Knowledge%20Bank/Attachments/18/Managing%20DCCBs_5_23_2008.pdf>
16. Business Standard (May 28, 2014), RBI asks urban co-operative banks not to lend to govt entities, <http://www.business-standard.com/article/ finance/rbi-asks-urban-co-operative-banks-not-to-lend-to-govt-entities-114052800655_1.html>
17. Anupam Mitra, NPA management of urban cooperative banks-A study of Hooghly district of West Bengal, Voice of Research Vol. 1,<http:// www.voiceofresearch.org/doc/V1_I2/V1_I2_11.pdf>
18. The Economic Times (Oct 23, 2013), Post offices, cooperative banks the next Amul success story in banking? <http://articles.economictimes. indiatimes.com/2013-10-23/news/43326641_1_foreign-banks-cooperativebanks-co-operative-banks>
19. The Economic Times (May 8, 2014), Co-operative banks offer higher rates on fixed deposits with higher risks, <http://economictimes.indiatimes.com/wealth/savings-centre/analysis/co-operativebanks-offer-higher-rates-on-fixed-deposits-with-higher-risks/articleshow/34800937.cms>
20. The Economic Times (Mar 19, 2014), RBI imposes Rs 5 lakh fine on District Co-op Bank in Andhra, <http://articles.economictimes. indiatimes.com/2014-03-19/news/48366387_1_lakh-fine-reserve-bankmonetary-penalty>
21. The Economic Times (April 24, 2014), Cooperative banks agree to finance women self help groups, <http://economictimes.indiatimes.com/news/ economy/finance/cooperative-banks-agree-to-finance-women-self-help-groups/ articleshow/34167395.cms>
22. The Economic Times (Mar 13, 2012), West Bengal State Cooperative Bank criticises government stance on mortgaged properties, <http:// articles.

economictimes.indiatimes.com/2012-03-13/news/31159568_1_wilfuldefaulters-cooperative-banks-nabard>

23. Tripura State Cooperative Bank Limited, <http://tscbank.nic.in/>
24. Nupur Singh, Short notes on Land Development Banks, <http://www.preservearticles.com/2012033129449/short-notes-on-land-developmentbanks.html>
25. Land Development Banks, <http://en.wikipedia.org/wiki/Land_development_bank>
26. Cooperative banking in India, Section II, <http://ietd.inflibnet.ac.in/ bitstream/10603/2031/11/11_chapter%202.pdf>
27. (Dr) E. Gnanasekaran, Dr. M. Anbalgan & N. Abdul Nazar, A study on the Urban Cooperative Banks Success and growth in Vellore District – Statistical Analysis, <http://www.ijarcsse.com/docs/papers/March2012/ volume_2_Issue_3/V2I30040.pdf>
28. Chapter 1, Introduction, cooperative bank, <http:// www.prsindia.org/uploads/media/vikas_doc/docs/bills/ 11674693 84/bill54_2007010354_Reportofthe>
29. Developments in Co-operative Banking, Chapter IV, <http:// rbidocs.rbi.org.in/rdocs/Publications/PDFs/81457.pdf>
30. Sachin R. Agrawal and Dr. S.S.Solanke, Problems faced by co-operative banks and perspectives in the Indian Economy, International Journal of Commerce, Business and Management (IJCBM), Vol. 1, No.2, October 2012, <http://www.iracst.org/ijcbm/papers/vol1no22012/4vol1no2.pdf>

Chapter - 6

Islamic Bank

"If you don't have a functioning financial system, the world economy won't be revived. All the major economies have their responsibility to assist at a pace, which is required to clean up the balance sheet of the banking system and to ensure that credit flows are resumed." — ***Manmohan Singh Dr.***

Introduction

According to Khan (2009), banking system in an economy works like the blood circulation system of a body. As only an efficient blood circulation system can ensure a healthy body, similarly an efficient and equitable banking system can dispense economic efficiency and justice. These basic concepts and objectives are common to any banking system, whether it be conventional or Islamic. Allah has forbidden taking interest and has guided everyone to do business, trade and profession. All'a'h in the following Quranic Verse, has also ordered that we should not consume usury in any shape.[1]

According to Saeed (2012), Islamic banking, an alternate to interest - based banking is not banking in the traditional sense of the word. It derives inspiration and guidance from the religious edicts of Islam and has to conduct operations strictly in accordance with the directives of Shar'i'ah. Islamic financial system employed the concept of participation in the enterprise, utilizing the funds at risk on a profit-and-loss-sharing basis.[2]

According to Ashraf and Giashi (2011), banking is no longer limited to specialized institutions and has expanded both geographically and in product richness, with structured credit finance receiving most of the attention. Greater importance of the General Council for Islamic Banking and Finance Institutions, the Islamic Financial Service Board, the Islamic International Rating Agency and the Accounting and Auditing Organization of Islamic Finance Institutions, will add consistency in accordance to Islamic laws (Shar'i'ah) interpretations by religious boards and the primacy of bankable governing law as a matter of form remain essential to further growth of Islamic banking.[3]

What is Islamic Banking?

According to Hameed and Ahamed (2012), Islamic Banking refers to a method of banking on Islamic Law (Shar'i'ah) which prohibits interest based banking' and permits only profit sharing based banking The concept is based on a verse of the Holy Quran that says – Alla'h has allowed only legitimate trade and prohibits interest. It is against the interest, as interest is believed to lead to exploitation and unproductive income. Islamic banking has the same purpose as conventional banking except that it operates in accordance with the rules of the Sha'r'iah, known as Fi'qh al-Mua'mal'at (Islamic rules on transactions).[4]

According to Singh and Yadav (2013), Islamic banking, also known as interest free banking or finance, is a banking system, which promotes profit sharing, but prohibits the charging and paying of interest. This system is based on the principles of Shar'i'a Islamic Law, which are derived from the Holy Quran and the "Had'eeth", a compilation of the noted sayings of Prophet Mohammad. Islamic Banks follow everywhere these principles in business. The productive activities alone promote entrepreneurship, trade, commerce and societal development are supported, while those which earn income sans risk, such as interest (Ri'ba) bearing transactions and unproductive activities like speculation or gambling are prohibited.[5]

The basic principles of Islamic banking are: (a) *Sharing of Profit and Loss*: The borrower and the lender share the profits as well as losses arising from the venture with the finances obtained from the lender. The general community is believed should benefit from such activities; (b) *Prohibition of Investing in Unlawful Businesses*: Islamic Law prohibits investing in unlawful businesses such as businesses involved in selling alcohol or pork; or businesses that produce media for instance, gossip columns or pornography; or gambling industry; and (c) *Prohibition of Ri'ba* (Interest): Islamic Law prohibits the receiving and giving interest.[6]

The Needs

According to Singh and Yadav (2013), Islamic [fi]nance is in many ways very similar to conventional [fi]nance. Some believe this similarity is an attempt to dilute the Islamic teachings to simplify our lives, while others may feel the Islamic Legal distinctions between Islamic and regular [fi]nance are artificial means of creating an industry where none is needed.[7] According to El-Gama (2000), an Islamic contract in which one side provides capital and other side provides labour. The profits are to be shared in proportions, agreed upon before implementation of the contract. The providers of capital bear net loss according to the contract, unless there has been a violation of contract terms or neglect from the part of the working partner.[8]

According to Ahangar (2009), The Islamic banking system possesses several benefits not found in conventional banking. For example, Islamic banks offer products with interest-free mechanisms. This is beneficial, especially in the current macroeconomic condition. Banking and other sectors are faced with managing high cost of funds, with a high interest rate, yielding a negative margin. The introduction of a non-interest-based system can, to some extent, alleviate this problem. Additionally, Islamic banking eliminates unproductive speculation, and introduces a system of partnership with a high level of moral principles.[9]

Historical Aspect

According to Siregar and Ilyas (2000), an early market economy and an early form of mercantilism, called "Islamic capitalism", were developed between the eighth and twelfth centuries.[10] The first Islamic Development Bank was founded in Dubai in 1975. In 1977, two private Banks in Egypt and Sudan, named the Faisal Islamic Bank were opened[1977]. Iran, Sudan, Pakistan, Indonesia and Malaysia often adopted new guidelines of Islamic Banking. About 280 interest free banking sectors are on in approximately 50 countries. Denmark, USA, Britain, Luxemburg and Switzerland have also adopted this special kind of banking system. South of London has developed as a centre of Islamic Banks Income Sources of Islamic Banks.[11]

Sources of Income

According to Shamshad (2011), the basic principle of Islamic banking is based on risk-sharing component of trade rather than risk transfer found in conventional banking. Islamic banking introduces concepts such as profit sharing, safekeeping, joint venture, cost plus, and leasing. In its mortgage transaction, a bank might buy the item itself from the seller, and re-sell it to the buyer at a profit, instead of lending the buyer money to purchase the item, while allowing the buyer to repay in installments. The profit cannot be made explicit and there were no additional penalties for late payment. The bank asks for strict collateral against default. The goods or land is registered in the name of the buyer from the transaction. This arrangement is called Mur'aba'h'ah. An innovative approach by some banks for home loans, called Mush'ar'aka al-Mut'an'aqisa, allows for a floating rate in the form of rental.

The bank and borrower form a partnership entity, either providing capital at an agreed percentage to purchase the property. The partnership entity rents the property out to the borrower against arrived value of rent. The duo will share from the proceeds, rent being based on the current equity, in case of default. share of partnership. They receive a proportion of the proceeds from the sale of property based on each party's current equity. Several approaches are being used in business transactions. Islamic banks lend money to companies through floating interest rate loans, pegged to their individual rate of return. The bank's profit on such loan is equal to a certain percentage of the company's profits. Once the principal loan amount is repaid, the profit-sharing arrangement finds closure. The practice is called Mush'ar'aka. Islamic banking is restricted to Islamically acceptable transactions, excluding those involving alcohol, pork, gambling, etc., to engage in only ethical investing, and moral purchasing.[12]

The sources of their financial resources owe to paid-up capital, reserves, funds raised through borrowings from the central Bank and government and other banks (inter-bank borrowing), and non-bank financial institutions, and the issue of different types of Islamic financial instruments, to attract the untapped savings of the people. The major part of operational financial resources, derived from deposits mobilized on the principles of Al-W'adia (safe custodianship) and mudâraba (trust financing).[13]

Global Perspectives

According to Sarkar (1999), Islamic financial institutions are now operating in over 75 countries. Estimates suggest the overall Islamic finance industry, includes Islamic banking, non-banking companies, mutual funds, leasing, real estate investment and stock market investment as well as charitable financial institutions, grown 40-fold since the 1980s. Accounting its 15 per cent annual growth during the last two decades, even a conservative estimate will put its finance sector size beyond $ 1,000 billion, in about 100 countries.

The first Islamic Bank was established in 1963, in Mt. Ghamr, Egypt, but could'nt last long. It was established by the Organization of Islamic countries in 1974, called Islamic Development Bank, explicitly based on Shar'i'ah principles.[14]

Islamic banking assets with commercial banks globally reached US$1.54 trln [2012]. It includes pure-play Islamic banks and windows. More banks were expanding into high potential markets to build regional brands. In Saudi Arabia, supply push has seen the share of Islamic banking cross 50 per cent of system assets.[15] According to Khan (2013), Malaysia, accounts for 25 per cent market share and is on the track to hit 40 per cent; in Indonesia, while the share is still low at 5 per cent, the growth rate is more than twice the rate of conventional banking, and market share could reach 15 per cent in the next seven to eight years.[16]

Increasing population across the Muslim world and the appetite for demand in investment for infrastructure therein has led to an increase in need for capital conforming to Islamic standards. Many of these countries, especially in the Middle East, Central Asia and South East Asia, where the oil and natural gas deposits pushed the need for companies to build extraction, transport and refining capacity. Developing countries such as those in Africa, Pakistan, and Afghanistan, finds an increasing need for electricity [production-distribution] and water desalination stations. These projects are capital intensive in nature.[17]

According to Camacho (2005), from Jakarta to Jeddah to Jordan, 280 Islamic banks operate in over 50 countries, with assets estimated between $250 billion and $300 billion. Some 35 per cent of the institutions are in the Middle East. Islamic banks will account for 40 to 50 per cent of the total savings of Muslims in eight to ten years. Moreover, according to the International Islamic Finance Forum, the banks' holdings grew by 15 per cent every year. The value of Islamic loans grew at an annual rate of 40 per cent, which is likely to increase. The number of banks offering Islamic products worldwide is expected to grow on demand 50 per cent by 2009.[18]

Islamic banking in Malaysia with Perbadanan Wang Simpanan Bakal-Bakal Haji [Sept '63]. was established. The first bank was established in 1983. Commercial banks, Merchant banks and finance companies were allowed to offer Islamic banking products and services under the Islamic Banking Scheme [1993].[19] The Indonesian Ula'ma' Council held its symposium on "Issues in Interest and Banking [1990]." A plan to amend the Banking Act 14 (1967) lead the government and parliament enact the Banking Act 7, providing opportunities to develop Islamic banks [1992]. The first Islamic bank, PT Bank Muam'al'at Indonesia, was established in Jakarta, in the same year. Some rural banks were also established in Java.[20]

According to Siregar and Nasirwan Ilyas (2000), Islamic banking commenced operations in Bangladesh [1983], with the establishment of "Islami Bank Bangladesh Limited." It was incorporated on March 14, 1983, went into operation on March 30, 1983 and a full package of banking services came in August 1983. It was considered as the first interest-free bank in Southeast Asia. IBBL is a public limited company with limited liability under the Companies Act, 1913. The second Islamic bank in the country, Al-Baraka Bank Bangladesh Limited commenced business on May 20, 1987, incorporated under the same Companies Act, with a registered office in Dhaka. Al-Arafah Islami Bank Limited was incorporated on June 18, 1995, and went into operation as the third bank in the private sector on September 27, 1995.

Social Investment Bank Limited was the fourth bank, incorporated on July 05, 1995, and with its operations on November 22, 1995. It is a venture bank, owned by international Islamic organizations and the Government of Bangladesh. Faysal Islamic Bank of Bahrain EC, Dhaka obtained permission to open a single branch in Bangladesh on March 06, 1997. Three Pakistani banks (Habib Bank Limited, National Bank of Pakistan, and Muslim Commercial Bank Limited) also have a branch each in Bangladesh. Two conventional banks, i.e. Prime Bank Limited and Dhaka Bank Limited, commenced limited Islamic banking activities within their present conventional set-up.[21]

According to Sarkar (1999), Islamic banking in Turkey dates back to

1985, when the late Turgut Özal led government passed the legislation for interest-free banking. The first "participation bank" was Alb'ar' aka Türk, established in February 1985. Islamic banks offer customers profit-sharing proceeds instead of interest, and charge borrowers participation-sharing, instead of loan interest.[22] Islamic Banking is flourishing dynamically in Pakistan like all other Muslim and non-Muslim countries since January, 1981 as a result of Islamization of banking sector through radical and structural developments made by the Government.[23]

Iranian Banks are operated under strict Islamic principles as the country's government mandates follow the strict Islamic principles. Running a traditional banking network would be considered as against the fundamental teachings of Qur'an. It became compulsory for the Central Bank of Iran to set up an Islamic Banking law in tune with the instructions of Quran, following the Islamic Revolution.[24]

Operation in India

According to Ashraf and Giashi (2011), Islamic banking seems an alien concept in India's conventional banking. Despite impressive growth elsewhere, such as the Middle East, South East Asia (which primarily include Malaysia and Indonesia) and Europe, it is yet to find favor with the Indian authorities. Former RBI Governor D Subbarao recommended its introduction and wrote to the government about amending the law to facilitate the system. A high level committee on financial sector reform of the Planning Commission of India (2008) headed by Dr. Raghuram Rajan, recommended the introduction of interest-free finance and banking as part of mainstream banking in the interest of inclusive, innovative growth. Many Indian institutions, including some government-owned banks, evinced interest in the growing niche opportunity.[25]

In India, the scope for Islamic banking is very large, owing to 140 million Muslims, making 15 per cent of the Islamic population around the world. According to Standard & Poor's Ratings Services, the potential market is $4 trillion worldwide; therefore this can be a tool for enhancing economic development. It will avail opportunities to Muslim laborers and the working class. Several foreign banks operate in India, like Citibank, Standard Chartered Bank, HBSC through interest-free windows in several West Asian countries, USA and Europe.

The growing awareness about the concept among Indian banks was felt about the huge potential market for Islamic banking in India.[26] According to Manzoor (2007), domestic economy grew, but paradoxically the rate of poor people is also on the rise. The state must endeavour to establish an egalitarian society. However, most of the Indian citizens do not have access to credit. The present banking system is not conducive for protecting the interests of all sections of the population. The banking system of Islam, based on Islamic law (Shar'i'ah), has been institutionalised in many parts of the world. Islamic banking is interest-free banking system based on the real asset. The risks are being shared between lender and borrower under mechanisms of partnership, joint ownership, lease and sale.[27]

Certain Islamic financial solutions exist in India, but are nowhere near the standard of global Islamic finance industry. Strictly speaking, there are no Islamic banks in India. However, there are various types of Islamic financial organisations that carry financial transactions on an interest-free basis. Several Baitul Mals work in cities as well as in villages. Ten to fifteen banks with deposits exceeding Rs.75 crore operate in various states. These are non-banking finance companies, working on profits-loss basis. Islamic banks, by and large, cater to the needs of local area, except a few operate across districts or states. The sources of funds are limited and as a result, these have to operate on small scale without enjoying the economies of scale.[28]

According to Singh and Yadav (2013), Indian banking laws do not explicitly prohibit Islamic banking. There are provisions that make Islamic banking an almost unviable option. Banks in India are being governed under the Banking Regulation Act 1949, Reserve Bank of India Act 1934, Negotiable Instruments Act 1881, and the state and central Co-operatives Acts. One of the distinguishable features of Acts is that they define banking as the mode to accept public deposits for further lending. Section 5 (b) and 5 (c) of the Banking Regulation Act 1949 prohibit them from investing on profit and loss sharing. Section 8 of the Banking Regulation Act 1949 envisages, "No banking company shall directly or indirectly deal in buying or selling or bartering of goods ..."[29]

According to Nihar (2012), RBI has allowed a Kerala-based firm to operate as a non-banking financial company under Islamic principles - a small step towards developing Sha'r'i'a-compliant finance in the country. An estimated million Muslims in India, the largest Muslim minority population in the world, are unable to use them, because laws covering the sector require banking to be based on interest, forbidden in Islam. Some companies, especially in Kerala has a larger Muslim population with an overseas diaspora, who remit money back from the Gulf, are nevertheless trying to develop Islamic financial products outside the banking sector.[30]

The Kerala government has got a go-ahead from the RBI for a financial institution following the principles of Islamic finance. In this direction, Cheraman Financial Services Limited will be floated by Kerala State Industrial Development Corporation to function as a non-banking finance company. The RBI, the Securities and Exchanges Board of India and the Waqf Board have given clearness. The Kerala State Industrial Development Corporation will be the single largest shareholder with 11 per cent Stake. Other individual shareholders can hold a maximum of nine per cent shares. The previous government had hoped to raise Rs 40,000 crore, upon the state's traditional Gulf link.[31]

India needs huge investments to restore economy and mobilize its ambitious infrastructure development plans. The Islamic finance is estimated to be a US$2.1 trillion industry. It is being seen as a small, but decisive step towards opening up the sector to interest-free banking. It was not allowed to accept deposits from the public or offer retail banking services, which needs suitable amendments in Indian laws. Ordinary citizens, making small investments are inaccessible at the moment.

A high-level committee on financial sector reforms headed by Dr Raghuram Rajan recommended interest-free finance and banking in the "interest of inclusive and innovative growth" and suggested measures "to permit the delivery of interest-free finance on a larger scale, including through the banking system[2008]". Islamic banking and finance is now present in over 75 countries including Australia, France, the UK, Hong Kong, Singapore, Luxembourg, South Africa, Sri Lanka and Malaysia, claiming to be its capital. In India, many Muslims do not claim interest on deposits or give them in charity. A 2009 study clais unclaimed interests worth Rs.50 bn is lying in Kerala banks alone.[32]

Infrastructure Development

Infrastructure financing is a desirable investment product for Islamic financial institutions. It is in line with the mission of Islamic banking and finance. Investments in highways, airports, power generation and distribution, telecommunication networks, oil and gas pipelines etc. in developing Muslim economies is believed to accelerate the process of economic development, as well as create value and wealth in these societies. Such desirable outcomes are directly in contrast to those of the Islamic equity funds, which generally involve an outflow of capital from these resource-starved economies into the developed ones.[33]

According to Obaidullah (1999), infrastructure is a social capital that is embodied in such forms in helping direct product activities in the economy. The term infrastructure includes transport, communication, energy and other public services like water supply, essential for increasing the lifestyle of the population. The country needs massive capital for its development, but the government has fund constraints in infrastructure facilities. Muslim nations have invested appreciably in US and European countries, perforce them withdraw the investment from those nations on the 9/11 and global financial crisis. Now, they are searching suitable haven for investing billions of dollars in some trusted nation.

Few states such as Kerala, Bihar and Maharashtra at home take efforts for Islamic banking availing capital for infrastructural development. The Kerala government has already completed the final process for an Islamic bank with the strong participation of the state financial corporation, against enormous criticisms from many parts of the country. The officials of National Committee on Islamic Banking, Indian centre for Islamic finance have discussed with the chief minister of the state of Bihar availing opportunities of Islamic finance in state's infrastructural development. They have persuaded with the chief minister about the liquidity problem, which could be solved through the appreciable inflow of capital from gulf nations. The states of Kerala and Maharashtra have taken major steps for Islamic finance to mobilize infrastructural development.[34]

Conclusion

The Islamic law prohibits accepting or allowing interest as essential feature of Islamic banking. The basic sources of Shar'i'ah principles are the 'Quran' and the 'Sunnah', followed by the consensus of the jurists and interpreters of Islamic law. Profit sharing and fee-based financing approaches were developed in compliance with the Shar'i'ah laws. The special modes of financing have emerged in retail, private and commercial banking for debt and capital markets, insurance, asset management, structured and project financing, derivates, etc. The purpose of Islamic banking resemble with the conventional banking. In an Islamic mortgage transaction, instead of lending the buyer money to purchase the item, a bank might straightaway, buy the item from the seller, and re-sell that to him at a profit, allowing him repay the bank in installments.

References

1. Agha Zohaib Ali Khan (2009), Growth of Islamic Banking in Pakistan, <http://www.kantakji.com/media/7519/c52.pdf>
2. Prof. Dr. Khawaja Amjad Saeed, Islamic Banking in Pakistan: A Review of Conventional and Islamic Banking, <http://umt.edu.pk/icobm2012/pdf/2C-95P.pdf>
3. Dr. S. Husain Ashraf, Mr. Ali Alizadeh Giashi, Islamic Banking in Iran - Progress and challenges, Kuwait Chapter of Arabian Journal of Business and Management Review Vol. 1, No.2; October 2011, <http://www.arabianjbmr.com/ pdfs/KD_VOL_1_2/4.pdf>
4. Dr. G. Shahul Hameed and Fayaz Ahamed, Development of Islamic banking with reference to UAE, <http://sukuk.fr/files/20100607_ Develo - pmentofislamicbanking.pdf>

5. Dr. Jeet Singh and Dr. Preeti Yadav, Islamic banking in India: Growth and potential, International Journal of Marketing, Financial Services and Management Research, Vol.2, No. 4, April (2013), <http://indianresearchjournals.com/pdf/ IJMFSMR/2013/April/6.pdf>
6. Why India needs Islamic banking? <http://www.infosys.com/finacle/solutions/ thought-papers/Documents/why-India-needs-islamicbanking.pdf>
7. Dr. Jeet Singh and Dr. Preeti Yadav, Islamic banking in India: Growth and potential, International Journal of Marketing, Financial Services and Management Research, Vol.2, No. 4, April (2013), <http://indianresearchjournals.com/pdf/ IJMFSMR/2013/April/6.pdf>
8. Mahmoud Amin El-Gama (2000), A Basic Guide to Contemporary Islamic Banking and Finance, <http://www.ruf.rice.edu/~elgamal/files/ primer.pdf>
9. Gowhar Bashir Ahangar, Mohd Ummer Jan Padder, and Ashaq Hussain Ganie, Islamic banking and its scope in India, IRACST – International Journal of Commerce, Business and Management(IJCBM), Vol. 2, No.5, October 2013, <http://www.iracst.org/ijcbm/papers/vol2no52013/7vol2no5.pdf>
10. Mulya E. Siregar and Nasirwan Ilyas, Recent Developments in Islamic Banking in Indonesia, Proceedings of the Fifth Harvard University Forum on Islamic Finance: Islamic Finance: Dynamics and Development Cambridge, Massachusetts. Center for Middle Eastern Studies, Harvard University. 2000. pp. 189-96, <http://ifp.law.harvard.edu/login/view_pdf/?file=Recent+ Developments+in+Islamic+Banking+in+Indonesia.pdf&type=Project_ Publication>
11. Islamic banks, <http://en.wikipedia.org/wiki/Islamic_banking>
12. Dr. A. Shamshad, "Interest Free Islamic Banking in India for Inclusive Growth and Social Uplift: Scopes and Challenges", International Journal of Business, Humanities and Technology, Vol. 1 No.1; July 2011, <http://www.ijbhtnet.com/ journals/Vol._1_No.1_July_2011/12.pdf>
13. Islamic Banking (2014), <http://en.wikipedia.org/wiki/Islamic_banking>
14. Md. Abdul Awwal Sarker, Islamic Banking in Bangladesh: Growth, Structure, and Performance, Proceedings of the Third Harvard University Forum on Islamic Finance: Local Challenges, Global Opportunities Cambridge, Massachusetts. Center for Middle Eastern Studies, Harvard University. 1999. pp. 271-90.
15. Khurram Ajaz Khan, Emerging Islamic Banking: Its Need and Scope in India, Pacific Business Review International Volume 5 Issue 7 (January 2013), <http:/ /www.pbr.co.in/Vol%205%20Iss%207/12.pdf>
16. World Islamic Banking Competitiveness Report 2013–14: The transition begins, <http://www.mifc.com/index.php?ch=28&pg=72&ac=58&bb=uploadpdf>
17. <http://www.themalaymailonline.com/money/article/islamic-bankingindustry-seeking-additional-growth-drivers>
18. Jasper Camacho, 2005, Islamic Financing for Large Infrastructure Projects, <http:/ /people.hbs.edu/mdesai/IFM05/Camacho.pdf>
19. Banking on Faith: Islamic Banking in the Middle East, <http://www.infosys.com/ finacle/solutions/thought-papers/Documents/Islamic-Bankingin-the-Middle-East.pdf>

20. Islamic banking in Malaysia, <http://en.wikipedia.org/wiki/Islamic_banking_in_Malaysia>
21. Mulya E. Siregar and Nasirwan Ilyas,Recent Developments in Islamic Banking in Indonesia, Proceedings of the Fifth Harvard University Forum on Islamic Finance: Islamic Finance: Dynamics and Development Cambridge, Massachusetts. Center for Middle Eastern Studies, Harvard University. 2000. pp. 189-96, <http://ifp.law.harvard.edu/login/view_pdf/??file=Recent+Developments+in+Islamic+Banking+in+Indonesia.pdf&type=Project_Publication>
22. Md. Abdul Awwal Sarker, Islamic Banking in Bangladesh: Growth, Structure, and Performance, Proceedings of the Third Harvard University Forum on Islamic Finance: Local Challenges, Global Opportunities Cambridge, Massachusetts. Center for Middle Eastern Studies, Harvard University. 1999. pp. 271-90.
23. Islamic banking in Turkey, <http://www.hurriyet.com.tr/english/ finance/10623462.asp>
24. Growth of Islamic Banking in Pakistan by Using AID Model, International Journal of Business and Social Science, Vol. 3 No. 23; December 2012, <http://ijbssnet.com/journals/Vol_3_No_23_December_2012/16.pdf>
25. Dr. S. Husain Ashraf , Mr. Ali Alizadeh Giashi, Islamic Banking in Iran - Progress and challenges, Kuwait Chapter of Arabian Journal of Business and Management Review, Vol. 1, No.2; October 2011, <http://www.arabianjbmr.com/ pdfs/KD_VOL_1_2/4.pdf>
26. Why India needs Islamic banking? <http://www.infosys.com/ finacle/solutions/thought-papers/Documents/why-India-needs-islamicbanking.pdf>
27. Manzoor K.P, Islamic Banking and Finance in India: Opportunities and Challenges, <http://ibtra.com/pdf/journal/v9_n1_article7.pdf>
28. Inclusive growth in India through Islamic banking, <http://www.sciencedirect.com/science/article/pii/S1877042812007574>
29. Dr. Jeet Singh and Dr. Preeti Yadav, Islamic banking in India: Growth and potential, International Journal of Marketing, Financial Services and Management Research, Vol.2, No. 4, April (2013), < http://indianresearchjournals.com/pdf/IJMFSMR/2013/April/6.pdf>
30. Dr Shariq Nisar, Challenges for Islamic banking in India, <http://www.shariqnisar.com/images/My_writings/Challenges%20for%20Islamic%20Banking%20in%20India.pdf>
31. RBI allows non-bank Islamic finance firm, <http://in.reuters.com/article/2013/08/20/islamic-finance-india-idINDEE97J07L20130820>
32. Kerala: India's first Islamic bank gets RBI approval, <http://www.coastaldigest.com/index.php/news/56490-kerala-indias-first-islamic-bankgets-rbi-approval>
33. India takes key step toward full-fledged Islamic banks, <http://www.arabnews.com/news/527476>
34. Mohammed Obaidullah, Designing Islamic Contracts for Financing Infrastructure Development, Proceedings of the Third Harvard University Forum on Islamic Finance: Local Challenges, Global Opportunities Cambridge, Massachusetts.

Center for Middle Eastern Studies, Harvard University. 1999. pp. 163-76, <http://ifp.law.harvard.edu/login/view_pdf/?file=Designing%20Islamic%20Contracts%20for%20Financing%20Infrastructure%20Development.pdf&type=Project_Publication>

35. Manzoor K.P, Islamic Banking and Finance in India: Opportunities and Challenges, <http://ibtra.com/pdf/journal/v9_n1_article7.pdf>

Chapter - 7

Microfinance

"When we want to help the poor, we usually offer them charity. Most often we use charity to avoid recognizing the problem and finding the solution for it. Charity becomes a way to shrug off our responsibility. But charity is no solution to poverty. Charity only perpetuates poverty by taking the initiative away from the poor. Charity allows us to go ahead with our own lives without worrying about the lives of the poor. Charity appeases our consciences."

— ***Dr. Muhammad Yunus***

Introduction

According to Okpara (2010), Poverty is a phenomenon that has generated a lot of interest in recent times. The issue of poverty has been a major concern to many nations, particularly the developing countries.[1] The term "poverty" does not lead to a straight forward definition. It is a complex universal phenomenon of multiple dimensions. World Bank (2004) defined poverty as a condition of insufficient resources or income, wherein its most extreme form is the lack of basic human needs, such as, health services, education, drinking water etc. Insufficient resources may include land, tools, supportive network of friends and families.[2]

According to Adu-Okoree (2012), many experts have defined poverty in their own ways.[3] According to Hoxhaj (2010), now-a-days, microfinance is demonstrating a great expansion specifically in poor developing countries. The financial intermediaries, microfinance institutions, represent a large range of institutions with different characteristics and ownership structures.[4] According to Maes and Foose (2006), microfinance has become a strategy for reducing poverty by providing small loans and savings facilities to people, who are excluded from commercial financial services. Access to credit and deposit services is a way to avail the poor with opportunities to take an active role in their respective economies through entrepreneurship, building income, bargaining power and social empowerment among poor women and men.[5]

According to Demont (2010), main challenges in identifying the causal impact of financial deepening and microfinance in particular are related to the self-selection of participants and the non-random placement of programs that makes simple comparisons impossible between clients and non-clients.[6]

What is Microfinance?

Microfinance as defined by Steel et al (2004) which refers to the small financial transactions with low-income households and micro enterprises (both urban and rural), using non-standard methodologies, such as character-based lending, group guarantees and short-term repeat loans. Fernando [2006] emphasized the scheme as some noble approach, to reach more people in anticipation of maximized commercial profits, to support those objectives. It has the potential, as a company, to facilitate core objective of being financially self-sufficient and deliver to larger market, focusing at the same time, mostly on their customer. The sector, as such, has been changing quickly.

According to William Grant (2000), all microfinance providers, whether non-governmental organizations, focussing on poverty lending or for-profit commercial institutions, concerned with maxima return on investment, realizing the crucial existence of a strong and permanent institution, for successful provision of such services.[7] According to Adjei et. al. (2009), microfinance programmes are known to support smooth consumption during an adverse shock for poor individuals or households . Access to credit may help them avoid distress through sales of assets, and replace productive assets destroyed in natural disasters.[8]

Microcredit

It is the extension of smaller loans to impoverished borrowers, lacking the collateral, steady employment and a verifiable credit history. It is part of microfinance, and provides a wider range of financial services, especially savings accounts, for the poor. It is ideally based on a unique set of principles, readily distinguished from trends in the wider credit market. Many organizations function now as independent banks. Bangladesh Grameen

Bank is the oldest and is probably the best-known microfinance institution in the world.[9]

SHG Group

According to Lopamudra and Suresh (2012),Self-help groups are small voluntary association of the poor and the marginalized, preferably from the same socio-economic background. It became the vehicle of change for the strata to release them from the clutches of poverty.[10] According to Baland et. al. (2011), RBI defines an SHG as: a registered[un] group of micro entrepreneurs with homogenous social and economic background, coming together voluntarily, to save small amounts regularly, mutually agree to contribute to a common fund and meet with the emergency needs on mutual help. The members use collective wisdom and peer pressure, to ensure proper end-use of credit and timely repayment thereof.[11]

SHGs focus on thrift and credit. These were being trained in different avocations and linked with banks to start microenterprises, either in groups, or individually based on their interests and viability of the avocation. The thrust of economic activities is to enhance the income from existing resources availing additional opportunities of employment to optimize local resources and skill.[12]

Microfinance Institutions

Microfinance institutions offer typically a variety of loan products and, increasingly, savings services as well. The institutions are quite heterogeneous. The term "microfinance" is still generally associated with them, but increasingly being used in the wider context of providing financial services for the currently excluded products, irrespective of the type of institutions providing them.[13] According to Herrington and Sutcliffe (2010), MFIs primarily provide small loans to clients. Unlike commercial banks, these do not require borrowers to provide collateral for loans. Some apply a creditworthiness standard based on the performance of a group of borrowers by initially extending loan to an individual and lending money to additional members of the group, if that individual proves to be a reliable borrower.[14]

NGOs

According to Mustafa et. al. (2000), an NGO is a body of people who come together to provide help to those failing to accumulate sufficient resources for survival. These have emerged in real numbers only after WW-II, concurrent with the dismantling of former colonies. Many such organizations have evolved from anti-colonial independence movements. These are dedicated to the uplift of the poor and implicitly recognize that government alone can ameliorate the poor and destitute. These are also effective mechanisms through which to disseminate valuable information on ways to improve the health, legal rights, sanitation and other relevant concerns of the poor. Experience shows that small credits play a significant role in poverty eradication. The benefits have been observed to include better education and food and health care for their families, when their loans are being used by women.[15]

Scene in South Asia

According to Moses (2011), modern concept of micro-finance can be traced out as Marshall Plan at the end of WW-II in the middle of 20th century.[16] According to Chaudhury (2012), in developing countries, the formal sector financial institutions exclude poor households through the collateral requirement, credit rationing, preference for high income clients, bureaucratic and lengthy procedures of loan sanctions. On the other hand, informal sector financial sources are exploitative in nature.[17]

According to Lee (2006), the member-owned institutions have been identified as the most viable means to reach the poorest and the most remote areas. These have the potential to push the rural frontier into more remote areas, because they are both self-replicating and adaptive. They could build on the best of the local and the most strategic of linked arrangements.

These can be distinguished from other microfinance institutions by their ownership structure. They have the responsibility for owning, managing and operating the financial institutions, as they are the main, sometimes only, customers of those same institutions.[18]

Microfinance Development Bank Limited is a national level microfinance development bank, licensed by Nepal Rastra Bank. Currently, FMDB provides wholesale services to MFIs to operate microfinance program for economically and socially disadvantaged and deprived people.[19] According to Shrestha (2009), the government launched in 1982, a women focused microfinance program i.e., 'Production Credit for Rural Women through the Women Development Section of the Ministry of Local Development with the support of the government owned commercial banks for credit, which has outnumbered 82,416 women. Similarly, the government made provision of credit component in several donor assisted rural development projects for supporting self-employment, promotion and income earning activities.[20]

According to Hussein (2009), the Nepal Rastra Bank, the Agricultural Development Bank of Nepal, the Rastriya Baniya Bank and the Grameen Banks are the formal financial sector that provides microfinance services through mandated government programmes.[21] The financial sector in Bhutan is very small and provides limited financial products and services. There are four major institutions, two commercial banks - (a) Bhutan National Bank and (b) Bank of Bhutan and two non-banking institutions –

(a) Bhutan Development Finance Corporation and (b) Royal Insurance

(b) Corporation of Bhutan. Non-bank financial institutions were set up as part of the economic modernization drive. The Agricultural Lending Department has considerably improved itsloan processing methodology.[22]

The poor people of Pakistan have relied upon informal sources for meeting their credit requirements. Microfinance services were initiated on a small scale by several NGOs running development programmes, when they realized credit as an essential input for enhancing productivity and income. The Aga Khan Rural Support Programme in the Northern Areas and the Orangi Pilot Programme in urban Karachi were the first to initiate a micro-finance programme.

The financing of NGOs from the established Pakistan Poverty Alleviation Fund provided a real impetus to the sector growth. The government [2000] under separate ordinance and with the ADB's financial support established the Khushali Bank for extending microfinance to the left out and underserved areas of the country.[23] According to Atapattu (2009), there are many practicing MFI models in Sri Lanka.. Historically, credit Co-operatives, Village Societies, also called community based organization and Village Revolving Funds were the most popular till 1990's. Many INGOs such as CARE International commenced village revolving funds and are yet popular in conflict areas where the UNHCR supports such autonomous village funds.[24]

According to Hussein (2009, Afghanistan's formal financial system at the end of 2001, was virtually non-operational, with insolvent public financial institutions without private banks. The models of micro-finance found from borrowed experiences gleaned elsewhere, were found to have developed indigenously. The predominant models combine the group lending approach with individual lending. Some use the solidarity group lending model, while one or two have experimented on the feasibility. WOCCU is the apex organization of the international credit union system which is assisting with the setup of credit unions. The Aga Khan Foundation and the Natural Resources Institution supported by the Research in Alternative Livelihoods Fund programme [on a pilot basis] have established SHG as an alternative approach to microfinance provision for the poor in Badakhshan province.[25]

NABARD brings out data on microfinance in India every year. The data finds compiled through stakeholders like partner NGOs, financial institutions, government departments, etc., which are based on returns submitted by participant banks covering commercial banks, RRBs and cooperative banks. The micro-finance Development and Equity Fund is being utilized for the promotion of various microfinance activities, such as formation and linkage of SHGs through SHPIs, training and capacity, building of stake holders, livelihood propagation, studies, documentation, etc.[26]

According to Sinha (2009), the Development Banking Cell within the Bank of Maldives in 1990 provides financial services to more distant atolls. The financial sector of Maldives consists of the Maldives monetary authority, six commercial banks, several NBFIs. Their regulations were being carried out under the guidelines of the MMA Act, 1981, which requires local and foreign financial institutions to obtain a license from the MMA. The companies are being registered under the Companies Act of Republic of Maldives and with absolute participation from the authorities in terms of the ownership in major financial institutions.[27]

Experience of Bangladesh

Bangladesh has record history on microfinance. Pilot programs and experiments conducted by Grameen Bank and BRAC, reflected steady improvement.[28] According to Alamgir (2009), the success of microcredit Bangladesh has led the country use the approach as a major tool in reducing national poverty strategy by the state authorities and NGOs. The mainstream loan product or microcredit for the moderately poor people, the original product introduced by Grameen Bank has became routine loan product in the market.[29]

According to Westover (2008), Dr. Muhammad Yunus, the country's

Economist was recipient of the Nobel Peace Prize for his pioneering sustained effort in addressing the problem of poverty, microfinance programs have continued to grow in usage and popularity. Numerous studies demonstrated the tremendous successes of such programs throughout much of the under- developed world.[30] According to Augsburg and Fouillet (2010), the focus of development strategies in the late 1980s and early 1990s can be singled out as one of the major determinants in the growing popularity of microfinance.[31] According to Alam (2009) rural-based micro entrepreneurs are compelled to borrow funds from local moneylenders at a high rate of interest. In recent years different Islamic banks in Bangladesh started lending interest-free microfinance to different rural-based micro enterprises.[32]

According to Matin (2003), Increasing depth of poverty outreach and enhancing poverty impact dominated microfinance discourses in Bangladesh. Urban micro- finance needs to be focused much more than it is now.[33] The government created a number of institutional set up to reach millions of rural populace with the support in the form of subsidized credit facilities, specially targeted for the agricultural sector. Besides credit operations, savings mobilization, micro insurance facilities, human resources development through different training and awareness program, health and hygiene program etc were also part of MFI operations.[34]

According to Khandker (2005), Grameen Bank is the best known and among the oldest, microfinance providers. Dr. Muhammad Yunus founded the project funded by commercial banks, to extend microcredit in the 1970s. Grameen Bank is best known for developing the solidarity lending system, which is now being utilized in over 43 countries. The Nobel Committee cited micro-credit as one way in which large population groups could potentially break out of poverty, thereby increasing the likelihood of peace and lasting stability for such people, as well as advancing democracy and human rights.[35]

According to Dr. Mohammad Yunus, founder of the Grameen Bank and one of the pioneers of microfinance, "the first microfinance principle of Grameen banking is that the clients should not go to the bank, it is the bank which should go to the people." He perceived that to alleviate other potential imbalances, financial services should be provided to poor people on their terms, in a manner that was respectful of their needs, activities and livelihoods. At the Grameen Bank, this means "12,000 staff serves 3.2 million clients in 45,000 villages spread out all over Bangladesh, every week".[36]

According to Ahmed (2011), it increases the economic well-being of poor families, besides [as well as] improving the food security and nutrition status, which ultimately contribute to good health. When the borrower families enjoy the financial solvency, they tend to invest higher in education for their children.[37]

According to Chowdhury (2012), Bangladesh has experienced exceptionally rapid growth in the sector since 1990. Earlier, only a handful of organizations were operating in the microcredit sector. Following the innovation and success of Grameen Bank in extending small collateral free loans to poor people for income generating activities, many NGOs adopted microcredit technology and started mobilizing the poor for microcredit activities.[38]

Experience of India

According to Rozycki (2006), microfinance services became increasingly important tools for financial and social intermediation in the lives of the world's poorest. This method of grassroots economic development has showed promise throughout the world, the number of microfinance institutions has increased rapidly, and borrowers are offered a range of lending alternatives.[39]

In India, the concern for poverty alleviation has always been high on the agenda of policy makers. With nearly a third of the population below the poverty line, the government has, over the past fifty years, initiated a number of steps in this direction. In response to the inadequacy of the formal financial institutions to meet the credit needs of the poor and non-availability of other financial services, an alternative financial services delivery mechanism started emerging in the villages and small towns of the country.[40]

India has many informal insurance schemes. These schemes are often small, run by cooperatives, churches and non-governmental organizations, which pool their members' contributions to create an insurance fund for a specific purpose, for example to cover funeral costs. Two central regulations have shaped micro insurance in India. The first is a set of regulations published in 2002 entitled the Obligations of Insurers to Rural Social Sectors.[41]

According to Abraham (2011), the government established NABARD [1982] for promoting, monitoring and refinancing the rural financial system in the country. The SHGs provide inspiration, provide financial inclusion for the small and marginal farmers, empower them and often assume political role.[42]

According to Raj (2004), under the SGSY, assistance is given to the poor families living below the poverty line in rural areas for taking up self employment. [known as '*Swarojgars*'].These may take up the activity either individually or in groups, called the Self-Help Groups. The SHGs enhance the status of women as participants, decision-makers and beneficiaries in the participants, decision- makers and beneficiaries in the democratic, economic, social and cultural spheres of life.[43]

According to Jain et. al. (2004), the SHGs enhance the equality of status of women as participants, decision-makers and beneficiaries in the democratic, economic, social and cultural spheres of life. They have uncalculated a great confidence in the minds of rural women to succeed in their day to day life.[44]

According to Sane and Thomas (2007), there are two models in India that link the formal financial sector with lending to low income households that cannot afford collateral. The first is the bank-led SHG model, promoted by the State through commercial banks, which lends to groups of 10 to 20 women called the Self-Help Groups. The other model is that of micro-finance institutions which private sector entities are lending to small groups similar to the SHGs.[45]

According to Snijders and Geske Dijkstra (2011), India has seen an impressive growth of microfinance activities over the past decade, of which the largest share belongs to the Self Help Group Bank Linkage programs that originated in the 1980s. The latter is an integrated approach to provide low-cost financial access combined with learning programs.[46]

According to Sane and Thomas (2012), Indian MFI is in the business of being a credit provider with obligations on two fronts: the consumer on one end and the formal financial sector on the other end from whom the MFI obtains resources.[47]

According to Ghadoliya (2013), a pilot project for linking SHGs with banks was launched by NABARD in 1992. The RBI persuaded commercial banks, RRBs and cooperative banks to partake in the linkage programme. Under the RBI's guidelines, banks were given permission to open saving banks account in the name of SHG, and relaxation of security requirements.[48] According to Krishnan (2012), spread of microfinance is uneven in the country. The performance was better in southern states, with other regions lagging behind. Eastern region is a distant second. Other regions have to do some catching- up-trials. The success of microfinance in southern region is because apart from banks, NGOs and Micro Finance Institutions were also active. In other regions especially in northern and north-eastern, the microfinance is predominantly through banking channels; there is lesser number of NGOs and MFIs are few and far between.[49]

Microfinance in India has brought number of people above the poverty line. But the coverage is uneven with large number of people in rural hinterland still remaining out of the ambit of the outreach programs.[50]

Microfinance and Poverty Eradication

According to Jayasuriya (2007), poverty is the state of being without associated with need hardship and lack of resources across a wide range of circumstances.[51] Poverty reduction via access to financial services has been heralded as the main mission of microfinance institutions.[52] The microfinance industry offers attractive opportunities to investors seeking to participate in alleviating poverty in developing countries.[53]

Poverty reduction has been an important development challenge over decades. One of the identified constraints facing the poor is lack of access to formal sector funds to enable them to take advantage of economic opportunities to increase their level of output, hence move out of poverty.[54]

According to Yeboah (2010), poverty reduction is unarguably the overarching objective for governments, NGOs and other developmental partners for investing in microfinance. Specialists advocated microfinance to efficiently and effectively provide sustainable financial services to poor households, inaccessible to conventional financial systems without collateral. Microfinance is not simply banking; it is a development tool.[55]

According to Kala et. al. (2010), creation of SMEs generates employment, but these enterprises are short –lived, making many lose jobs irrespective of their poverty status. Banks do not lend them for they do not have what was required for the banking services.[56] According to Sarangi (2007), evidence from social programmes in developed and developing countries have divided outcome , even among those eligible, whose participation rates vary widely and are sensitive to programme design.[57]

Millions of rural poor are inaccessible to basic savings and credit services Traditional ways of saving, such as investing into livestock or jewellery, can leave them where they were. Liquid cash is far more convenient.[58]

Microfinance supports mainly informal activities with low return and low market demand. Its aggregate poverty impact remain modest or even nonexistent.[59] It won't maximize profits, nor reimburse but is intended to ameliorate the poor, provided some element of subsidy to enable effectively.[60]

Poor people can earn more, build assets, and cushion selves against external shocks. The households use microfinance to move from everyday survival to future planning, invest in better nutrition, housing, health, and education.[61] According to Bakhtiari (2006), poor need to borrow, save, and invest, and protect their families against adversity. Developing couldn't satisfy the credit needs of poor. Microfinance is believed to reduce the inadequacies of formal and informal financial institutions, an important credit partner to the poor therein.[62]

According to Dunford et. al. (2010), in the past few years, microfinance has been widely heralded as a successful contributor to the alleviation of poverty and a valuable tool for achieving the MDG. Its impact on clients' ability to repay, flourish, build assets and pull themselves out of poverty, some microfinance institutions have added nonfinancial services, such as dialogue-based education and linkages to health products and providers, to impressive effect.[63]

Microfinance and Women Empowerment

Microfinance become the panacea for reaching poor women. There are good reasons to target women.[64] A life of dignity is the right of every citizen. Poverty is an obstruction to such dignified life. About 70 per cent of the 1.3 billion population around the world are women.[65] Women empowerment is a process wherein they challenge the existing norms and culture, to effectively improve their well-being within the south Asian context.. Some argue about them as the most vulnerable among the underprivileged. Others believe investing in their capabilities empowers them make choices, for economic growth and development.[66] According to Agrawala and Carraro (2010), women make up a large section of informal businesses and microfinance. It involves self-employment in the informal sector. Quite often, they have been viewed as more conservative in their investment strategy, more responsive to peer pressure for repayments, and ultimately more responsible in repaying loans. Targeting loans to women fosters their empowerment.[67]

According to Swain and Wallentin (2007), access to credit has received greater attention in the context of poverty reduction and women's empowerment. There has been an increasing expectation on the impact on women empowerment under MDG. Majority of programs target women with the explicit goal to empower with different premises.[68] According to Garikipati (2010), an SHG typically consists of around 10-15 women from poor communities, who come together to save and access credit. The existing institutional structure is linked to individual SHGs. It is being referred to as the SHG-bank linkage programme. It uses the extensive state banking apparatus extending credit to rural poor, along innovations such as joint liability and peer-monitoring to cultivate borrower discipline.[69]

According to Lopamudra and Singh (2012), micro finance and Self Help Group intervention have brought tremendous change in the life of women at the grassroots level by empowering women.[70] The status of women in India has been subject to many great changes over the past few millennia. Self-help groups intermediated by micro credit have had positive effects. They have played valuable roles in reducing the vulnerability of the poor through asset creation, income and consumption smoothing, provision of emergency assistance, empowering and emboldening women through assets control, increased self-esteem and knowledge.[71]

According to Mayoux and Hartl (2009), gender equality and empowerment goals depended on the specific types of financial services by different types of institutions or programmes.[72] India offers a lot of opportunities to women, to hear their a voice in everyday life, Nevertheless, India continues as male-dominated society, where women subordinate them and remain inferior forever.[73]

Empowerment of Women

According to Suja (2012), women at home were oppressed culturally, socially, economically and politically for centuries. They were exploited at home, in the families, in the society and in the country. In the multi-ethnic and multi-cultural society exploitation assumes various forms. They shoulder sundry responsibilities, but were not given adequate participatory or decision making power in the family or elsewhere. They can gain such power, if their economic status, cultural and social status improves. Women empowerment is their overall improvement of power.[74]

According to Bijli (2012), the neglect of women's education to handle her finances is particularly disturbing in the context of globalization. It requires them understand the macro-situation, develop skills and abilities anew to survive development. SEWA Bank play a positive role in expanding the knowledge about money management practices through an awareness drive. Educational processes ought to be expanded as they are critical in enabling them understand micro-credit programmes, for negotiating interests for empowerment.[75] According to Loomba (2010), majority of microfinance programmes focus women for empowerment. Some argue them to vary amongst the poor and the most underprivileged. A more feminist point of view stresses them an increased access to financial services. Such organizations explicitly perceive microfinance as the essential tool in their fight for women's rights and independence. An increasing number of microfinance institutions prefer women members as they believe them to be more reliable borrowers.

Self-help groups intermediated by microcredit have had positive rippling effects on women. They have played valuable roles in reducing the vulnerability of the poor, through asset creation, income and consumption smoothing, provision of emergency assistance, and empowering and emboldening women by giving them control over assets and increased self-esteem and knowledge[76]

The process of empowerment of the beneficiaries is not automatic, but depends upon their abilities; environment, initiative and status of women as group.[77]

According to Sharma (2012), the women micro entrepreneurs in rural areas continue to produce traditional designs for local markets. Women in SHGs produce variety of essential products, village crafts and home made snack foods. Many are being engaged in retail trading of groceries and textiles[78] According to Venkatesh and Kala (2011), microfinance has gained recognition in development conversation the world over as a tool of poverty mitigation and women empowerment.[79] Many institutions could identify their poor clients and trace their poverty levels through lending cycles to help design products and financial services attuned to their needs.[80]

Women in southern India ran viable businesses and contribute to family income. Hundreds of thousands of them opened up grocery shops, engage in poultry and livestock, pappad or pickle making, pottery, vegetable vending, bangle or trinket shops, and beauty parlours. Microfinance is a social finance system designed for bottom of the pyramid customers.[81] According to Mayoux (2005), the system finds promoted as an entry point in the context of a wider strategy for women's economic and socio-political empowerment emphasizing upon gender awareness and feminist organization.[82]

According to D'Espallier (2009), supply and demand for microcredit arguments explain the targeting of women by microfinance organizations. Demand for its services is probably higher among women for a number of reasons. In many countries, women are more credit constrained than men.[83] According to Mayoux (2012), their access to savings and credit facilitates them greater economic role in decision-making through savings and credit components. Women optimize their own and the household's welfare through such decisions.[84] The facilitators must also be cautious to avoid any possible negative outcome.[85] According to Anand (2002), the status of women is intimately connected with their economic position, and depends on opportunities for participating in economic activities.[86]

Conclusion

Microcredit and microfinance have received extensive recognition as the strategy for poverty reduction and economic empowerment. It is a way to fight poverty, particularly in rural areas, where the world's appreciable poor live.[87] Microfinance gives access to financial and non-financial services to the low-income strata in their efforts to access money for starting or developing an income generation activity.[88]

Microfinance has demonstrated its potential to assist the poor in making significant strides towards reducing their exposure, improve the purchasing power, pay for basic health care and bear the educational expenses for their children.[89] Microcredit and micro insurance are often referred to as important and effective ex -post natural hazard risk coping mechanism.[90] In most cases, the provision of savings services in 'microcredit' schemes simply involves the collection of compulsory deposit amounts, designed to collateralize those loans.[91]

Most of the poor people cannot get good financial services. There are not enough strong institutions in this direction, extending such services. The institutions ought to charge enough to cover their costs.[92] Microfinance has contributed in improving the access to credit for consumption and productive purposes. Most (formal) institutions have regarded low-income households as "too poor to save".[93]

References

1. Godwin Chigozie Okpara (2010), Microfinance banks and poverty alleviation in Nigeria, Journal of Sustainable Development in Africa, Volume 12, No.6, <http://www.jsd-africa.com/Jsda/V12No6_Fall2010_B/PDF/ Microfinance%20Banks%20and%20Poverty%20Alleviation%20in%20Nigeria.pdf>

2. Analysis of Micro-finance Impact on Poverty Reduction in Adamawa state, Nigeria (2010),<http://www.fspublishers.org/jass/past-issues/JASSVOL_6_NO_4/5.pdf>
3. Benzies Isaac Adu-Okoree (2012), Peri-urban poverty: Can micro-finance be a panacea?, <http://www.academicjournals.org/ijsa/abstracts/ abstracts/Abstracts2012/Jun/Adu-okoree.htm>
4. Rezart Hoxhaj(2010), Regulation and supervision of microfinance in Albania, <http://academicpublishingplatforms.com/docs/BEH/Volume2/09_V2_BEH_ALBANIA_Rezart_Hoxhaj_Albania_d.pdf>
5. Jan Maes and Laura Foose (2006), Microfinance Services for Very Poor People: Promising Approaches from the Field and The US Law's Mandate to Reach Very Poor People: What Strategies are MFIs Developing, and What do they Mean for the Rest of the Field? -A Practitioner Survey, <http://p31.itcilo.org/entdev/synergies/en/graduation-programs/microfinance-servicesfor-very-poor-people-promising-approaches-from-the-field-jan-maes-2006>
6. Timothée Demont (2010), The impact of microfinance: a study of Self-Help Groups in India, <http://econ.lse.ac.uk/staff/bandiera/demont_slides.pdf>
7. What is Microfinance?, <http://wikimemoires.com/2011/06/whatis-microfinance/>
8. Joseph Kimos Adjei, Thankom Arun and Farhad Hossain (2009), The Role of Microfinance in Asset-Building and Poverty Reduction: The Case of Sinapi Aba Trust of Ghana, <http://www.bwpi.manchester.ac.uk/resources/Working-Papers/bwpi-wp-8709.pdf>
9. Microcredit (2013),<http://en.wikipedia.org/wiki/Microcredit>
10. Sahu Lopamudra and Singh Suresh K (2012), A qualitative study on role of self help group in women empowerment in rural Pondicherry, India, <http://njcmindia.org/uploads/3-3_473-479.pdf>
11. Jean-Marie Baland, Timothée Demont and Rohini Somanathan (2011), Microfinance mechanisms: evidence from observational panel data about SelfHelp Groups in India, <http://www.econ.yale.edu/conference/neudc11/papers/paper_215.pdf>
12. Empowering women through self help groups (2010),Yagna.
13. "Including Africa – beyond microfinance": A new CSFI report, by Mark Napier Sponsored by Citi/DfID, <http://www.creativemetier.com/news/ csfi-report-published-including-africa-beyond-microfinance/>
14. Orrick, Herrington & Sutcliffe LLP (2010), At a glance guide microfinance, <http://www.a4id.org/sites/default/files/user/documents/003%20-%20Guide%20to%20Micrtofinance%20%2830%20Aug%2011%29.pdf>
15. Khalid Mustafa, Zulfiqar Ahamad Gill and Toseef Azid (2000), NGOs, Microfinance and Poverty Alleviation: Experience of the Rural Poor in Pakistan, The Pakistan Development Review,39 : 4 Part II, <http://pide.org.pk/ pdr/index.php/pdr/article/viewFile/1774/1747>
16. Emerlson Moses (2011), An overview of microfinance in India, International Referred Research Journal, <http://www.ssmrae.com/admin/ images/a9899d99b70fc26da4d85961755b8a59.pdf>

17. M. Jahangir Alam Chowdhury, Does Access to Finance Reduce Inequality? Evidence from Bangladesh, <http://jourdev.gretha.u-bordeaux4.fr/ sites/jourdev.gretha/IMG/pdf/5e_chowdury.pdf>
18. Nanci Lee (2006), Rural Remote Microfinance and Selfish Genes, <http://www.ruralfinance.org/fileadmin/templates/rflc/documents/ 1164106672796_Rural_remote_microfinance_and_selfish_genes.pdf>
19. First Microfinance Development Bank Limited.(2013), <http://www.fmdb.com.np/>
20. Shankar Man Shrestha (2009), State of Microfinance in Nepal, <http://www.rmdcnepal.com/form/state_of_microfinance_in_nepal_2011.pdf>
21. Rural Banking and Microfinance, 1st edition, (Hyderabad: The ICFAI University Press, 2006), at 331.
22. Maliha Hamid Hussein (2009), State of Microfinance in Bhutan, Retrieved from <http://www.inm.org.bd/publication/state_of_micro/Bhutan.pdf>
23. Maliha Hamid Hussein (2009), State of Microfinance in Pakistan, <http://www.inm.org.bd/saarc/document/Pakistan.pdf>
24. Anura Atapattu (2009), State of Microfinance in Sri Lanka, <http://www.inm.org.bd/publication/state_of_micro/Sri%20Lanka.pdfhttp://www.inm.org.bd/publication/state_of_micro/Sri%20Lanka.pdf>
25. Maliha Hamid Hussein (2009), State of Microfinance in Afghanistan, < http://www.inm.org.bd/publication/state_of_micro/Afghanistan.pdf>
26. Status of micro finance in India 2011-12,<http://www.nabard.org/departments/pdf/status%20of%20microfinance%202011-12%20full%20book2.pdf>
27. Frances Sinha (2009), State of Microfinance in Maldives, <http://www.inm.org.bd/publication/state_of_micro/Maldives.pdf>
28. Mohamed Yunus and Microfinance in Bangladesh, <http://www.bangladesh.com/blog/mohamed-yunus-and-microfinance-in-bangladesh>
29. Dewan A. H. Alamgir (2009), State of Microfinance in Bangladesh, < http://www.inm.org.bd/publication/state_of_micro/Bangladesh.pdfhttp://www.inm.org.bd/publication/state_of_micro/Bangladesh.pdf>
30. Jon Westover (2008), The Record of Microfinance: The Effectiveness/Ineffectiveness of MicrofinancePrograms as a Means of Alleviating Poverty, Electronic Journal of Sociology, <http://www.sociology.org/ content/2008/_westover_finance.pdf>
31. Britta Augsburg and Cyril Fouillet (2010), Profit Empowerment: The Microfinance Institution's Mission Drift, <http://www.rume-ruralmicrofinance.org/IMG/pdf_PGDT_9_3-4_327-355.pdf>
32. Mohammed Nurul Alam (2009), Interest-Free Microfinance to Micro Entrepreneurs in Rural Bangladesh,Paper to presented at the First International Microfinance Conference on Microfinance held at ULB Brussels on June 2-4, 2009, <http://www.researchgate.net/publication/233547734_Profit_Empowerment_The_Microfinance_Institution's_Mission_Drift>
33. Imran Matin (2003), Poverty Impact and Outreach of Microfinance in Bangladesh: Current Knowledge, Practices and Moving Ahead, [Retrieved from –Missing]

34. Resource Mobilization by the MFIs in Bangladesh, <http://www.esrc.ac.uk/my-esrc/grants/RES-544-28-5001/outputs/read/20186030-db2c-4397-b186-19c64b1a6b0d>

35. Shahidur R. Khandker (2005), Microfinance and Poverty: Evidence Using Panel Data from Bangladesh, The World Bank Economic Review Advance Access published September 8, 2005, <http://wber.oxfordjournals.org/content/19/2/263.abstract>

36. Tapan Parikh, Rural Microfinance Service Delivery: Gaps, Inefficiencies and Emerging Solutions, <http://ieeexplore.ieee.org/xpl/ login.jsp?tp=&arnumber=4085536&url=http%3A%2F%2Fieeexplore.ieee.org%2 Fxpls%2Fabs_all.jsp%3Farnumber%3D4085536>

37. Ferdoushi Ahmed1, Chamhuri Siwar1 Nor Aini Hj. Idris and Rawshan Ara Begum (2011), Impact of microcredit on poverty alleviation among rural women: A case study of Panchagarh District in Bangladesh, <http://www.academicjournals.org/ajbm/pdf/pdf2011/18Aug/Ahmed%20et%20al.pdf>

38. M. Jahangir Alam Chowdhury, Poverty and Microfinance: An Investigation into the Role of Microcredit in Reducing the Poverty Level of Borrowing Households in Bangladesh and the Philippines, The Whitehead Journal of Diplomacy and International Relations, <http://blogs.shu.edu/diplomacy/files/archives/04%2520Chowdhury.pdf>

39. Valerie Rozycki (2006), Credit Information Systems for Microfinance in India: Developing solutions to manage anticipated boom in sector growth, Centre for Micro Finance Working Paper Series, <http://www.microfinancegateway.org/gm/document-1.9.26696/33422_file_CreditInformation Systems_for_MFG_doc.pdf>

40. Micro Finance in India- Transformation of MFIs and Role of SIDBI, <http://www.apraca.org/2012/upload/book/50/10-13%20paper%20forum%20ngotrans%20cambodia%20sidbi.pdf>

41. Anne-Claire Siliki, Why people dropout from Microfinance institutions? Case study of an MFI in Mali, <http://www.rug.nl/research/globalisationstudies-groningen/research/conferencesandseminars/conferences/eumicrofinconf2011/papers/1new.15a.siliki.pdf>

42. Jaya Anitha Abraham (2011), Measurement of social empowerment of farmers in SHGS: Evidence from India, International NGO Journal Vol. 6(12), pp. 255-61.

43. D. Sunder Raj (2004): "SHGs and Women's Empowerment", Social Welfare, January, p. 40.

44. Ritu Jain, R.K.Kushawaha and A.K.Antony (2003): "Socio-Economic Impact through Self-Help Groups", Yojana, July——, p. 11.

45. Renuka Sane and Susan Thomas, A policy response to the Indian micro-finance crisis, <http://www.igidr.ac.in/pdf/publication/WP-2011-007.pdf>

46. Anna-Larisa Snijders and Geske Dijkstra, Microcredit and women's empowerment in South India, <http://www.rug.nl/research/globalisation-studiesgroningen/research/conferencesandseminars/conferences/eumicrofinconf2011/ papers/1new.12.dijkstra.pdf>

47. Renuka Sane and Susan Thomas, What should regulation do in the field of microfinance?, <http://www.igidr.ac.in/pdf/publication/WP-2012-012.pdf>
48. Prof. M.K.Ghadoliya, Empowering Women Through Self -Help Groups: Role Of Distance Education, <http://www.wojde.org/FileUpload/ bs295854/File/ 01_13.pdf>
49. Dr. Mahalaxmi Krishnan, Micro Finance through Self Help Groups for Inclusive Growth, <http://www.abhinavjournal.com/images/Arts_&_Education/Jan12/3-Maha.pdf>
50. Dr. Mahalaxmi Krishnan, Micro Finance through Self Help Groups for Inclusive Growth, <http://www.abhinavjournal.com/images/Arts_&_Education/Jan12/3-Maha.pdf>
51. Prasansha Kumari Jayasuriya, Impact of the Micro Finance on Poverty Alleviation in Sri Lanka: Special Reference to Sammurdhi Programme, <http:// www.kln.ac.lk/uokr/ARS2007/2.7.pdf>
52. Beatriz Armendáriz, Bert D'Espallier, Ariane Szafarz & Marek Hudon (2011), Subsidy Uncertainty and Microfinance Mission Drift, <http://www.unifr.ch/ controlling/seminar/2012-2013/Szafarz%20Ariane_Subsidy% 20Uncertainty% 20and%20Microfinance%20Mission%20Drift%202011.pdf>
53. Marie Brière and Ariane Szafarz (2011), Investment in Microfinance Equity: Risk, Return, and Diversification Benefits, <https://dipot.ulb.ac.be/ dspace/ bitstream/2013/100398/1/wp11050.pdf>
54. Appah Emimobowei, John M.Sophia and Soreh Wisdom (2012), An analysis of microfinance and poverty reduction in Bayelsa State of Nigeria, Kuwait Chapter of Arabian Journal of Business and Management ReviewVol. 1, No.7; <http:// www.arabianjbmr.com/pdfs/KD_VOL_1_7/3.pdf>
55. Eric H. Yeboah, Achieving poverty reduction and institutional sustainability through a contextual sustainability approach, <http://erd.eui.eu/ media/2010/ Yeboah-201006.pdf>
56. K. Nithya Kala, K. Vidya Kala and S. Poornima, Microfinance: An anti poverty vaccine for rural India, <http://www.abesit.in/pdfs/Micro-Financeas-an-Anti.pdf>
57. Niranjan Sarangi (2007), Microfinance and the Rural Poor: Impact Assessment Based on Fieldwork in Madhya Pradesh, India, <http://www.hss.iitb.ac.in/ties07/ paper/ts4/psB/2.pdf>
58. Microfinance and poverty reduction (2013). <http://www.ifad.org/media/pack/ microfinance.htm>
59. Role of Self Help Groups through Micro-finance for poverty alleviation and Micro entrepreneurship of women (2011). <http://www.academia.edu/2053940/ Role_of_Self_Help_Groups_through_Micro-finance_for_ poverty_alleviation_ and_Micro-Entrepreneurship_of_women>
60. <http://ifmr.ac.in/cmf/mrap/wp-content/uploads/2009/04/grammen-bank-groupsand-self-help-groups.pdf>
61. Microfinance and Poverty eradication: Some international evidence, Sadegh Bakhtiari, (Bakhtiari_Sadegh@yahoo.com), Isfahan University, Iran, International Business & Economics ResearchJournal- December 2006, Volume 5, No.12.

62. Sadegh Bakhtiari (2006), Microfinance And Poverty Reduction: Some International Evidence, Journal International Business & Economics Research, <http://www.ijbssnet.com/journals/Vol_2_No_21_Special_Issue_November_2011/16.pdf>
63. Christopher Dunford, Sheila Leatherman, Myka Reinsch Sinclair, Marcia Metcalfe, Bobbi Gray and Ellen Vorder Bruegge, How microfinance can work for the poor, <https://www.freedomfromhunger.org/howmicrofinance-can-work-poor-case-integrating-microfinance-education-andhealth-services>
64. Susy Cheston and Lisa Kuhn, Empowering Women Through Microfinance, <http://www.wikigender.org/index.php/Empowering_Women_ through_Microfinance:_Evidence_from_India>
65. Britta Augsburg, Ralph De Haas,Heike Harmgart, and Costas Meghir (2010), Microfinance, poverty and education, <http://www.povertyactionlab. org/publication/microfinance-poverty-and-education>
66. Empowering women through microfinance: Evidence from India, <http://www.wikigender.org/index.php/Empowering_Women_through_Microfinance:_Evidence_from_India>
67. Shardul Agrawala and Maëlis Carraro (2010). "Assessing the role of microfinance in fostering adaptation to climate change", OECD Environmental Working Paper No. 15, 2010, OECD publishing.
68. Ranjula Bali Swain and Fan Yang Wallentin (2007), Does microfinance empower women? Evidence from Self Help Groups in India, <http://www.nek.uu.se/pdf/wp2007_24.pdf>
69. Supriya Garikipati (2010), Microcredit and Women's Empowerment: Have We Been Looking at the Wrong Indicators?, <https://dipot.ulb.ac.be/dspace/bitstream/2013/57623/1/wp10030.pdf>
70. Sahu Lopamudra and Singh Suresh K (2012), A qualitative study on role of self help group in women empowerment in rural Pondicherry, India, <http://njcmindia.org/uploads/3-3_473-479.pdf>
71. Chapter 5, Women empowerment and micro credit system, <http://shodhganga.inflibnet.ac.in/bitstream/10603/3936/6/06_contents.pdf>
72. Linda Mayoux and Maria Hartl (2009), Gender and rural microfinance: Reaching and empowering women: Guide for practitioners, <http://www.ifad.org/gender/pub/gender_finance.pdf>
73. Women situation in India, <http://www.saarthakindia.org/womens_situation_India.html
74. Dr. S. Suja, Women empowerment through Self-Help group: An evaluative study, <http://www.sonamgmt.org/gmr-may-2012.pdf>
75. Heena K. Bijli (2012). Financial Literacy: An Essential Tool for Empowerment of Women through Micro-finance, Stud Home Com Sci, 6(2): 77-85.
76. Dr. Shuchi Loomba, Role of microfinance in women empowerment in India, <http://jms.nonolympictimes.org/Articles/Article1.pdf>
77. Impact of Microfinance on Women Empowerment, Chapter: 6, <http://shodhganga.inflibnet.ac.in/bitstream/10603/3031/14/14_chapter%206.pdf>

78. Dr. Ranjana Sharma (2012), Microfinance: A platform for the empowerment of women, <http://www.wissen.allianz.at/?97/microfinance-aplatform-for-the-empowerment-of-women>
79. Dr. J. Venkatesh and Ms. K.Kala (2011), Upholding of microfinance self-help groups, <http://www.jmijitm.com/papers/1300824009172-175.pdf>
80. Utilising the Palestine Simple Poverty Scorecard: Baseline Poverty Study of UNRWA Microfinance Clients in the West Bank(February 2011), <http://www.unrwa.org/userfiles/2011050234417.pdf>
81. Microfinance and women empowerment, <http://www.gdrc.org/ icm/wind/magic.html>
82. Linda Mayoux (2005). Women's Empowerment through Sustainable Microfinance: Rethinking 'Best Practice' <http://www.sed.manchester.ac.uk/research/iarc/ediais/pdf/WomensEmpowerment throughSustainable Microfinance.pdf>
83. Bert D'Espallier, Isabelle Guérin and Roy Mersland (2009). Women and Repayment in Microfinance, <http://www.microfinancegateway.org/gm/document-1.9.40253/Women%20and%20Repayment%20in%20Microfinance.pdf.>
84. Linda Mayoux, Micro-finance and the empowerment of women: A review of the key issues, <http://www.ilo.org/wcmsp5/groups/public/@ed_emp/ documents/publication/wcms_117993.pdf>
85. Small change, Big changes: Women and Microfinance, <http://www.gjournals.org/GJSC/GJSC%20PDF/2013/May/022613502%20Ocholah%20et%20al.pdf>
86. Jaya S. Anand (2002). Self-Help Groups in Empowering Women: Case study of selected SHGs and NHGs, Microfinance and Poverty Reduction: Some International Evidence
87. Dr.AjitKumarBansal and Ms.Anu Bansal (2012), Microfinance and poverty eradication in India, Integral Review- A Journal of Management, <http://www.integraluniversity.ac.in/12052010/Ajit_Anu.pdf>
88. A guide to Gender sensitive microfinance (2002), <http://www.fao.org/docrep/012/ak208e/ak208e00.pdf>
89. Muhammad Akram and Imtiaz Hussain (2011), The Role of Microfinance in uplifting Income Level: A study of District Okara – Pakistan, <http://connection.ebscohost.com/c/articles/61067874/role-microfinanceuplifting-income-level-study-district-okara-pakistan>
90. Sonia Akter and Naureen Fatema, The role of microcredit and micro insurance in coping with natural hazard risks, <http://www.webmeets.com/ eaere/2011/m/viewpaper.asp?pid=546>
91. Sadegh Bakhtiari (2006), Microfinance And Poverty Reduction: Some International Evidence, Journal International Business and Economics Research, <http://www.microfinancegateway.org/p/site/m/template.rc/1.1.9467/http://www.ijbssnet.com/journals/Vol_2_No_21_Special_Issue_November_2011/16.pdf>

92. Sadegh Bakhtiari (2006), Microfinance And Poverty Reduction: Some International Evidence, Journal International Business and Economics Research, <http://www.ijbssnet.com/journals/Vol_2_No_21_Special_Issue_ November_ 2011/16.pdf>

93. Naveen K. Shetty, The Microfinance Promise in Financial Inclusion and Welfare of the Poor: Evidence from India, <http://www.igidr.ac.in/money/ mfc-13/mfc_08/Copy%20of%20Copy%20of%20Naveen% 20K%20Shetty_ submission_23.pdf>

94. http://www.researchgate.net/publication/228455159_Microfinance_ mechanisms _evidence_from_observational_panel_data_about_Self-Help_Groups_in_India.

Chapter - 8

National Bank for Agriculture and Rural Development [NABARD]

"Rather than justice for all, we are evolving into a system of justice for those who can afford it. We have banks that are not only too big to fail, but too big to be held accountable."
— ***Joseph E. Stiglitz***

Introduction

Bank is a financial intermediary. It accepts deposits and channels them into lending activities, either directly by loaning or indirectly through capital markets. A bank links together capital deficits and customers with capital surpluses. Their importance in the financial system and the influence on national economies, have made banks highly regulated in most countries. Banking, in its modern sense evolved in the14th century in the rich cities of Renaissance, but in many ways was a continuation of ideas and concepts of credit and lending that had its roots in the ancient world.[1] They are the most important segment of any country where money and its necessity is utmost. A developed financial system ensures development. A modern bank provides valuable services to a country. Capital is one of the offshoot of any business or industry, life blood. Banks increase capital formation by collecting deposits from depositors and convert those advanced loans to industries.[2/3]

NB: Authors- your third quotation finds some repetition. So, I've changed the quotation 2 as 2/3.

The businesses have a need for a line of credit or other financing with a bank. It will be so, when business slows down or the company is under struggles, strained relations with the banker. Commercial banks play a key role in the economy at the national and global level. Their importance include the fact that they serve as a trusted and safe place, where the funds of people and businesses can be safeguarded, reducing the necessity to park enormous sums of money on the private or business premises.[4]

What Is Nabard?

NABARD is an apex Development Bank with a mandate for facilitating credit flow for promotion and development of agriculture, small scale industries, cottage and village industries, handicrafts and other rural crafts. It supports allied economic activities in rural areas, promote integrated and sustainable rural development and secure prosperity of rural areas.[5] According to Mohanaiah (2010), It targets (a) promoting sustainable and equitable agriculture and rural prosperity through effective credit support, related services, institution development and other innovative initiatives; (b) ensures integrated development of rural areas through single window approach.[6]

The main objectives of the NABARD, while placing the bill before the Lok Sabha were categorized as: (a) The National Bank will be an apex organisation in respect of matters relating to policy, planning operational aspects in the field of credit for promotion of agriculture, small scale industries, cottage and village industries, handicrafts, rural crafts and allied economic activities, (b) It will serve as a short [long]-term refinancing institution for institutional credit in rural areas, (c) It will lend directly to the government at the Centre approved institution and (d) will have have organic links with the RBI and maintain a close link from within.[7]

Its History

The Committee to Review Arrangements for Institutional Credit for Agriculture and Rural Development (CRAFICARD), set up by the Reserve Bank of India under the chairmanship of B. Sivaraman, conceived and recommended the establishment of the National Bank for Agriculture and Rural Development (NABARD). It was established on July 12, 1982 by a special act of the parliament. Its main focus was to uplift rural India by increasing the credit flow for elevation of agriculture and rural non farm sector. It has completed 25 years of service as on July 12, 2007. CRAFICARD found it prudent to integrate short, medium and long-term credit structure for agriculture sector by establishing a new bank. NABARD is being the result of the recommendation. It was set up with an initial capital of Rs 100 crore, enhanced later to Rs 2,000 crore, fully subscribed by the government of India and the RBI. NABARD will be vested with the assets and liabilities pertaining to the RBIs National Agricultural Credit (Long Term Operations) Fund and the National Agricultural Credit (Stabilisation) Fund, while assimilating with Agricultural Finance and Development Corporation. It would create correspondingly and maintain The Rural Credit (Long-term Operations) Fund and the National Rural Credit (Stabilisation) Fund, respectively. It will take over the liability of SCBs and RRBs in respect of loans and advances extended already by RBI at the time of establishment under Section 17 (excluding sub-section (4) of the RBI Act, 1934 with rights to recover the said dues.[8]

Its Functions

NABARD, headquartered at Mumbai, is an apex institution looking after the development of cottage, small and village, and rural industries. Its refinance is available to State Cooperative Agriculture and Rural Development Banks (SCARDBs), State Co-operative Banks (SCBs), Regional Rural Banks (RRBs), Commercial Banks (CBs) and other financial institutions approved by RBI. Its ultimate beneficiaries of investment credit can be individuals, partnership concerns, companies, state-owned corporations or co-operative societies, production credit is generally given to individuals.[9]

Its other activities include:

(a) it is the inspecting authority, combining the responsibilities envisaged for developmental and statutory inspections;

(b) It will receive such returns and other data concerning regional rural Banks, state cooperative banks to keep close watch over the performance, health and viability of the institutions;

(c) RBI is being empowered to verify any of its certificate whether any state cooperative or a regional rural bank satisfies the requirements about the share capital and reserves and whether their affairs are being conducted in a manner not detrimental to the interests of depositors. It would be in a position to issue such certificate, while auditing those banks;

(d) It is vested with the responsibility to coordinate with other rural development Institutions;

(e) It will extend facilities for training, dissemination of information and promotion of research in the field of rural banking, agriculture and rural development;

(f) It may also collect such credit information when called for and share the same with the Central Government and RBI.[10]

Rural Development

NABARD is being entrusted with: (a) refinances to lending institutions in rural areas; (b) bring about or promote institutional development and (c) evaluate, monitor and inspect client banks from time to time. Potential Linked Credit Plans [PLPs] were being prepared by NABARD annually for districts across the country. It maps the potential available for development in agriculture and rural sectors in those districts and projects the credit requirements, accounting for the long-term physical potential, available infrastructure and planned extension services, marketing support, credit absorption capacity besides the strength and capabilities of the Rural Financial Institutions (RFIs). The PLPs form the basis for preparation of Annual Credit Plan at the district level by banks. The state governments in completing such rural infrastructure projects often take up new infrastructure projects.

Rural Infrastructure Development Fund (RIDF) was set up with NABARD in 1995-96 for providing term loans at concessional rates to state governments. At present, 31 activities cover the institution in every aspect of rural infrastructure under RIDF. The institution provides policy support for farm sector initiatives in accelerating ground level credit flow by rural credit agencies for farm related activities, under investment credit. It shall increase agricultural productivity, generate employment, manage natural resources and alleviate the sector through credit and support grant. It supports in natural resource management through unique models, which become the benchmark in the respective fields.[11]

The institution, established as the premiere development bank, was envisaged to provide credit for development, and publicity of small-scale industries, handicrafts, rural crafts, village industries, cottage industries, agriculture, etc. It supports economic related operations in rural sector and looks after promoting its sustainable growth.

The institution promotes institutional development, facilitate, refinance loan providers in rural sector, inspect, monitor, and evaluate client financial corporations. It assists the RBI with other organizations concerned with the development of rural sector, and the government of India, coordinates with the functions of rural loan providers, aids those state governments in assisting rural developmental institutions, besides training facilities for cooperatives, banks, and other organizations.[12]

The institution will start livelihood projects in 19 Maoist-hit districts of Odisha [under pipeline], through an MoU with the Sir Dorabji Tata Trust (SDTT). As NABARD and SDTT, would jointly undertake integrated developmental programme in agriculture, health, sanitation and safe drinking water in rural areas. Some partner organizations like NGOs would promote farming through producers' cooperatives and SHGs and SHG federation, for which the institution will extend credit support. The collaboration would also promote Diversion-based Irrigation [DBI] projects vegetable cultivation, anganwadi development, scaling up of System of Rice Intensification (SRI)/System of Crop Intensification, seed production, aggregation of crop produce and market linkages, establishing agriculture implements bank, watershed development with improved crop production techniques, improved agriculture and poly house/net house.[13]

The Hindu (May 29, 2014) reported on the institution's warning to the state of Odisha that sanction for development projects under Rural Infrastructure Development Fund will be withdrawn, on its failure to implement projects at faster rate. NABARD's report [As on March 31, 2014], 189 projects with the RIDF loan of Rs.380.09 crore have not been grounded, out of which 20 projects and 169 projects were completed within a period of 12 months and 18 months, respectively from the date of sanction letter. As per existing guidelines, any project isconsidered as non-starter, if it is not grounded within 12 months from the date of sanctioned letter. The sanction would lapse, if the state government fails to ground the projects within a period of 18 months from the date of sanctioned letter. The apex rural development bank urged the government to ensure a quick review of projects. Of the 1,27,060 projects sanctioned under RIDF XII to XVIII, 75,682 projects were completed, where completion reports for 46,195 projects were received thereupon.[14]

The State Focus Paper for the year 2014-15 focuses on two important aspects viz., estimation of sectoral potential for credit on a scientific and rational basis besides suggesting an incisive coverage of critical infrastructure requirements and gaps to be bridged for development in each of the sectors.[15] The Business Standard (June 2, 2014) reported what NABARD claimed in the state of Madhya Pradesh agriculture sector, as increasingly unviable owing to yield and price risks as well as lack of risk mitigation mechanism for small and marginal farms.

The bank has emphasized on some alarming issues like dwindling land holding much below the national average and poor credit vis-a-vis other states. About 50 per cent of the 90 lakh operational land holdings were covered with credit and the per hectare agriculture credit was lower than that of many states, pointing at the need for concerted efforts of the banks in improving farm credit scenario in the state. It has projected that a whopping Rs.75, 000 crore to the state as bank credit, primarily to its agriculture and allied sectors. The fragmentation of land has been challenging issue, as evidenced by the increasing number of small land holding in the state. The average land holding declined from 2.02 hectare [2005-06] to 1.78 hectare [2010-11] as against all India average of 1.16 hectare. Marginal and small farmers, accounted for more than two third (71 per cent) holding around one-third (34 per cent) of total area. The stern measure restricts farm mechanization, affecting production and productivity.[16]

The Economic Times (May 15, 2014) quoted the, Banks' outstanding deposits under the Rural Infrastructure Development Fund and some funds with NABARD to be treated as priority sector lending under indirect agriculture category. It has been decided to include the outstanding deposits by banks under Rural Infrastructure Development Fund and certain other funds established with NABARD, on account of the shortfall in lending to priority sector, as part of indirect agriculture, under priority sector classification. Loans to corporate, including the farmers' producer companies of individual farmers, partnership firms and their co-operatives, directly engaged in agriculture and allied activities, such as dairy, fishery, animal husbandry, poultry, bee-keeping and sericulture (rearing up to cocoon stage) were amongst the indirect agriculture lending. Credit to dealers/ sellers of fertilisers, pesticides, seeds, cattle feed, poultry feed, agricultural implements, construction and running of storage facilities, setting up of agriclinics and agribusiness centres were amongst the indirect agriculture lending. Agriculture, small scale industries, education, housing and export credit were categorised as priority sector lending for which the domestic banks are expected to lend about 40 per cent of their advances.[17]

NABARD has been implementing Natural Resource Management projects (Watershed Development and Wadi Development Programmes) for the past 18 years under Indo-German collaboration with the support from German Development Corporation (GDC). NABARD and GDC have now launched the Umbrella Programme on Natural Resources Management (UPNRM). The objective of the package was to improve rural livelihood through Community-based and sustainable NRM interventions. It envisages a shift from grant-based to loan based funding support.[18]

The Times of India (June 09, 2014) reported on the bank's desire raise Rs. 5,000 crore through tax-free bonds, in augmenting resources and boost lending to protect farming and the dairy sector to counteract food inflation. The institution has written to the government, seeking higher fund allocation and clearance for the bond issue in the central Budget. A tax-free status would make its bonds more attractive to investors and help reduce funding cost, the daily justified.

The previous UPA government had allowed a few infrastructure finance institutions to issue tax-free bonds. It has initiated a pilot project to fund protected agriculture in Maharashtra for onion, in West Bengal for potatoes and in Haryana for tomatoes. Warehouse funding for efficient use of milk, eggs and meat were to be encouraged. Nabard expects an allocation of about Rs. 5,000 crore for above activities. Any shortage in rains could leave a big impact on agriculture and farmers' income, making it difficult for them to repay loans since more than 60 per cent of the country's farm land is rain fed. Nabard has reduced refinance rates on long-term loans by 20-basis points, or 0.2 per centage point, in an attempt to incentivise the capital formation in agriculture. The new rates of refinance was 9.50 per cent for five years and above, and 9.70 per cent for 3-5 years.[19]

NABARD [Amendment] Bill

The NABARD (Amendment) Bill, 2013 was introduced in the Lok Sabha on May 06, 2013. It seeks to amend the earlier Act, 1981. It has been referred to the Standing Committee on Finance (chair person, Yashwant Sinha) on May 09, 2013 for examination [which was expected to submit report by August 9, 2013]. The government at the Centre and the RBI, as per the Act, were to hold its capital, and its share is being valued at Rs. 20 crore, to be transferred to the central government. The Act requires the central government to consult with the RBI on steps (i) guiding the institution on matters of policy, (ii) removal of its chairman and the managing director, besides (iii) approving the establishment of offices, branches or agencies outside India. The Bill, envisaged the centre not to consult RBI on such measures, including the requisite capital enhancement to Rs. 100 crore. Additionally, the Act has a provision for the central government to notify an increase in the capital up to Rs. 5,000 crore in consultation with the RBI. The Bill requires the institution to establish a fund to be known as the National Rural Credit (Short Term Operations) Fund. This fund is to include sums of money that may be contributed by the centre and state governments, the RBI and the Board of NABARD. The Bill specifies that the amount in the National Rural Credit (Short Term Operations) Fund is to be used for providing financial assistance by way of refinance, loans and advances for periods not exceeding 18 months. The Bill merges the posts of the chairman and the managing director of NABARD.[20]

The institution commenced the SHG-Bank Linkage Programme (SHG-BLP) in 1992 for providing the SHGs with Bank credit. It foresees the SHGBLP, as part of an overall arrangement for providing financial services to the poor in a sustainable manner and also as an empowerment process for the members of this SHGs. It has instituted dedicated Funds as also Departments at Head Office and Regional Offices to pursue various developmental initiatives in micro finance related activities.[21]

Conclusion

NABARD is being set up as an apex development bank with a mandate for facilitating credit flow for promotion and development of agriculture, small scale industries, cottage and village industries, handicrafts and other rural crafts. The mandate supports allied economic activities in rural areas, promote integrated and sustainable rural development and secure prosperity of rural areas. It had had a portfolio of Natural Resource Management Programmes involving fields like Watershed Development, Tribal Development and Farm Innovation through dedicated Funds. The role of the institution in overall development of India in general and rural and agricultural sector in specific is highly pivotal. It has been instrumental in grounding rural, social innovations and social enterprises in the rural hinterlands.

References

1. Bank (2014), <http://en.wikipedia.org/wiki/Bank>
2. Importance of bank, <http://icv.hubpages.com/hub/IMPORTANCE-OF - BANKS-IN-THE-DEVELOPMENT-OF-THE-COUNRTY>
3. <http://icv.hubpages.com/hub/IMPORTANCE-OF-BANKS-IN-THEDEVELOPMENT-OF-THE-COUNTRY>
4. <http://www.wisegeek.com/what-is-the-importance-of-commercial-banks.htm>
5. National bank for agriculture and rural development, <http:// kandhamal.nic.in/ km-nbrd/nbrd-1.pdf>
6. Paladi Mohanaiah, Role of NABARD in Promoting, Supporting and Regulating Agriculture Finance, <http://www.agrifinfacility.org/sites/ agrifinfacility.org/files/ NABARD.pdf>
7. About NABARD, <http://oldsite.nabard.org/objectives.asp>

8. Role of NABARD in Rural Development, <http://www.enabl ersi ndia.com/ banker/ibfsa03a.pdf>

9. National bank for agriculture and rural development, <http:// en.wikipedia.org/ wiki/National_Bank_for_Agriculture_and_Rural_Development>

10. Role of NABARD in Rural Development, <http://www.enabler sindia.com/ banker/ibfsa03a.pdf>

11. National bank for agriculture and rural development, <http:// kandhamal.nic.in/ km-nbrd/nbrd-1.pdf>

12. National Bank for Agriculture and Rural Development, <http:// business. mapsofindia.com/rural-economy/development/national-bankagriculture.html>

13. NABARD to start livelihood project in 19 Maoist-hit districts of Odisha, <http:/ /www.orissadiary.com/CurrentNews.asp?id=50430>

14. The Hindu (May 29, 2014), NABARD warns Odisha on pending projects, <http:/ /www.thehindu.com/todays-paper/tp-national/tp-otherstates/ nabard-warns-odisha-on-pending-projects/article6059585.ece>

15. <http://www.indiaenvironmentportal.org.in/content/387332/nabards-statefocus-paper-2014-15-for-madhya-pradesh/>

16. Business Standard (June 2, 2014),NABARD paints a sordid picture of Madhya Pradesh's agriculture sector, <http://www.business-standard.com/ article/ economy-policy/nabard-paints-a-sordid-picture-of-madhya-pradesh-sagriculture-sector-114013001299_1.html>

17. The Economic Times (May 15, 2014), Outstanding deposits under Rural Infrastructure Development Fund under priority lending, <http:// economictimes. indiatimes.com/industry/banking/finance/banking/outstandingdeposits-under-rural-infrastructure-development-fund-under-priority-lending/articleshow/ 35164659.cms>

18. <http://www.bombaychamber.com/uploads/NABARD-%20Umbrella%20 Programme%20for%20Natural%20Resource%20Management.pdf>

19. The Times of India (June 09, 2014),Nabard plans to raise Rs 5,000 cr via taxfree bonds, <http://articles.economictimes.indiatimes.com/2014-06-09/news/ 50447981_1_nabard-harsh-kumar-bhanwala-tax-free-bonds>

20. National Bank for Agricultural and Rural Development (Amendment) Bill, <http:/ /www.prsindia.org/billtrack/the-national-bank-foragriculture-and-rural-development-amendment-bill-2013-2736/>

21. <http://slbckarnataka.in/userfiles/NABARD/Nabard%20&%20%20GOI %20Schemes.pdf>

PART - II

FUNCTIONS AND ACTIVITIES

Chapter - 9

Nationalization of Indian Banks

"The rich run a global system that allows them to accumulate capital and pay the lowest possible price for labour. The freedom that results applies only to them. The many simply have to work harder, in conditions that grow ever more insecure, to enrich the few. Democratic politics, which purports to enrich the many, is actually in the pocket of those bankers, media barons and other moguls who run and own everything." — ***Charles Moore***

Introduction

Bank is a financial institution that provides banking and other financial services to customers. A bank is generally understood as an institution, which provides fundamental banking services, such as accepting deposits and providing loans. A banking system referred as a system provided by the bank, offers cash management services for customers, reporting the transactions of their accounts and portfolios, round-the-clock the day. Before their establishment, the financial activities were handled by money lenders and individuals. The interest rates levied were very high. There was no security of public savings nor uniformity about the offered loans.[1]

Bank of Hindustan (1770-1829) and The General Bank of India [1786] are now defunct. Banking in India was generally fairly mature in terms of supply, product range but access to poor still remains a challenge. The government has developed initiatives to address this problem through the State Bank of India. It is expanding the branch network and through NABARD in extending things like microfinance.[2]

According to Chakrabarti (2012), banking is an ancient business in India., with some references in the writings of Acharya Manu. Bankers played an important role during the Mogul period. During the early part of the East India Company era, agency houses were involved in banking. Modern banking (i.e. in the form of joint-stock companies) may be said to have had its beginnings in India as far back as in 1786, with the establishment of the General Bank of India. Three Presidency Banks were established in Bengal, Bombay and Madras in the early 19th century. These banks functioned independently for about a century, before they were being merged into the newly formed Imperial Bank of India [1921].[3]

India has a long history of public and private banking. Modern banking in India began in the 18 century, with the founding of the English Agency House in Calcutta and Bombay. Early 19 century, enabled to surface. After the 1860, introduction of limited liability, private banks with foreign banks entered the market. Early 20 century saw the introduction of joint stock banks. The presidency banks were merged to form the Imperial Bank of India [1935], subsequently renamed as the State Bank of India. India's central bank, the Reserve Bank of India, began operation in the same year. Following the independence, the RBI was given broad regulatory authority over commercial banks in India. In 1959, the State Bank of India acquired the state-owned banks of eight former princely states. Thus, by July 1969, approximately 31 per cent of scheduled bank branches throughout India were government-controlled as part of the State Bank of India.

The Reasons behind!

The main aim of nationalizing the banks in India was to make it reach its clients in rural areas with quality services. Only 14 more banks were nationalized [1969] and seven more banks entered the fray [1980]. The state bank is always the best commercial bank in India, among the top five banks in the whole world.[5]

According to Singh (2013), the nationalisation of commercial banks increased the role of public sector banks. The reasons accountable are: (1) the removal of control by a few; (2) provision of adequate credit facilities to agriculture, small industry and exports; (3) encourage of professional bent to bank management; (4) encourage of new classes of entrepreneurs, (5) adequate training as well as reasonable terms of service for bank staff; (6) march forward towards socialism; (7) greater stability of banking structure; (8) greater control by the Reserve Bank; (9) balanced regional development; and (10) help extended to agriculture. Nationalisation of banks creates great interest among various sections of the public. Many hopes were raised in the middle class and poor people with regard to the financial assistance.[6]

The drive in India

Nationalised banks dominate the system in India. The history dates back to mid-20 century, when Imperial Bank of India was nationalised (under the SBI Act of 1955) and re-christened as the State Bank of India [July 1955]. On July 19, 1960, its seven subsidiaries were also nationalised with deposits over Rs. 200 crore, was the occasion, when the subsidiaries of SBI were State Bank of Bikaner and Jaipur, State Bank of Hyderabad, State Bank of Indore, State Bank of Mysore, State Bank of Patiala, State Bank of Saurashtra, and State Bank of Travancore.[7] In a major process of nationalization, seven subsidiaries of the State Bank of India were nationalized by the Indira Gandhi regime.

The subsequent drive took place in two phases. The first phase commenced in 1955, when the erstwhile Imperial Bank of India became the State Bank of India with an Act of parliament. During 1959, seven subsidiaries were nationalized and associated with the State Bank of India, one after another..This heralded a new beginning in Indian banking system. The State Bank group became the largest bank in India serving 90 million customers with a network of over 9,000 branches in every nook and corner of the country. The second phase of the drive was commenced in 1969 with 14 major commercial banks entering the fray. In 1980, six more commercial banks were nationalized and became public sector banks. After this period the Public Sector Undertaking banks expanded their reach and grew in leaps and bounds.[8]

Following the exercise, 14 major private commercial banks were nationalized. [1969] These banks were as follows: Central Bank of India, Bank of Maharastra, Dena Bank, Punjab National Bank, Syndicate Bank, Canara Bank, Indian Bank, Indian Overseas Bank, Bank of Baroda, Union Bank, Allahabad Bank, Union Bank of India, UCO Bank, and Bank of India. In the subsequent phase of nationalization [1980], the government of India acquired the ownership of six more banks (i.e. Andhra Bank, , Corporation Bank, New Bank of India, Oriental Bank of Commerce, Punjab & Sindh Bank, Vijaya Bank), thus bringing the total number of nationalised banks to 20. The private banks at that time were allowed to function side by side with them and the foreign banks were allowed to work under surveillance. After the two major phases of nationalization in India, the 80 per cent of the sector came under the public sector / government ownership.[9] According to Deolalkar (2012), the government in 1969, arranged the nationalization of 14 scheduled commercial banks in order to expand the branch network, followed by six more in 1980. A merger reduced the the number from 20 to 19. The state bank group and nationalized banks are together referred to as the public sector banks (PSBs).[10]

Nationalised banks in India were of higher quality, because they were strong, clean and have very transparent balance sheets than other ordinary banks and the main aim of these banks was to manage volatility, with a fixed exchange rate. Nationalized banks in India offer great and quality services to customers, they also offer insurance services like health insurance which enables a person to save money for any unexpected accidents.[11] According to Cole (2008),nationalized banks remained corporate entities, retaining most of their staff, with the exception of members of the board of directors, replaced by appointees of the central government.

The political appointments included the representatives from government, industry, agriculture, as well as the public. Nationalization was accompanied by a series of government regulations that sought to affect lending decisions. The government enacted priority sector targets, which required banks to lend a certain share of credit to agriculture, small-scale industry, and other sectors. Banks falling short of this target were required to lend the shortfall amount of the to the government at penalty (very low) rates.[12] It was proposed that nationalization will enable to direct the credits to priority fields of agriculture, small scale and exports, in whom banking units could not expand in rural areas on the enhancement of public confidence. Indian commercial banks catered only to the large and medium scale industry, to repay the money at a higher interest rate in comparison to rural areas.[13]

Liberalization in 1990s

In the early 1990s, the then Narsimha Rao government embarked on a policy of liberalisation, licensing a small number of private banks. These came to be known as New Generation tech-savvy banks, and included Global Trust Bank (the first of such new generation banks to be set up), which later amalgamated with Oriental Bank of Commerce, Axis Bank (earlier as UTI Bank), ICICI Bank and HDFC Bank. This move facilitated the growth in Economy, revolutionized the banking sector, with contribution of banks from three sectors, namely, government, private and foreign.

The RBI allowed [March '66] Warburg Pincus to increase its stake in Kotak Mahindra Bank (a private sector bank) to 10 per cent. This is the first time an investor has been allowed to hold more than 5 per cent in a private sector bank since the RBI announced norms in 2005 that any stake exceeding 5 per cent in the private sector banks would need to be voted in.[14]

The RBI Review Panel

The Times of India (May 15, 2014) quoted P J Nayak, the chairman of the RBI panel to review, the governance in banking boards, the Bank Nationalisation Act of 1969 is too primitive and irrelevant to cope with the needs of corporate governance. The new government that takes charge at the Centre will have to decide whether to discard with the four-decade-old law introduced by Indira Gandhi as recommended by the panel. Nayak said, "The Bank Nationalisation Act of 1969 was necessary at that time and its enactment was for government ownership of the banks. But 45 years after the Act was promulgated, it is important for us to ask if this is the best legislative structure, under which the banks should now function. For a long time, we had an unreformed Companies Act, but in 2013 we got the new Companies Act which creates good governance structure at the level of the board."

The Companies Act provides more relevant way of governing banks than the Bank Nationalisation Act as a whole. In fact, in comparison, the later Act appears irrelevant, almost primitive today. It (Bank Nationalisation Act) was not created to govern banks; but to take them over. The time has come to move them under a company law responsibility framework. This could be done, if the legislation find introduced. The former finance minister Pranab Mukherjee had hailed the legislation in his Union Budget for 2009. Nayak said that the panel's recommendation was aimed at empowerment of the boards of public sector banks. It sought to bring in accountability by 168 suggesting that there should be rollback of bonuses if banks, if banks hid bad loans through "ever greening".[15]

Conclusion

Nationalization of Indian banks is the main turning point in the history. All banks were under the control of central government. The domestic banking system has several outstanding achievements. The government took major steps in the banking sector reform after independence. In 1955, it nationalized the Imperial Bank of India with extensive banking facilities on a large scale, especially in rural and semi-urban areas. The government's regular policy since 1969 has paid rich dividends with the nationalization of 14 major private banks. The sector reform was carried out subsequently, with seven more banks, enabling 80 per cent of the segment under government ownership.

References

1. An overview of banking sector, Chapter 1, <http://shodhganga. inflibnet.ac.in/bitstream/10603/2031/10/10_chapter%201.pdf>
2. Banking in India, <http://en.wikipedia.org/wiki/Banking_in_India>
3. Rajesh Chakrabarti, Banking in India – Reforms and Reorganization, <http://unpan1.un.org/intradoc/groups/public/documents/apcity/ unpan025796.pdf>
4. Banking reforms in India, <http://www.brookings.edu/~/media/ research/files/articles/2004/3/india%20policy%20forum/2004_banerjee_cole_ duflo.pdf>
5. Nationalised Banks of India, <http://dpprsystems.in/products/27/ manual.pdf>
6. Nupur Singh, 12 main Reasons for Nationalisation of banks, <http://www.preservearticles.com/2012033129398/12-main-reasons-fornationalisation-of-banks.html>
7. Nationalised Banks in India, <http://www.iloveindia.com/finance/ bank/nationalised-banks/>
8. Bank Nationalization in India, <http://pnbsu.com/news/ banking_finance/bank_nationalization.pdf>
9. Brief history of banking in India, <http://www.gktoday.in/briefhistory-of-banking-in-india-3/>
10. G. H. Deolalkar, The Indian Banking Sector: On the Road to Progress, <http://aric.adb.org/pdf/aem/external/financial_market/India/india_bnk.pdf
11. Nationalised Banks of India,Retrieved from http://dpprsystems.in/products/27/manual.pdf>
12. Shawn A. Cole (2008), Financial Development, Bank Ownership, and Growth. Or, Does Quantity Imply Quality? <http://www.hbs.edu/faculty/Publication%20Files/09-002.pdf>
13. Nationalisation Of Banks In India The Economic Effect Economics Essay, <http://www.ukessays.com/essays/economics/nationalisation-ofbanks-in-india-the-economic-effect-economics-essay.php>
14. An overview of banking sector, Chapter 1, <http:// shodhganga.inflibnet.ac.in/bitstream/10603/2031/10/10_chapter%201.pdf>
15. The Times of India (May 15, 2014),Bank Nationalisation Act primitive today: P J Nayak, <http://timesofindia.indiatimes.com/business/indiabusiness/Bank-Nationalisation-Act-primitive-today-P-J-Nayak/articleshow/>35128006.cms

Chapter - 10

Private Sector Banks

"I sincerely believe that banking establishments are more dangerous than standing armies, and that the principle of spending money to be paid by posterity, under the name of funding, is but swindling futurity on a large scale."

— ***Thomas Jefferson***

Introduction

Bank is a financial intermediary accepting deposits and channelizing them into lending activities, directly by loan or indirectly through capital markets. A bank links deficit customers with those having capital surpluses. Modern banking practice, including fractional reserve banking and the issue of bank notes, emerged in the 17 century and 18 century. The Bank of England was the first to begin the permanent issue of bank notes in 1695. Banks provide different payment services. A bank account is considered indispensable by businesses and individuals. These can create new money when they avail some loan. New loans throughout the banking system could generate new deposits elsewhere in the system.

Bank can generate revenue in different ways, including interest, transaction fees and financial advice. The main method is via charging interest on the capital it lends out to customers. The bank profits form the difference between the level of interest it pays for deposits and other sources of funds, with that of interest it levies on lending. These face a number of risks in their business. There has been a huge reduction to the barriers of global competition in the industry. Increases in telecommunications and other financial technologies, such as Bloomberg, have allowed them extend their reach all over the world.

They no longer have to be near customers to manage their finances and risk.[1]

What is Private Bank?

Private Banks are banks owned by an individual or a general partner(s) with limited partner(s). These are not incorporated. The creditors can look on the "entirety of the bank's assets" as well as that, of the sole-proprietor's/ general-partners' assets. These can refer to non-government owned banks in general, in contrast with the government-owned banks, prevalent in communist, socialist and some social democratic states in the 20 century.[2]

Private banking is banking, investment and other financial services. The banks provide the services to private individuals, who enjoy high levels of income or invest sizable assets. The term private refers to customer-service rendered on a personal basis than in mass-market retail banking, usually via dedicated bank advisers, non-incorporated banking institution, can't be a private bank.[3]

Significance of Private Banks

The system is being accorded to build geographically spread infrastructure for resource mobilization towards pre-determined economic priorities for planned economic development.[4]

According to Singh (2010), the private sector banks play a vital role in the Indian economy. They indirectly motivate the public sector banks through a healthy competition. They: (a) offer higher degree of professional management; (b) creates healthy competition; (c) encourages foreign investment; (d) helps to access foreign capital markets; and (e) develop innovation for expertise.[5]

Private scene in India

The private-sector banks in India form part of the banking sector, made up of both private and public sector banks. The "private- sector banks" are those banks, where appreciable stake or equity is being held by the private shareholders alone. These are split into old and new by financial regulators. The old ones existed prior to the 1969-nationalisation drive. These have their independence. They were either too small or specialized for nationalisation. The new banks were those that have had their banking license since the liberalisation in the 1990s.

The banks ignored during 1969 and 1980 nationalized drive, are known as the old private-sector banks. Smaller size and regional focus kept them out of nationalization. We have 19 such banks under original category.

City Union Bank

City Union Bank is an Indian bank. The Kumbakonam Bank Limited was incorporated as a limited company on October 31, 1904. The bank initially preferred the role of a regional bank in the Thanjavur District, Tamil Nadu. It often preferred the role of a regional bank built slowly but steadily at a place in the Delta District Thanjavur. The first branch was opened at Mannargudi on January 24, 1930. The branches were later opened at Nagapattinam, Sannanallur, Ayyampet, Tirukattupalli, Tiruvarur, Manapparai, Mayuram and Porayar within a span of twenty five years. It was included in the Second Schedule of the Reserve Bank of India Act, 1934, on March 22, 1945. It took over the assets and liabilities of the Common Wealth Bank Limited [1957] and annexed to the five branches of Common Wealth Bank Limited at Aduthurai, Kodavasal, Valangaiman, Jayankondacholopuram and Ariyalu. [7]

Dhanlaxmi Bank

It is an old private sector bank headquartered in Thrissur City, Kerala. It focused mostly on Southern states like Karnataka, Tamil Nadu, Andhra Pradesh and Kerala. It went for a pan-India presence since the last few years[November 14, 1927]. Dhanalakshmi Bank Ltd was incorporated with a capital of 11,000 and mere seven employees. It became a Scheduled Commercial Bank [1977], now has 275 branches. It has changed its name from Dhanalakshmi Bank to Dhanlaxmi Bank on August 10, 2010.[8]

Federal Bank

It is a major Indian commercial bank in the private sector, headquartered at Aluva, Kochi, Kerala. It is the fourth largest bank in India in terms of capital base. it has 1150 branches spread across 24 states[As of February 09, 2014]. Travancore Federal Bank began operations [1931] at Pattamukkil Varattisseril house off Nedumpuram, near Thiruvalla, Kerala. Federal Bank took over Chalakudy Public Bank [1963~70] Cochin Union Bank (1963) in Trichur, Alleppey Bank (1964) in Alappuzha, St. George Union Bank (1965) in Puthenpally, and Marthandam Commercial Bank (1968) in Thiruvananthapuram. It became a scheduled commercial bank [1970] and came out with its initial public offering [1994]. It was the principal sponsor of Kochi Tuskers Kerala. The bank opened its first overseas office in Abu Dhabi [January 2008].[9]

ING Vysya Bank

It is a privately owned Bangalore headquartered Indian multinational bank, with retail, wholesale, and private banking platforms. It was formed from an equity stake in Vysya Bank by the Dutch ING Group [2002]. ING Vysya is the seventh largest private sector bank in India, with assets totaling Rs. 54, 836 crore (US$9.3 billion) and operating a pan-India network of over 1,000 outlets, including 527 branches, which service over two million customers. Vysya Bank was formally incorporated in the city of Bangalore, Karnataka. Vysya Bank built its banking business organically in southern India. Vysya Bank established two independently operating subsidiaries, providing equipment leasing and home mortgaging services (Vysya Bank Leasing Ltd and Vysya Bank Housing Finance Ltd, respectively). Vysya Bank entered into a long-term strategic alliance with Belgian bank Bank Bruxelles Lambert (BBL).[10]

Jammu and Kashmir Bank

The Jammu and Kashmir Bank was founded on October 01, 1938 under letters patent issued by the then Maharaja Hari Singh of Jammu and Kashmir. It commenced business on July 04, 1939. It was considered the first of its nature and composition as a state-owned bank. It had to face serious problems at the time of independence. Two out of ten branches branches of Muzaffarabad, Rawalakot and Mirpur fell to the other side of the line of control (now Pakistan- administered Kashmir) along with cash and other assets. The bank celebrated its platinum jubilee [2013]. J&K Bank operates on the principle of 'socially empowering banking'and seeks to deliver innovative financial solutions for household, small and medium enterprises.[11]

Karnataka Bank

Karnataka Bank Limited is a private sector banking institution. It is being based in the coastal city of Mangalore - Karnataka. It has a national presence with a network of some 587 branches across 20 states and two Union territories. The bank was incorporated on February 18, 1924, as the Karnataka Bank Limited with business on May 23, 1924. Its founders have established the bank at Mangalore, a coastal town in the Dakshina Kannada district of erstwhile Madras Presidency. The bank acquired three smaller banks [1960s] . Itsigned an MoU with Infosys Technologies [2000], to develop a core-banking solution called FINACLE.[12]

Karur Vysya Bank

Karur Vysya Bank is a private-sector Indian bank, headquartered in Karur in Tamil Nadu. It was set up in 1916 by M. A. Venkatarama Chettiar and Athi Krishna Chettiar. The bank has 551 branches and 1,277 ATMs covering 17 States and 2 Union Territories and added 100 branches and 457 ATMs[2012-13] . KVB offers several deposit and loan products, tailor-made to cater to the specific needs of customers. It offers NRE/FCNR deposits and remittance services and "KVB Gruhapravesh" home loans to NRIs. The bank distributes the Mutual Fund products of UTI, SBI MF, Reliance MF, Sundaram BNP Paribas MF, Birla Sun life MF, Franklin Templeton MF and LIC MF.[13]

Lakshmi Vilas Bank Limited

The bank was incorporated on November 03, 1926 under the Indian Companies Act, 1913. It has obtained the certificate to commence business on November 10, 1926. It obtained the requisite license from the RBI on June 1958 and became a Scheduled Commercial Bank by August 1958. LVB took over nine banks and raised its branch network [1961-65] considerably. At present, with a network of 362 branches and eight extension counters, spread over 15 states and the union territory of Pondicherry, it focus on customer delight, through high standards of customer service and finds progressing admirably.[14]

The Nainital Bank

It is a private Indian bank based in Nainital and has expanded later on to Uttar Pradesh. Govind Ballabh Pant and a few prominent men from the Shah/Sah community of Kumaon have founded the bank. National Insurance Company signed an agreement with the bank [April 10, 2004] for distribution of general insurance products through its branches across the states of Uttarakhand, Haryana and New Delhi. The bank is associated with Bank of Baroda, HDFC Bank, LIC, National Insurance Company Limited etc.[15]

Development Credit Bank

It is a private sector scheduled commercial bank in India. Its financial products and services range from loans for Small and medium enterprises, wealth management, banking for Non-Resident Indians, Internet banking, Mobile Banking, Business Finance, Home Loans. It was founded in 1930.[16]

South Indian Bank

It is a private sector bank headquartered at Thrissur City in Kerala. South Indian Bank has 802 branches across more than 26 states and union territories in India. It had with a new logo and its image marches on. The bank is considered one of the most proactive banks in India with a competent tech savvy team of professional at the core of services.[17]

Tamilnad Mercantile Bank

Tamilnad Mercantile Bank is being headquartered in Tuticorin -Tamil Nadu. It was founded as the Nadar Bank [1921], but changed its name to Tamilnad Mercantile Bank [November 1962] to widen its appeal beyond the Nadar community. The bank was originally registered as Nadar Bank Limited under the Indian Companies Act, 1913 [May 11, 1921]. M.V.Shanmugavel

Nadar was elected as the first chairman on November 04, 1921. It adopted modernization drive, as early in the year 1983. Computerization of its branches has added a new dimension in rendering quality service to clients. The bank is constantly coming up with better schemes and sops for costumers.[18]

The Catholic Syrian Bank

It was founded on 26 November 1920 in Thrissur city. CSB commenced business on January 01, 1921. It has a strong foothold in rural India with a snowballing presence in semi-urban and urban areas. It is one of the selected few old generation banks to be considered under The Indian Banks Bipartite Settlement following the nationalised pay scale and norms.[19]

HDFC Bank

The Housing Development Finance Corporation Limited (HDFC) was amongst the first to receive an 'in principle' approval from the RBIs Liberalisation Drive -1994. The bank was incorporated on August 1994 in the name of 'HDFC Bank Limited', with its registered office in Mumbai. The bank commenced operations as a Scheduled Commercial Bank in January 1995.[20]

ICICI Bank

It is an Indian multinational banking and financial services company headquartered at Mumbai. It was established by the Industrial Credit and ·Investment Corporation of India (ICICI), an Indian financial institution, as a wholly owned subsidiary in 1955. It was a joint-venture of the World Bank [1955]. India's public sector banks and public-sector insurance companies to provide project financing to Indian industry. It is the second largest bank in India by assets and by market capitalization, [As of 2014]. It is one of the *Big Four banks* of India, along with the State Bank of India, Punjab National Bank and Bank of Baroda. The bank has subsidiaries in the United Kingdom, Russia, and Canada; branches in United States, Singapore, Bahrain, Hong Kong, Sri Lanka, Qatar and Dubai International Finance Centre; besides the representative offices in United Arab Emirates, China, South Africa, Bangladesh, Thailand, Malaysia and Indonesia.[21]

Kotak Mahindra Bank

It is an Indian bank and financial service firm established [1985]. It was previously known as Kotak Mahindra Finance Limited, a non-banking financial company. RBI gave the licence for banking business to its flagship company [February 2003]. Kotak Mahindra Finance Ltd. is the first company in the domestic banking history to convert to a bank.[22]

Axis Bank

It is the third largest private sector bank. It offers financial services to customer segments covering large and mid-corporates, MSME, Agriculture and Retail Businesses. Axis Bank has its headquarters in Mumbai, Maharashtra. It began operations in 1994, after the government of India allowed new private banks to be established. Axis Bank operates in four segments: Treasury operations, Retail banking, Corporate/Wholesale banking and other banking business.[23]

YES Bank

It is being a private bank headquartered in Mumbai. Ppromoters Ashok Kapur and Rana Kapoor founded the bank [2004]. It deals in corporate investment services, for a fee, financial advice to customers, generally corporate or individual investors. It also competes in the South Asian commercial banking market. Commercial banking is essentially the equivalent of retail banking for commercial entities. The bank had 560 branches and 1,139 ATMs[As on March 31, 2014].[24]

IndusInd Bank

It is a Mumbai based Indian new generation bank [1994]. It offers commercial, transactional and electronic banking products and services. It was the first among the new-generation private banks in India. It has specialized in retail banking services and upgrades support system continuously by introducing innovative technologies. It is on expansion drive of branches across the country meeting with global benchmark.[25]

New Private Sector Bank

The banks, in operation post-1991, on financial sector reforms are called "new private sector banks". Banking Regulation Act was amended in 1993. It permitted the entry of new private-sector banks under the RBIs norms in the Indian banking sector. The banking regulator has licensed twelve such banks in the private sector over the past two decades in two phases. Ten banks were licensed on the basis of January 1993 guidelines.

Fresh applications were invited on revised 2001 January guidelines based on the gained experience Two more licenses were issued on the vetting of a RBI constituted high-level advisory committee. The then Union Finance Minister announced on the floor of both Houses of parliament in 2010-11 Budget, the desire to issue some additional banking licenses to private sector players. He said that non-banking financial companies could also be considered, if they meet the RBI's eligibility criteria. The draft guidelines on 'Licensing of New Banks in the private sector' were framed taking into account the experience gained from the bank functioning licensed under 1993 and 2001-guidelines with the feedback and suggestions received in response to the Discussion Paper.[26]

The Weekly India Today (Dec 09, 2012) reported about the scenario, when the new generation private sector banks started operations in 1993, they had to compete against the established players, some of whom had been in business for over a century. The market was dominated by the state-owned banks, which had strong branding as well as a widespread branch network. There were also foreign banks operating in India. The new generation private sector banks had to carve out a niche for themselves within this framework. Today, they have a market share of 20 per cent in deposits and advances. This has been achieved in a growing market, indicating that private sector banks have successfully capitalised on the growth of the Indian economy. The new banks developed the concept of direct selling agents, who reached out to customers with credit products, taking loans to the customer's doorstep. Not only did the private sector banks expand in this manner, their example forced public sector banks to also adopt similar strategies. The Indian market is a growing market and to keep succeeding one has to explore the existing opportunities well. The banking sector is expected to grow at 2.5 to three times the country's GDP growth rate.[27]

Private to National Bank

Nationalised banks dominate the banking system at home. Their history dates back to mid-20 century, when the Imperial Bank of India was nationalised (under the SBI Act of 1955) and re-christened as State Bank of India in July 1955. Its seven subsidiaries were also nationalised with deposits over Rs. 200 crores [July 19, 1960]. These subsidiaries were State Bank of Bikaner and Jaipur, State Bank of Hyderabad, State Bank of Indore, State Bank of Mysore, State Bank of Patiala, State Bank of Saurashtra, and State Bank of Travancore.[28] In a major process of nationalization, seven subsidiaries of the State Bank of India were nationalized by the Indira Gandhi regime.

The drive was done in two subsequent phases. The first phase commenced in 1955 when the erstwhile Imperial Bank of India became the State Bank of India under ratified Act of parliament. Seven subsidiaries were nationalized and associated with State Bank of India one after another [1959]. This heralded a new beginning in the domestic banking system. The State Bank group became the largest bank in India serving 90 million customers with a network of over 9,000 branches in every nook and corner of the country. The second phase nationalized 14 major banks [1969]. Six more commercial banks were added to the kitty [1980]and became public sector banks. The Public Sector Undertaking banks expanded their reach and grew in leaps and bounds in the aftermath.[29]

Consequently, seven subsidiaries of the State Bank of India were nationalized by the Indira Gandhi regime. 14 major private commercial banks were nationalized [1969]. These were - Central Bank of India Bank of Maharastra Dena Bank Punjab National Bank Syndicate Bank Canara Bank Indian Bank Indian Overseas Bank Bank of Baroda Union Bank Allahabad Bank Union Bank of India UCO Bank Bank of India. The second phase of nationalization [1980] sustained when the government of India acquired the ownership of six more banks (i.e. Andhra Bank, Corporation Bank, New Bank of India, Oriental Bank of Commerce, Punjab & Sindh Bank,Vijaya Bank), thus bringing the total number of nationalised banks to 20. The private banks were allowed to function side by side with those nationalized banks and the foreign banks were allowed to work under strict surveillance. Eighty per cent of the banking sector came under the public sector /government ownership following two major phases of nationalization.[30]

Conclusion

Private banking is banking, investment and other financial services provided by banks to private individuals, enjoying of these higher levels of income or invest sizable assets. Private banking forms an important, more exclusive, subset of wealth management. It defines their value proposition along one or two dimensions, and meet the basic needs across others. The private-sector banks in India represent part of the Indian banking sector of private and public sector banks. The private sector banks are being split into two groups - old and new. The old private sector banks existed prior to the 1969 nationalisation drive remain Independent, because they were either too small or specialised to be included in the package. The new private sector banks gained their banking license following the 1990 liberalisation drive.

References

1. Bank (2014),<http://en.wikipedia.org/wiki/Bank>
2. Private bank (2014), <http://en.wikipedia.org/wiki/Private_bank
3. Private banking (2014), Retrieved from http://en.wikipedia.org/wiki/> Private_ banking
4. See <http://www.informationweek.in/informationweek/white-papers/286559/ licensing-banks-indian-private-sector-implications-recommendations>
5. Nupur Singh, What is the Importance of Private Sector Banks in India? <http:// www.preservearticles.com/2012033129402/what-is-the-importanceof-private-sector-banks-in-india.html>
6. City Union Bank (2014), <http://en.wikipedia.org/wiki/City_Union_Bank>
7. City Union Bank (2014), <http://www.cityunionbank.com/english/About Us.aspx>
8. Dhanlaxmi Bank (2014), <http://en.wikipedia.org/wiki/Dhanlaxmi_Bank>
9. Federal Bank (2014), <http://en.wikipedia.org/wiki/Federal_Bank>
10. ING Vysya Bank, <http://en.wikipedia.org/wiki/ING_Vysya_Bank>
11. Jammu and Kashmir Bank, <http://en.wikipedia.org/wiki/Jammu_%26_ Kashmir_Bank>
12. Karnataka Bank (2014), <http://en.wikipedia.org/wiki/Karnataka_Bank>
13. Karur Vysya Bank (2014), <https://www.kvb.co.in/global/ bank_profile.html>
14. Lakshmi Vilas Bank Limited (2014), <http://www.lvbank.com/ aboutus.aspx>

15. Nainital Bank (2014), <http://en.wikipedia.org/wiki/Nainital_Bank>
16. Development Credit Bank (2014), <http://en.wikipedia.org/wiki/Development_Credit_Bank>
17. South Indian Bank (2014), <http://www.southindianbank.com/>
18. Tamilnad Mercantile Bank (2014), <http://en.wikipedia.org/wiki/Tamilnad_Mercantile_Bank_Limited>
19. The Catholic Syrian Bank (2014), <http://en.wikipedia.org/wiki/Catholic_Syrian_Bank>
20. HDFC Bank (2014), <http://www.hdfcbank.com/aboutus/general/ default.htm>
21. ICICI Bank (2014), <http://en.wikipedia.org/wiki/ICICI_Bank>
22. Kotak Mahindra Bank (2014), <http://en.wikipedia.org/wiki/Kotak_Mahindra_Bank>
23. Axis Bank (2014), <http://en.wikipedia.org/wiki/Axis_Bank>
24. Yes Bank (2014), <http://en.wikipedia.org/wiki/YES_Bank>
25. IndusInd Bank (2014), <http://en.wikipedia.org/wiki/IndusInd_Bank>
26. See <http://rbi.org.in/scripts/bs_viewcontent.aspx?Id=2651>
27. India Today (Dec 09, 2012),Transforming the Way Banking Is Done, <http://businesstoday.intoday.in/story/new-generation-private-banks-settrend-indian-banking-space/1/189972.html>
28. Nationalised Banks in India, <http://www.iloveindia.com/finance/ bank/nationalised-banks/>
29. Bank Nationalization in India, <http://pnbsu.com/news/ banking_finance/bank_nationalization.pdf>
30. Brief history of banking in India, <http://www.gktoday.in/briefhistory-of-banking-in-india-3/>

Chapter - 11

Public Sector Banks

"If you followed this economic crisis and you do not think that the world is getting flatter, you are not paying attention. We saw the entire global economy at one time acting totally in sync. The real truth is the world is even flatter than I thought. Our mortgage crisis is killing Deutsche Bank. You still don't think the world is flat?" — ***Thomas Friedman***

Introduction

A good bank is not only the financial heart of the community, but also one with an obligation of helping in every possible manner to improve the economic conditions of the common people. A bank is a financial intermediary that accepts deposits and channels those deposits into lending activities. Banks are a fundamental component of the financial system, and are active players in financial markets. The essential role of a bank is to connect those who have/seek capital.[1]

According Rathe (2013), The Indian banking can be broadly characterized as nationalized (government owned), private banks and specialized banking institutions. The RBI monitored any discrepancies and shortcoming in the system, as the centralized body. Nationalization of banks took place in 1969. The public sector or the nationalized banks became prominent place and witnessed tremendous progress. The Indian banking has finally taken up challenges under competitive scenario. The sector has been addressing the relevant issues to take on the multifarious challenges of globalization.[2]

According to Sanyal and Shankar (2008), the 1991 balance of payments crisis led to wide ranging reforms. Policymakers chose to gradually implement financial deregulation, with changes spread over almost the entire decade of 1990s. One of the primary goals of restructuring was enhancing efficiency of the sector. Ascertaining the measures of performance it was clear that the liberalization has had some positive outcomes. Regulation, administered interest rates, poor asset quality, and market segmentation had severely compromised banking profitability in the pre-reform era. Many banks had low capital adequacy and earn less than reasonable rates of return. The constrained nature of the central bank's role lead to slow reform. .It lead to manage the government debt and the monetize the government's fiscal deficit.[3]

What is Public Bank?

A public bank is a financial institution, wherein a state or public actors are the owners. It is a company under state control. The government holds majority stake in them (i.e., more than 50 per cent) with NSE and BSE performance indicators. The shares of 21 PSBs also find listed on stock exchange. The term public sector banks are used commonly in India. They can also be termed as government owned banks.[4]

Its Importance

Banks are commercial institutions. These help in regulation and supply of funds in the economy. They are lenders to the needy and accept deposits of the worthy to return at higher rate. Practically speaking, it helps in balanced growth of economy. Indian Economy is mixed, needing the public-private presence. Public banks have more of a socialistic approach. They lend and accept funds from people of different strata of the society. They help in capital accumulation for the country and facilitate faster economic growth. They attract more FDI and FII in the economy. They are the infrastructural pillars of the country. Public and Private Banks play a vital role in economic development. It would be lopsided without the presence of either category.[5]

The adequacy of any public service will be contingent on safeguarding the quality provided to the consumer. It is important to ensure that cost changes are properly balanced with any change in the quality of service. Public ownership of banks, besides preventing the system from plunging into periodic crises, delivers many growth and welfare benefits. Public ownership of banks, besides preventing periodic economic crises, can subordinate the profit motive to social objectives and fashion a system of inclusive finance.

Bank Nationalisation drive

The central government entered the banking business with the nationalization of the Imperial Bank of India in 1955. RBI had a A 60 per cent stake and the new bank was named as the State Bank of India. The seven other state banks became the subsidiaries of the new bank, when nationalised on July 19, 1960. In the subsequent drive, the government of India, under Prime Minister Indira Gandhi, nationalised an additional 14 major banks.

Rs. 50 crore worth was found in them [1969]. The drive increased the presence of nationalized banks with 84 per cent of the total number of branches virtually coming under the government control. The subsequent drive nationalized six banks with deposits worth Rs. 200 crore (1980 April). This move led to a further increase in the number of branches in the market, increasing to 91 per cent of the total branch network of the country.[6]

Public Banking in India

According to Chaudhary (2011), the public sector banks are divided into two groups i.e. Nationalized Banks and State Bank of India and its associates. Among them, there are 19 nationalized banks and 8 State Bank of India associates. Public Sector Banks dominate 75 percent of deposits and 71 percent of advances in the banking industry. Public Sector Banks have dominated commercial banking India. These can be further classified into: State Bank of India; Nationalized banks and Regional Rural Banks.[7] Public sector in the banking industry emerged with the nationalization of Imperial Bank of India (1921) and creating the State Bank of India (1955) as a part of integrated scheme of rural credit proposed by the All India Rural Credit Survey Committee (1951). The Bank is unique in several respects. It enjoys a position of preeminence as the agent of RBI wherever RBI has no branches.

The public sector in the Indian banking got widened with two rounds of nationalization drive - first in July 1969 of 14 major private sector banks each with deposits of Rs. 50 crore or more, and thereafter in April 1980, 6 more banks with deposits of not less than Rs. 2 crore each. Over a period of time, their financial healths deteriorated, resulting in efficiency decline. It was thought, that their performance should not be judged merely in terms of profits, following imposition of many obligations – social and economic. The government earmarked budgetary provisions regularly for for recapitalization of nationalized banks [1984-85] their capital base has eroded. Indian banking system is predominantly branch-banking system.

For nearly have decades there had been massive branch expansion, primarily with the objective of covering the unbanked centers in rural and semi-urban centers, coupled with intensive branch network in urban metro centers to sustain profitability.[8] The liberalisation of the Indian economy brought paradigmatic shift in several sectors. One of them, the financial sector underwent structural changes with immediate effect .[9] Let us discuss the functioning of public sector banks in India.

Allahabad Bank

Allahabad Bank is a nationalised bank headquartered at Kolkata. It is the oldest joint stock bank in India. A group of Englishmen at Allahabad founded the bank on April 24, 1865. In the early 20 century, Allahabad Bank witnessed a spurt in deposits, with the start of Swadeshi movement,. It acquired United Industrial Bank [1989], a Calcutta-based bank [Estd 1940]. Two years later, it established All Bank Finance Ltd, a wholly owned Merchant Banking subsidiary. It opened its first office outside India in Shenzen, Mainland China [June 2006]. It opened its first overseas branch, in Hong Kong [February 2007]. Its equity shares are listed on Bombay Stock Exchange and the National Stock Exchange of India.[10]

Andhra Bank

Dr. Bhogaraju Pattabhi Sitaramayya founded Andhra Bank [1923] in Machilipatnam, Andhra Pradesh. The bank provided products and services categorized into businesses of Retail, Corporate, NRI, MSME, and Agricultural industries. The Bank introduced Internet Banking Facility (AB INFI-net) cluster linked branch customers. The representative offices in Dubai [May 2006] and Jersey City, New Jersey (USA) [June 2009] were opened. A foothold in New Jersey is strategic for the bank as the state has a large number of Indians from Andhra Pradesh. The bank entered an MoU with Bank of Baroda and Legal and General Group of UK to form a joint venture life insurance company IndiaFirst Life Insurance Company.[11]

Bank of Baroda

Bank of Baroda is an Indian state-owned banking and financial services company headquartered at Vadodara (earlier known as Baroda) in Gujarat. It is the second-largest bank in India, after State Bank of India, and offers a range of banking products and financial services to corporate and retail customers through its branches and specialised subsidiaries and affiliates. The bank was founded by the Maharaja Sir Sayajirao Gaekwad III of Baroda,

[July 20, 1908] in the princely state of Baroda, in Gujarat. The bank followed followed the Indian diaspora, especially Gujaratis, through has a joint venture in Zambia with 16 branches. The Bank of Baroda has received permission or in-principle approval from host country regulators to open new offices in Trinidad and Tobago and Ghana, where it sought to establish joint ventures or subsidiaries.[12]

Bank of India

Bank of India is an Indian state-owned commercial bank headquartered at Mumbai. A group of eminent businessmen from Mumbai found the bank [Sept 07,1906]. The bank was under private ownership and control and got nationalised with 13 other banks. The bank has 4,545 branches in India spread over all states/union territories including some specialized branches. The branches are being controlled through 50 zonal offices. It has overseas presence in 20 foreign countries spread over five continents with 53 offices including four subsidiaries, four representative offices and one joint venture, at the key banking and financial centres viz., Tokyo, Singapore, Hong Kong, London, Jersey, Paris and New York.[13]

Bank of Maharashtra

Bank of Maharashtra is a major public sector bank. A group of visionaries led by the late V. G. Kale and the late D. K. Sathe found the bank. It was registered as a banking company on September 16, 1935 at Pune. It attained autonomous status 188 in 1998. As a result, the bank has limited interference with bureaucracy in decision making and internal affairs. It has 15 million customers across the country, serving more than 1,825 branches. It has the largest network of branches by any public sector bank in the state of Maharashtra.[14]

Bharatiya Mahila Bank

Bharatiya Mahila Bank is an Indian financial services banking company based at New Delhi. Prime Minister Dr. Manmohan Singh inaugurated the bank on the 94th birth anniversary of former Indian premier Indira Gandhi [November 19, 2013]. It will emphasise on funding for skill developments to help in economic activity. Moreover, the products will be designed in a manner to women on loan rates. It has initial capital of Rs 1,000 crore. The government plans to have 25 branches of the said bank [March 2014] and 500 branches by fourth year of operation (2017). The government choose the iconic Air India building at Nariman Point in Mumbai for its first branch, but the position is unclear.[15]

Canara Bank

Canara Bank is an Indian state-owned bank headquartered at Bangalore, Karnataka. It is one of the oldest banks in the country [Estd 1906]. It had a network of 4,600 branches and over 5,500 ATMs spread across the country [As on February 28,2014]. The bank established its international division in 1976. In 1983, the first oversea branch came in London. It has offices abroad in London, Hong Kong, Moscow, Shanghai, Doha, and Dubai. It established a joint venture with the SBI in Moscow, and Commercial Bank of India LLC.[16]

Central Bank of India

Central Bank of India is one of the oldest and largest commercial Banks. It is based in Mumbai. Sir Sorabji Pochkhanawala with Sir Pherozeshah Mehta were its chairman [Estd. Dec 21, 1911]. It acquired the Tata Industrial Bank in the wake of the failure of the Alliance Bank of Simla [1923]. The 1969 nationalization drive facilitated the bank with 13 others. At present, Central bank has overseas offices at Nairobi, Hong Kong and a joint venture with the Bank of India, Bank of Baroda, and the Zambian government.[17]

Corporation Bank

Corporation Bank is a public sector banking company headquartered in Mangalore. It was founded in the Temple Town of Udupi [March 12, 1906]. The need to start the bank was felt, because there was no such facility at Udupi, an important trading centre next to Mangalore in South Canara district. The bank opened its branch at Kundapur [1923]. The second branch was opened in Mangalore at Car Street [1926]. It graduated into a regional bank [1945], when its branches stood at 28. The Corporation Bank was the first public sector bank, other than State Bank of India associates, to achieve 100 per cent CBS (Core Banking Solutions)developed and implemented by Laser Soft Info systems Limited, Chennai.[18]

Dena Bank

Dena Bank is one of the earliest banks in India, headquartered at Mumbai. The family of Devkaran Nanjee under the name Devkaran Nanjee Banking Company Ltd founded the bank [May 26, 1938]. The 1969 nationalization drive got the bank nationalized with 13 other major banks.

It is now a public sector bank constituted under the Banking Companies (Acquisition & Transfer of Undertakings) Act, 1970. Under the provisions of the Banking Regulations Act 1949, in addition to the business of banking, it can undertake other business as specified under Section 6 of the Banking Regulations Act, 1949. Its logo depicts Goddess Lakshmi, the Goddess of Wealth, according to Hindu mythology. It was the desire of founding fathers that the bank should be a symbol of prosperity for all clients, and the logo thenceforth represents the promise.[19]

IDBI Bank

IDBI Bank is an Indian financial service company headquartered at Mumbai. RBI has categorised the bank as 'another public sector bank'. It was established by an Act of Parliament [1964] to extend credit and other facilities for the development of fledgling industry. IDBI provided financial assistance, both in rupee and foreign currencies, for green-field projects in their drive to expand, modernize and diversify. IDBI provides indirect financial assistance by way of refinanced loans extended by the state-level institutions and banks and by way of rediscounting of bills of exchange arising out of sale of indigenous machinery on deferred payment terms.[20]

Indian Bank

Indian Bank is an Indian state-owned financial services company headquartered at Chennai. It was established on 15th August 1907 as part Swadeshi movement lead its establishment [August 15,1907]. After the war, in 1948, it reopened its branch in Colombo. It also reopened branches in Burma, Malaya and Singapore [1962]. The Burmese government nationalised foreign banks, including Indian Bank's branch [1963]. It has overseas branches in Singapore, Colombo including a foreign currency banking unit at Colombo and Jaffna. It rescued [1991] the Bank of Tanjore (Bank of Thanjavur; Est. 1901), with 157 branches in Tamil Nadu. A case of malpractice was exposed [1992], when the then chairman M. Gopalakrishnan lent 13 billion to small corporate and exporters from the south, which the borrowers never repaid.[21]

Indian Overseas Bank

Indian Overseas Bank is a major bank based in Chennai (Madras). Thiru.M. Ct. M. Chidambaram Chettyar established the Indian Overseas Bank (IOB) [1937] to facilitate the oversea banking and foreign exchange operations. The bank offers internet Banking (E-See Banking) and Mobile

Banking. The government of India has approved the bank for online payment of taxes, whose business has doubled more in the past four years.[22]

Oriental Bank of Commerce

Oriental Bank of Commerce is an India-based bank. It was one of the public sector banks at Lahore in the undivided Indian peninsula. Late Rai Bahadur Lala Sohan Lal, the founding father was its first chairman. It offers features such as internet banking, phone banking NRI banking etc. However, it does not allow online banking access from outside India. Global Trust Bank Limited (GTB) was amalgamated into OBC [August 14, 2004].[23]

Punjab National Bank

Punjab National Bank was registered under the Indian Companies Act, with office in Anarkali Bazaar, Lahore [May 19, 1894]. The founding board was drawn from professionals of different backgrounds/faiths, however, had common objective of providing the services of truly a national bank in the economic interest of the country. PNB is one of the Big Four banks of India, with the State Bank of India, ICICI Bank and Bank of Baroda. It is the third largest bank in India, in terms of asset size (US$6.6 billion by the end of FY 2012-13). It has a banking subsidiary in UK, as well as branches in Hong Kong, Dubai and Kabul. It has representative offices in Almaty [Kazakhstan], Dubai, Shanghai (China), Oslo (Norway) and Sydney (Australia).[24]

Punjab & Sind Bank

Punjab & Sind Bank (P&SB) is a major public sector bank in Northern India and work 100 per cent on CBS platform. Some peers in Amritsar such as Bhai Vir Singh, Sir Sunder Singh Majitha and Sardar Tarlochan Singh founded the bank, to help weaker sections of the society. The bank was among six banks nationalized in the subsequent drive [April 1980]. The bank established its branch in London [decade 1960s]. The Bank of Baroda acquired the bank's London branch at the behest of the RBI, following following its involvement in the Sethia fraud [1987]. The bank sponsored Setluj Gramin Bank.[25]

Syndicate Bank

Syndicate Bank is one of the oldest and major commercial banks. Peers and social workers T M A Pai, Upendra Pai and Vaman Kudva founded the bank at Udupi, in Dakshin Kannada district of erstwhile Mysore state [1928].

It secured membership as a clearing house at Mumbai [1937]. It sponsored the first regional rural bank in India under name Prathama Bank, in Moradabad district of the state of Uttar Pradesh[October 02, 1975]. The bank stocks are being listed on Bombay Stock Exchange, National Stock Exchange, Mangalore Stock Exchange and Bangalore Stock Exchange.[26]

UCO Bank

UCO Bank is one of the oldest and major commercial banks of India. It was formerly United Commercial Bank [Est.1943] in Kolkata. Ghanshyam Das Birla, an eminent Indian industrialist, conceived the idea of organising such bank [1942 Quit India movement], with requisite Indian capital and management, which helped the bank make its presence through the United Commercial Bank Limited. The 1969 nationalization drive accommodated the bank with 13 major commercial banks. The year 1985, the name 'United Commercial Bank' was changed into UCO Bank under an Act of Parliament. Over the years, UCO Bank been regarded as one of the familiar and vibrant banks within the country.[27]

Union Bank of India

Union Bank of India was registered on 11 November 1919 as a limited company in Mumbai and was inaugurated by Mahatma Gandhi. At the time of India's Independence in 1947, UBI only had four branches - three in Mumbai and one in Saurashtra, all concentrated in key trade centres. Shortly after nationalisation, UBI merged in Belgaum Bank, a private sector bank established in 1930 that had itself merged in a bank in 1964, the Shri Jadeya Shankarling Bank. Then in 1985 UBI merged in Miraj State Bank, which had been established in 1929. In 1999 the Reserve Bank of India requested that UBI acquire Sikkim Bank in a rescue after extensive irregularities had been discovered at the non-scheduled bank. At present, the offshore banking operations of Union Bank of India are led by its branches in Hong Kong and newly opened branch in Dubai at Dubai International Financial Centre.[28]

United Bank of India

United Bank of India is a state-owned financial services company headquartered in Kolkata, West Bengal. UBI was the result of the merger in 1950 of four Bengali banks: Comilla Banking Corporation, Bengal Central Bank, Comilla Union Bank and Hooghly Bank. After nationalisation, the Bank expanded its branch network in a big way and actively participated in the developmental activities, particularly in the rural and semi-urban areas in conformity with the objectives of nationalisation. In recognition of the role played by the Bank, it was designated as Lead Bank in several districts and at present it is the Lead Bank in 30 districts in the States of West Bengal, Assam, Manipur and Tripura. UBI played a significant role in the spread of banking services in different parts of the country, more particularly in Eastern and North-Eastern India. UBI has sponsored 4 Regional Rural Banks one each in West Bengal, Assam, Manipur and Tripura. These four RRBs together have over 1000 branches. UBI is also known as the 'Tea Bank'because of its age-old association with the financing of tea gardens. It has been the largest lender to the tea industry.[29]

Vijaya Bank

Vijaya Bank is a medium sized public sector bank. Shri. Attavar Balakrishna Shetty established the bank at Bunts Hostel in Mangalore [October 23, 1931]. It was named 'Vijaya Bank' owing to commencing of operation on Navaratri, Vijaya Dasami. The objective was to promote banking habits, thrift and entrepreneurship among the farming community of Dakshina Kannada district in erstwhile Mysore state. The bank became a scheduled bank [1958]. It is one among the few banks in the country to get principal membership of VISA International and MasterCard International.[30]

Challenges Ahead!

India's public sector banks continue to face several challenges in mobilizing capital and meeting the higher Basel III international banking reforms. It includes insufficient market appetite to fill the regulatory requirement, which has raised the dependence on the state-owned Life Insurance Corporation for private placement of PSBs' Basel III-compliant capital instruments.[31]

According to Choudhary and Tandon (2011), the future of these banks rests on their capability to continuously build good quality assets in an increasingly competitive environment, maintaining capital adequacy and stringent prudential norms. Consolidation and competition may be the key factors impacting their future performance. A need was realized not only to increase profits, but also to reduce the nonperforming assets of banks.[32] The Business Standard (Feb 10, 2014) reported over the loss of United Bank of India, to the extent of Rs 1,238 crore [3rd quarter of 2013-14], with Rs 489 crore [previous quarter], or wiping closer to 30 per cent of funds - capital, reserves and surplus - with which it the financial year arose. UBI's problems were deep-rooted, being historical and systemic, partly from its presence in the country's economically most backward region. It is the lead bank in most of the districts of West Bengal with relatively higher share of agricultural advances, problematic most of the time. It also suffers from systemic shortcomings and remain traditionally weak in monitoring but difficult to pinpoint non-compliance, owing to non-availability of manuals for procedures and defined policies.[33]

The Hindu (Feb 21, 2014) exposed, two sets of related problems confronting policy makers. First, the question of recapitalising PSBs to offset the impaired capital, especially at a time when the banks were asked to move towards global norms of capital adequacy. Second, the disadvantages of government ownership extending to recovery. The bankers were found to have lesser flexibility in dealing with problem loans.[34]

Conclusion

Banks are the commercial institutions for regulation and supply of funds in the economy. They are lenders to the needy and accept deposits worthy to return at higher rate. The banks have more of a socialistic approach. They lend and accept funds from people of different strata of the society. Public ownership of banks, besides preventing the system from plunging into periodic crises, delivers many growth and welfare benefits. The central government entered the banking business with the nationalization of the Imperial Bank of India in 1955. The subsequent drive took place in 1969 when the government of India, under premier Indira Gandhi, nationalised an additional 14 major banks. The third round of nationalisation took place in April 1980, when the government nationalized six banks.

References

1. Financial performance of selected public sector banks in India, International Journal of Multidisciplinary Research,Vol.2 Issue 1,January 2012, <http://zenithresearch.org.in/images/stories/pdf/2012/Jan/ZIJMR/18%20M%20DHANABHAKYAM%20financial%20performance.pdf>
2. Dr. Raja M. Rathe, Assessment and Comparison of Indian Public and Private Sector Banks through Customers' and Customers' Satisfaction Survey Experience, Pacific Business Review International, Volume 5 Issue 12 (June 2013), <http://www.pbr.co.in/Vol%205%20Iss%2012/11.pdf>
3. Paroma Sanyal and Rashmi Shanka (2008), Ownership, Competition and Bank Productivity: An Analysis of Indian Banking in the Post-Reform Period, <http://people.brandeis.edu/~psanyal/India_Bank_Productivity.pdf>

4. Financial performance of selected public sector banks in India, International Journal of Multidisciplinary Research, Vol.2 Issue 1,January 2012, <http://zenithresearch.org.in/images/stories/pdf/2012/Jan/ZIJMR/18%20M%20DHANABHAKYAM%20financial%20performance.pdf>
5. See <https://in.answers.yahoo.com/question/index?qid=20081104053900AAZke8J>
6. Public Sector Banks in India (2014), <http://en.wikipedia.org/ wiki/Public_sector_banks_in_India>
7. Kajal Chaudhary and Monika Sharma, Performance of Indian Public Sector Banks and Private Sector Banks: A Comparative Study, International Journal of Innovation, Management and Technology, Vol. 2, No. 3, June 2011, <http://workspace.unpan.org/sites/internet/Documents/UNPAN92671.pdf>
8. Performance analysis of public sector banks in India, <http:// shodhganga.inflibnet.ac.in/bitstream/10603/3712/12/12_chapter%205.pdf>
9. Ravi K. Dhar and Silky Vigg Kushwah, Service Quality Expectations and Perceptions of Public and Private Sector Banks in India: A Comparative Study, <http://www.iimidr.ac.in/iimi/images/IMJ/Volume1_Issue3/Service%20Quality%20Expectations%20and%20Perceptions%20of%20Public%20a nd%20Private%20Sector%20Banks%20in%20India.pdf>
10. Allahabad Bank (2014), <http://en.wikipedia.org/wiki/Allahabad_Bank>
11. Andhra Bank (2014), <http://en.wikipedia.org/wiki/Andhra_Bank>
12. Bank of Baroda (2014), <http://en.wikipedia.org/wiki/Bank_of_Baroda>
13. Bank of India (2014), <http://www.bankofindia.co.in/english/history3.aspx>
14. Bank of Maharashtra (2014), <http://en.wikipedia.org/wiki/Bank_of_Maharashtra>
15. Bharatiya Mahila Bank (2014), <http://en.wikipedia.org/wiki/Bhartiya_Mahila_Bank>
16. Canara Bank (2014),<http://en.wikipedia.org/wiki/Canara_Bank>
17. Central Bank of India (2014), <http://en.wikipedia.org/wiki/Central_Bank_of_India>
18. Corporation Bank (2014), <http://en.wikipedia.org/wiki/Corporation_Bank>
19. Dena Bank (2014), <http://www.denabank.com/viewsection.jsp?id=0,1,12>
20. IDBI Bank (2014), <http://en.wikipedia.org/wiki/IDBI_Bank>
21. Indian Bank (2014), <http://en.wikipedia.org/wiki/Indian_Bank>
22. Indian Overseas Bank (2014), <http://en.wikipedia.org/wiki/Indian_Overseas_Bank>
23. Oriental Bank of Commerce (2014), <http://en.wikipedia.org/wiki/Oriental_Bank_of_Commerce
24. Punjab National Bank (2014), <http://en.wikipedia.org/wiki/Punjab_National_Bank>
25. Punjab & Sind Bank (2014), <http://en.wikipedia.org/wiki/Punjab_%26_Sind_Bank>
26. Syndicate Bank (2014), <http://en.wikipedia.org/wiki/Syndicate_Bank>

27. Uco Bank (2014),<http://en.wikipedia.org/wiki/UCO_Bank>
28. Union Bank of India (2014), <http://en.wikipedia.org/wiki/Union_Bank_of_India>
29. United Bank of India (2014), <http://www.unitedbankofindia.com/English/AboutOverview.aspx>
30. Vijaya Bank (2014), <http://en.wikipedia.org/wiki/Vijaya_Bank>
31. Indian public banks struggle to raise Basel III Capital: Fitch, <http://asianbankingandfinance.net/wholesale-banking/news/indian-public-banksstruggle-raise-basel-iii-capital-fitch>
32. Dr. Vikas Choudhary and Suman Tandon, Performance emulation of public sector banks, <http://www.skirec.com/images/download/vol-1-issue-1-%20final/vol-1-issue-1-art-1.pdf>
33. Business Standard (Feb 10, 2014),UBI in trouble, <http://www.b usiness-standard.com/article/opinion/ubi-in-trouble-114021001362_1.html>
34. The Hindu (Feb 21, 2014),The challenge of bad loans, <http:// www.th eh in d u .co m/o p in io n /ed ito r ial/th e- ch allen ge- o f- b ad - lo an s/ article5710442. ece>

Chapter - 12

Development Banks

"Money has never made man happy, nor will it; there is nothing in its nature to produce happiness. The more of it one has the more one wants."

— ***Benjamin Franklin***

Introduction

Economic development is the sustained, concerted actions of policy makers and communities that promote the standard of living and economic health of a specific area. The scope of economic development includes the process and policies by which a nation improves the economic, political, and social well-being of its people. Essentially, a country's economic development is related to its human development, which encompasses, health and education, among other things.[1]

The Banking Sector has been for centuries the pillars of economic prosperity. Indeed, the history supplements us with some information regarding how the banks have provided finance for imperialist ventures in newly acquired colonies. Over time, the banks have formed an important part in providing an avenue for both savings and investments. Banks provide the facility of transferring funds from one place to another, which leads to the growth of trade. A country's economic prosperity depends on the development of trade, commerce industry, agriculture, transport and communication etc. These sectors are financed by the commercial banks and employment opportunities are increasing.[2]

What is Development Bank?

Development Banks or Development Finance Institutions as these are normally called in the financial world are a post World War II phenomenon.

Such banks are basically providing loans for economic development of the nation. Their establishment in Africa, Asia and other developing countries in most cases have coincided with the attainment of independence.

Importance of Development Bank

According to Chandrasekhar (2011), the development banks lend and invest. They leverage lending to influence the investment decisions and monitor the performance of borrowers. They undertake entrepreneurial functions, such as determining the scale of investment, the choice of technology and the markets to be targeted by industry, and extension functions, such as offering technical support.

Stated otherwise, they are a component of the financial structure that could ensure sustained lending for productive investment in accelerating growth, despite a significant role as finance providers, development banks have adopted a passive role with respect to technological or managerial decisions of private borrowers, avoiding a role that such institutions are expected to play.[3] According to Kesava Varma (2010), it is vested with the responsibility of coordinating the working of those institutions engaged in financing, promoting and developing industries. It has evolved an appropriate mechanism for the purpose.[4]

Development Bank in India

According to Chandrasekhar (2011), a series of industrial credit institutions were promoted, for establishing the Industrial Finance Corporation [July 1948] for rendering term-financing for traditional industries apart from Industrial finance department within the RBI [1957] and administering the Credit guarantee scheme for small scale industries [July 1960].

In addition, State Financial Corporations were created under an Act wth effect from August 1952, to encourage the state-level medium size industries with industrial credit. In January 1955, the Industrial Credit and Investment Corporation of India, the first development finance institution in the private sector, became functional with the support of support of the World Bank. The Industrial Development Bank of India become as an apex term-lending institution and the Unit Trust of India as an investment institution, [operations in July 1964] as subsidiaries of the Reserve Bank of India.[5] Let us discuss about some 13 developmental banks at home.

State Financial Corporation

A Central Industrial Finance Corporation was set up under the Industrial Finance Corporation Act, 1948 (XV of 1948) for extending medium and long-term credit to industrial undertakings outside the purview of commercial banks. The state governments wished similar corporations in their states, to supplement the Industrial Finance Corporation. Their objective was to facilitate the state corporations confine to finance medium and small scale industrial enterprises and subject to consider those cases outside the scope of the Industrial Finance Corporation.[6]

According to Chand (2012), State Finance Corporations (SFCs) are the integral part of institutional finance structure in the country. These promote small and medium industries within the states. Besides, SFCs are helpful in ensuring balanced regional development, higher investment, employment generation and broad ownership of industries. There are 18 state finance corporations (out of which 17 SFCs were established under SFC Act 1951). Tamil Nadu Industrial Investment Corporation Ltd. established under Company Act, 1949, is also working as state finance corporation. The SFCs grant loans mainly for acquisition of fixed assets like land, building, plant and machinery. The authorised capital of a SFC is being fixed by the state government within the minima and maxima limits of Rs 50 lakh and Rs. 5 crore, respectively, and is being divided into the shares of respective state governments of equal value of the RBI, scheduled banks, co-operative banks, other financial bodies, such as insurance companies, investment trusts and private parties.[7]

State Industrial Development Corporation

It is the industrial and investment promotion agency for the promotion and development of medium and large scale units in the state. As the Nodal Agency for foreign and domestic investments, SIDC provides support for investors, besides processing various incentive schemes and facilitating interaction between the government and the industrial sector. It assists in identifying the state infrastructure needs, structuring projects to bridge the gaps and spearheading a balanced growth of core competencies of the state.

National Industrial Development Corporation [NIDC]

The National Industrial Development Corporation Limited was set up as the foremost PSU from ministry of commerce and industry under the government at the Centre. It is a consultancy outlet for providing inputs to country's industrialization requirements.[8] The government finds the corporation affecting industrial development [Estd. Oct 20, 1954].

It can also render assistance for the modernization of industries. It promotes industries, builds up ingenious scheme or collaborates with industries, besides modernization. Initially, it extended finance to cotton, jute, and sugar industries and for modernization and remains a consultation outlet for public-private sector. The NIDC extends assistance to cotton, jute, and sugar industries for modernization. It has established a consultancy in private and public sector.[9]

Industrial Finance Corporation of India [IIFC]

It is an Indian government owned development bank to cater to the long-term finance needs of the industrial sector. It was the first Development Financial Institution established by the Indian government after independence. The main objective of IFCI is to provide medium and long term financial assistance to large scale industrial undertakings, particularly when ordinary bank accommodation does not suit the undertaking or finance cannot be profitably raised by the concerned by the issue of shares. IFCI has fulfilled its original mandate as a DFI by providing long term financial support to all segments of Indian Industry. It has also been chiefly instrumental in translating the government's development priorities into reality.[10]

Industrial Investment Bank of India [IIBI]

The Industrial Investment Bank of India is a 100 per cent government of India-owned financial investor. The Parliament of India u/s 617 of the Companies Act ratified the bank [1971] for rehabilitation of sick industrial companies. It was reconstituted as the Industrial Reconstruction Bank of India [1985] under the IRBI Act, 1984. IIBI offered a wide range of products and and services, including term loan assistance for project finance, short duration non-project asset-backed financing, working capital/other short-term loans to companies, equity subscription, asset credit, equipment finance and investments in capital market and money market instruments.[11]

The Industrial Development Bank of India [IDBI]

The Industrial Development Bank of India is one of the familiar public financial institutions in India. It is also known as IDBI and is the fourth largest bank in terms of ratings. The main aim of its formation was to provide easy loans and financial support to industrial sector. IDBI under an act of parliament, aims to provide more financial impetus to industrial sector in order to add to the country's GDP. It has become familiar financial body in the country extending the state-of-the-art higher class facilities and services.[12]

Industrial Reconstruction Bank of India [IRBI]

The Industrial Reconstruction Bank of India [Estd.1985] under the Industrial Reconstruction Bank of India Act 1985. It is the principal credit and reconstruction agency for rehabilitation of sick and closed industrial units. It assists industrial concerns by extending loans and advances, underwriting of stocks, shares, bonds and debentures and guarantees for loans/deferred payments. Its range of services includes the provision of infrastructural facilities, consultancy, managerial and merchant banking facilities and making available machines and other equipments on lease or hire-purchase terms.[13]

According to Chand (2013), it was converted into a statutory corporation called the Industrial Reconstruction Bank of India [March 1985] with an authorised capital of Rs. 200 crore and a paid-up capital of Rs. 50 crore. It will function as the principal credit and reconstruction agency for industrial revival and co-ordinate with the activities of other institutions engaged in the revival of industries, to assist and promote industrial development and rehabilitation of industrial concerns. The IRBI is empowered to take over the management of assisted sick industrial units, lease out or sell them as running concerns or prepare schemes for reconstruction-by scaling down liabilities with the approval of the government of India.[14]

Unit Trust of India [UTI]

Unit Trust of India is a financial organization in India, under the UTI Act ratified by the Parliament [Dec 30, 1963]. It remained the sole vehicle for investment in the capital market for over two decades. The special undertaking of Unit Trust of India (SUUTI) was formed, specifically to take over the regular income schemes of the UTI. The cabinet committee on Economic Affairs decided often to encash some of the blue chip shares, reversing an earlier decision on the asset management company [2014].

Export-Import Bank of India [EXIM BANK]

The Export-Import Bank of India is the lead export finance institution under the Export Import Bank of India Act 1981 [1982]. It is also known as the Exim Bank of India. The government of India launched its operation to augment exports from India and combine the country's foreign trade and investment for growth in economy. It extends financial assistance to importers and exporters, beside financing oversea investment, export credit, for export-oriented units, films and agricultural and SMEs.[15]

EXIM bank took over the operations of the International Finance Wing of the IDBI. It acts as the apex agency in coordinating with the activities of other institutions engaged in the financing of exports and imports of goods and services.[16] It is about to set up a project development company with the African Development Bank, to encourage public-private partnership projects in Africa. It is working with a number of African regional banks and institutions to facilitate available credit for those projects. The financial institutions associating with African counterparts are the Economic Community of West African States, Western African Development Bank and African Development Bank.[17]

The Bank proactively seeks to enhance the competitive edge of Indian companies through a comprehensive range of financing programmes, advisory and support services at par with global trade environment encompassing various stages of export business cycle. It involved in creating export capability in small and medium enterprises, grassroots business enterprises and agro industries.[18]

Exim Bank extends Lines of Credit to overseas financial institutions, regional development banks, sovereign governments and other entities facilitating buyers therein, to import goods and services from India on deferred credit terms. The Indian exporters can obtain payment of eligible value from Exim Bank, without recourse against negotiable shipping documents.[19] The Bank, in order to help Indian companies in their internationalization efforts, provides a comprehensive programme covering equity finance, term loans, guarantees as advisory services. Besides, Exim Bank of India also takes direct equity stake in Indian ventures abroad, to enable them supplement their equity with the bank's equity. It has sought sought consciously to create a network of alliances with multilateral agencies, export credit agencies, development banks, besides trade and investment promotion bodies, enabling an environment for economic cooperation.[20]

According to Prabhu (2012), the Exim Bank also extends non-funded facility to Indian exporters in the form of guarantees. Its diversified lending covers various stages of exports, i.e., from the development to expansion of production capacity for exporters, production for exports and post-shipment financing. It focuses on the export of manufactured goods, project exports, export of technology services and computers software.[21]

The Export-Import Bank of India (Amendment) Bill, 2011 was introduced in the Lok Sabha [December 08, 2011] by the Union Minister of Finance, Pranab Mukherjee. The Bill was found passed by the Lok Sabha [December 21, 2011] and by the Rajya Sabha [December 27, 2011]. The Bill amends the Export-Import (EXIM) Bank of India Act, 1981 and establishes the bank as a corporation, promoting international trade by financing exporters and importers. It proposes to increase the authorized capital from Rs 2,000 crore to Rs. 10,000 crore, in meeting with the capital requirements arising from significant business growth. It also proposes the appointment of two whole-time directors to the bank's board by the central government. At present, its board has only the chairman and the managing director.[22]

National Bank for Agriculture and Rural Development [NABARD]

NABARD as the apex institution looks after the development of cottage and small industry, besides village and rural industries. It reaches out to allied economies, supports and promotes an integrated development. Its main focus was to uplift rural India by increasing the credit flow for elevation of agriculture and rural non-farm sector. It replaced the Agricultural Credit Department and Rural Planning and Credit Cell of the RBI, and Agricultural Refinance and Development Corporation. It is one of the premier agencies extending credit in rural areas.

NABARD is India's specialised bank. Its refinance is available to the state co-operative agriculture and rural development banks, state cooperative banks, regional rural banks, commercial banks and other financial bodies. It is also known for its *'SHG Bank Linkage Programme'* facilitating domestic banks lend SHGs.[23]

Land Development Banks [LDBs]

The long term credit needs of agricultural sector are being met by another type of co-operative institutions known as Land Development Banks. These are two-tiered banks, functioning – at as the Central Land Development Banks and primary Land Development Banks [at the state level]. LDBs Banks meet with the requirements of farmers for developmental purposes viz., provision of equipments like pump sets, tractors and machinery besides land improvement in the form of leveling, bundling, reclamation, fencing, sinking of new wells and repairs to old wells.[24]

LDB desires to promote the development of land, agriculture and increase production. It extends long-term finance to members directly through branches. The first LDB functioned at Jhang - Punjab [1920]. Its real progress climaxed when the LDB was established in Chennai [1929]. LDBs provides long-term term funds for agriculture-related projects, besides the development of land and business.[25]

Small Industries Development Bank of India [SIDBI]

It is a non-independent financial institution facilitating growth and development of MSMEs. It was incorporated initially as a wholly-owned subsidiary of IDBI, under an Act of Parliament [April 02,1990]. It refinances industries on short-term lending. It is the principal financial institution for the promotion, financing and development of MSMEs and coordinates with those institutions engaged in similar activities.[26]

SIDBI Venture Capital Ltd. is a subsidiary of SIDBI [July,1999]. It is an asset management company, managing two venture capital funds. Credit Guarantee Fund Trust for MSMEs [July 2000] and SIDBI, credit- guarantee supporting collateral free/third-party guarantee free loans extended by banks and lending institutions for MSMEs. The SME Rating Agency of India Ltd. [September 2005], as an MSME dedicated third-party rating agency to provide comprehensive, transparent and reliable ratings and risk profiling. India SME Technology Services Limited [November 2005], provides a platform for MSMEs to tap the opportunities at global level for acquisition of modern technologies.[27]

Industrial Credit and Investment Corporation of India [ICICI]

ICICI Bank is an Indian multinational banking and financial services company headquartered at Mumbai. It is a wholly-owned subsidiary [1955] established by ICICI. The parent company was a joint-venture of the World Bank, India's public sector banks and the public-sector insurance companies for project financing of the Indian industry. It launched internet banking operations [1998]. It was initially known as the Industrial Credit and Investment Corporation of India Bank, before changing its name to the abbreviated ICICI Bank.[28]

Conclusion

Development bank is a financial institution. It focuses on creating and delivering projects of a development and economic impact. They invest in infrastructure, public, and financial administration systems, as well as healthcare services. The banks include multibillion-dollar entities like the World Bank. Most of them are smaller regional and local lenders spread throughout the world. They exist to fund projects improving the material well-being of people, particularly those under abject poverty.

The Industrial Credit and Investment Corporation of India, the first development finance institution in the private sector, found established, with encouragement and support of the World Bank. Two other major steps in institution building were the setting up of the Industrial Development Bank of India as an apex term-lending institution and the Unit Trust of India as an investment institution, commencing operations as the RBI subsidiary [July 1964].

References

1. Economic development (2014), <http://en.wikipedia.org/wiki/Economic_development>
2. Role of Commercial Banks in Economic Development, <http:// wordsense1.hubpages.com/hub/Role-of-Commercial-Banks-in-EconomicDevelopment>
3. C.P. Chandrasekhar, Development Banks: Their role and importance for development, <http://www.networkideas.org/alt/apr2011/ development_banks.pdf>
4. Kesavavarma (2010), Functions of development banks, <http://www.studymode.com/essays/Functions-Of-Development-Banks-449986.html>
5. C.P. Chandrasekhar, Development Banks: Their role and importance for development, <http://www.networkideas.org/alt/apr2011/ development_banks.pdf>
6. State financial corporation (2014), <http://smallb.in/node/689>
7. Smriti Chand, India's State Finance Corporations: Management, Functions and Working of SFCs, <http://www.yourarticlelibrary.com/finance/ indias-state-finance-corporations-management-functions-and-working-of-sfcs/23507/>
8. National Industrial Development Corporation Limited, <http:// business.mapsofindia.com/sectors/public/national-industrial-developmentcorporation-limited.html>
9. National Industrial Development Corporation of India, <http:// www.yourarticle-library.com/organization/national-industrial-developmentcorporation-of-india-nidc/26208/>
10. Industrial Finance Corporation of India (2014), <http:// en.wikipedia.org/wiki/Industrial_Finance_Corporation_of_India>
11. Industrial Investment Bank of India (2014), <http:// en.wikipedia.org/wiki/Industrial_Investment_Bank_of_India>
12. The Industrial Development Bank of India, <http:// business.mapsofindia.com/banks-in-india/industrial-development-bank-ofindia.html>

13. The Industrial Reconstruction Bank of India (2014), <http:// www.bms.co.in/industrial-reconstruction-bank-of-india-irbi/>
14. Smriti Chand, Functions of Industrial Reconstruction Bank of India, <http://www.yourarticlelibrary.com/banking/functions-of-industrialreconstruction-bank-of-india-irbi/24814/>
15. Export-Import Bank of India (2014), <http://business. mapsofindia.com/banks-in-india/export-import-bank-of-india.html>
16. Export-Import Bank of India (2014), <http://agritech.tnau.ac.in/ banking/crbank_exim.html>
17. Export-Import Bank of India to start project development firm with African Development Bank, <http://www.dnaindia.com/money/reportexport-import-bank-of-india-to-start-project-development-firm-with-africandevelopment-bank-1968512>
18. Overview of Export-Import Bank, <http://www.eximbankindia.in/ sites/default/files/ANR_FULL.pdf>
19. Export-Import Bank of India, Export lines of credit, <http:// newsletters.cii.in/Newsletters/mailer/LAC_Newsletter/february/Opportunities/ locbooklet.pdf>
20. Exim bank of India, <http://www.ibef.org/download/ exim_bank.pdf>
21. Parvata Raj Prabhu,A study on role of Exim bank in export trade, <http://apjor.com/files/1374773690.pdf>
22. The Export-Import Bank of India (Amendment) Bill, 2011, <http://www.prsindia.org/billtrack/the-export-import-bank-of-india-amendment-bill-2011-2097/>
23. National Bank for Agriculture and Rural Development, <http:// en.wikipedia.org/wiki/National_Bank_for_Agriculture_and_Rural_Development>
24. Land development banks, <http://www.citeman.com/5872-landdevelopment-banks.html>
25. Land development bank, <http://en.wikipedia.org/wiki/Land_development_bank>
26. Small Industries Development Bank of India, <http:// en.wikipedia.org/wiki/Small_Industries_Development_Bank_of_India>
27. Small Industries Development Bank of India, <http://smallb.in/ small-industries-development-bank-india-sidbi>
28. Industrial Credit and Investment Corporation of India, <http:// en.wikipedia.org/wiki/ICICI_Bank>

Chapter - 13

Bank Balance Sheet

"Investment banking has, in recent years, resembled a casino, and the massive scale of gambling losses has dragged down traditional business and retail lending activities as banks try to rebuild their balance sheets. This was one aspect of modern financial liberalisation that had dire consequences."

— ***Vince Cable***

Introduction

The book of ICFAI University Press defines - accounting as a system of information for organizations and parties outside the organization to make judgments about the organization. Accounting is more important in business matters. It has existed for many centuries. The exact years or the period in which accounting was practiced is unknown, but symbols recording transactions between tribes have been found to date back 5000 BC.

In Greece, accounting became prestigious; the records of construction costs of government building were carved on the structures. Financial accounting consists of creation of financial information and the consequent use of such information, Creation involves *recording*, *classifying* and *summarizing* , which are dealt as:

1. *Recording of Transactions*: Journal.
2. *Classifying of Transactions*: Ledger.
3. *Summarizing of Transactions*: The trial/general balance sheet of business.

The recording commences when a business transaction occurs and gets quantified. All the events and transactions affecting the business ought to be recorded, in accordance with the principles of accountancy. Sales of goods cannot be registered in account books, when the goods are merely intended to be sold, but recorded only after such sale is complete and property in the goods were transferred to the buyer.[1] According to Bank accepted bills: FAQs (2010), Journal records the daily transactions of the business in an order of occurrence. The first step of recording is being done in the Journal in the chronological order. Thus, Journal is the book of original records. The Journal precedes the Ledger. The process of recording in the Journal is called the *Journalizing*.

The financial statements for banks present a different analytical problem than those for manufacturing and service companies. As a result, the analysis of a bank's financial statements requires some distinct approach recognizing the bank's unique risks. The banks accept deposits from savers and pay interest on them. They pass these funds on to borrowers and receive interest on loans. Their profits are derived from the spread between the rate they pay for funds and what rate they receive back from borrowers. The ability to pool up deposits from sources alike can be lent to different borrowers for flow of funds inherent in the system.

Banking is a highly leveraged business. It requires the regulators dictate minimal capital levels to help ensure the solvency of each bank and the very banking system. The banks as financial intermediaries, assume two types of risk when they manage with the flow of money through business. Interest rate risk is the management of spread between the interest paid on deposits and that received on loans over time. Credit risk is the likelihood that a borrower will default on a loan or lease, causing the bank to lose any potential interest earned as well as the principal amount lent to the borrower. In the simplest definition, *Bank Bills* are a form of an IOU with the exception that *these* have a specific date in future when payable. Their makeup is very similar to that of a cheque apart from the specific maturity date.[2]

According to Wagner (2012), the primary business of any bank is managing with the spread between deposits (liabilities, loans and assets). The bank generates a positive interest spread or net interest income, when the earned interest exceeds that payable on deposits. As a result, the net interest income varies on the differences in timing of the accrual change and the changing rate and yield curve relationship. The changes in the general level of market interest rates may also cause changes in the volume and the mix of a bank's balance sheet products. The banks, in the normal course of business, assume financial risk by availing loans at interest rates differing from those rates payable on deposits.

The deposits often have shorter maturities than loans. These ought to adjust with current market rates faster than loans. The result is a balance sheet mismatch between assets (loans) and liabilities (deposits). The credit risk is simply defined as the potential of a bank borrower [counter-party] failing on its obligations, in accordance with the agreed terms. The bank will often experience some loss [all of the credit provided to customer], and maintain an allowance for such loan and lease losses. The actual losses find written off from *the balance sheet account* "allowance" for such loan and lease losses. The allowance for loan and lease losses finds replenished through the income statement line item "provision" for loan losses.[3]

A financial snapshot shows the current health of business, as measured in terms of assets and liabilities. The assets include items such as cash, inventories and accounts receivable. The liabilities include bank's indebtedness and payable accounts. The balance sheet forecasts the financial health ensuring healthy business, i.e. that it is funded adequately. It would be useful for any banker or investor in assessing about the risk and collateral issues.[4]

According to Basu (2013), the balance sheet summarizes a company's assets and liabilities, with the equity of shareholders. The term "owner's equity" refers to the equity of owners and partners for certain small businesses, such as the sole proprietorships and partnerships. The quarterly amounts and historical trends of balance sheet accounts are important metrics for management and investment community, similar to the financial ratios expressing relationship between those accounts. Assets and liabilities are the main components of any balance sheet. The third component, owner's or shareholders' equity is the difference between assets and liabilities. Assets include the current assets any company desires to use within a year, such as cash and inventory, and fixed or long-term assets, such as equipment. The liabilities include the payable current liabilities within a year, such as payable accounts and payable short-term debt and long-term liabilities, such as bonds.[5]

Balance sheets need to be prepared by businesses as part of the annual exercises, leading up to the year-end financial records. The owner of the business and shareholders ascertain through it on the company's financial health. A balance sheet is written documentation of assets or capital owned by [owing to] the business. It is a representation of the amount of money owned by the business to third parties. It is important to remember that the total net asset value should be at par with the capital and the net profit of business. It is also vital that business owners understand the balance sheet to ascertain about the financial state of business, although the balance sheets drafted by qualified accountants and financial controllers are worthier. *QuickBooks Accounting* software gives the business owners, the benefit of hands-on accounting, without necessitating years of accounting experience. Every balance sheet is unique; while the business may experience a high profit account, or simultaneously can have a poor balance sheet, if the net asset value is low and vice-versa. The balance sheets determine the financial strengths of any business and leave room for the future financial planning.[6]

According to Russell (2013), the balance sheet summarizes a company's Assets, Liabilities and Owners' Equity (net worth) at a specific point in time, usually at the end of an accounting period. The purpose of a Balance Sheet is to give users an idea of the company's financial condition along with displaying what the company owns and owes. It helps the business owners quickly get a handle on the financial strength and capabilities of business. The Balance Sheet for accounting is an extremely important and often used statement of entity condition. It shows the extent of entity ownership of assets, liability and equity at any given point in time. This point is the date on the statement. It is a physical representation of the 'accounting equation.' The equation states that the assets of any business are equal to the sum of liabilities and owner's equity, at any point of time. The equation forms also the basis of statement structure, which mirrors three aspects of such an equation, viz.,. (1) assets, (2) liabilities and (3) owner's equity. The assets are anything that the business owns.[7]

Explanation- General Balance Sheet Categories

Assets: Everything of value that the company owns

(a) Current Assets – can be converted into cash within a year – cash, receivables, inventory, etc.

(b) Fixed Assets – permanent in nature – land, buildings, machinery, equipment, etc.

(c) Other Assets – intangibles such as patents and goodwill

(d) Total Assets – aggregate of above assets

Liabilities: All the debts that the company owes

(a) Current Liabilities – debts due within one year from the date of Balance Sheet – payables, loans etc.

(b) Long Term Liabilities – debts due more than one year from date of Balance Sheet – loans, etc.

(c) Total Liabilities – aggregate of above Liabilities

Net Worth: Assets minus Liabilities – book value of the company

(a) Owner's Equity Investment – Owner's investment (cash and equipment) in the company

(b) Retained Earnings – Prior years' Net Profits/(Net Losses) "retained" in the business

(c) Net Profit – Current year's Net Profits (or Net Loss)

Total Net Worth: Total of all above Net Worth accounts (Total Owner's Equity)

Total Liabilities and Net Worth: Aggregate of up to the same amount as Total Assets; Assets therefore are in "balance" with the total of Liabilities and Net Worth.[8]

Assets

The properties and possession of business is known as Asset. Assets can be classified as:

(a) Fixed Assets: Assets used in the conduct of business operation, but not for for and not for reselling earn profit in order. These assets are not easily converted into cash in the normal course of business operation. Examples are, land and building, plant and machinery, furniture and fittings etc.

(b) Current Assets: All assets which are acquired for reselling purpose during the course of business are treated as current assets. They are acquired through cash and easily convertible into cash. Examples are cash and bank, debtors, inventory or stock, bills receivable etc.

(c) Intangible Assets: The latent assets but their real value depends upon the earning capacity of the business concern. Example, goodwill.

(d) Other Assets: The assets in tangible form, but are not used directly in the business operation.[9]

Liabilities

Liabilities is the amount payable to outsiders by the business. It is the claim of outsiders on business assets. These are:

(a) *Fixed Liabilities*: The liability paid or redeemed on the termination of Business. Example. capital.

(b) Lon-Term Liabilities: Obligations met after a period of an year is long-term liabilities. These are also known as non-current liability. Examples: debenture, long-term loans etc.

(c) Current Liabilities: Liabilities payable within one year. Examples: creditors, bills payable etc known as short-term liabilities

Contingent Assets and Contingent Liabilities

According to the Dictionary for Accountants, Contingent assets refers to an asset "the existence, value and ownership of which depends upon the performance [non-performance] of any specific act." For example, the pending decision of the court. The *contingent liability* is to pay on the happening [non-happening] of an uncertain event. It is not the actual liability, therefore shown as a footnote in the balance sheet. For example, the unpaid liability on the party-paid shares, claims not acknowledged as debt, etc.[10]

Bank Assets

Bank assets are its physical and financial property. It has commonly owned physical property (buildings, land, furniture, equipment), the bulk of its assets are financial, legal claims on the property or the wealth of others. The two most notable asset categories are loans (which generate interest revenue) and reserves (which keep deposits safe). It consists mainly of various kinds of loans and marketable securities and reserves of base money, held either as actual central bank notes and coins or in the form of a credit (deposit) balance at the central bank. The resource of a modern bank is borrowed money, which it loans out as profitably as is prudent. Banks hold cash reserves also for interbank settlements as well as to provide depositors with cash on demand, maintaining thereby a safe ratio of cash-to- deposits. The latter may be established by convention or by some statute.[11]

Capital and liquidity are distinct, but related concepts. Each plays an essential role in understanding the bank's viability and solvency. Liquidity is a measure of the ability and ease with which assets could be converted to cash. The *liquid assets* could be converted to cash quickly, if needed to meet financial obligations; examples of *liquid assets* generally include cash, central bank reserves, and the government debt. A financial institution must have enough *liquid assets* to meet its near-term obligations, such as withdrawals by depositors, to remain viable. The capital acts as a financial cushion absorbing unexpected losses and is the difference between the firm's assets and its liabilities. The value of a firm's assets must exceed its liabilities, to remain solvent.[12]

Commercial bank assets like assets of other companies bring value to the bank. Each commercial bank creates a monthly, quarterly, or annual balance sheet that lists in detail about the owned assets owned. The major asset categories include cash, securities, and loans, with several subcategories or other classes possible under the larger groups. In short, the commercial bank assets represent items that make up the economic wealth of the institution, with net economic wealth being total bank assets less liabilities.[13]

Money at call and short notices appear in the balance sheet of any bank. It includes funds lent to discount houses, money brokers, the stock exchange, bullion brokers, corporate customers, and increasingly to other banks. 'At call' money is repayable on demand, whereas 'short notice' money implies the notice to repay up to 14 days. Money at call and short notice are the banks' most liquid assets. They are usually interest-earning secured loans, but their importance lies in providing banks with an opportunity to use surplus funds and adjust their cash and liquidity requirements.[14] Money at call means a short-term loan without any set repayment schedule, but immediately payable on full upon demand. Money-at-call loans give banks a way to earn interest, retaining liquidity. Investors might use the money at call notice, to cover a margin account. The interest rate on such loans is called the call-loan rate.[15]

Cash and Investment

Current assets include cash and other assets converted into cash within the operating cycle. For example, a manufacturing enterprise uses cash to acquire inventories of materials. The latter are being converted into finished products and sold to customers. Cash is collected from customers. This circle from cash-back-to cash is called an operating cycle. In a merchandising business, one part of the cycle is eliminated. Cash is simply the money on hand and/or on deposit available for general business. It is always listed first on a balance sheet.

Cash held for some designated purpose, [such as the that held in a fund for eventual retirement of a bond issue], is excluded from current asset. The investments are temporary arising from excess funds that do not immediately need to conduct operations. Simply stated, accounts receivables are the amounts owed and are evidenced on balance sheet by promissory notes. Accounts receivable are the amounts billed to customers and owed to the balance sheet's date. Investments are cash funds or securities that hold for a designated purpose for an indefinite period of time. Investments include stocks or the bonds you may hold for another company, real estate or mortgages that are holding for income-producing purposes. Investments also include money that may be holding for a pension fund. Often classified as fixed assets, or as plant and equipment, plant assets include land, buildings, machinery, and equipment that are to be used in business operations over a relatively long period of time.[16]

Fixed Assets

Fixed assets are a term used in accounting for assets and property that cannot easily be converted into cash. This can be compared with current assets such as cash or bank accounts, which are described as liquid assets. Moreover, a fixed/non-current asset can also be defined as an asset not directly sold to a firm's consumers/end-use. It is a long-term tangible piece of property a firm owns and uses in the production of income and is not expected to be consumed or converted into cash no sooner than at least one year's time. Fixed assets sometimes are collectively referred to as "plant". Buildings, real estate, equipment and furniture are its good examples. Generally, intangible long-term assets such as trade marks and patents are not categorized as fixed assets but are more specifically referred to as "fixed intangible assets".[17] It is an asset that is not consumed or sold during normal course of business, such as land, buildings, equipment, machinery, vehicles, leasehold improvements, and other such items.[18]

A *fixed asset* is an asset of a business *intended for continuing use*, rather than a short-term, temporary asset such as stock. These must be classified in a company's balance sheet as *intangible*, *tangible* or *investments*. The examples of intangible assets include goodwill, patents, and trademarks. The examples of tangible fixed assets include land and buildings, plant and machinery, fixtures and fittings, motor vehicles and IT equipment. The benefits that a business obtains from a fixed asset extend over several years.[19] *Fixed assets* are included in the balance sheet at their initial cost, and depreciated throughout useful life until sold, replaced or recorded at their residual value on the balance sheet. The depreciation of a fixed asset is the initial cost less the residual value. It is recorded as an expense since it diminished the value of a company's total holdings.[20]

Fixed assets may be sold anytime during their useful life. This gives rise to the need to derecognize the asset from balance sheet and recognize any gain or loss resulting in the income statement.[21] Fixed assets are shown on the balance sheet at historical cost less depreciation. The depreciation is calculated to write off the cost less residual value of each asset over its expected useful life. Fixed assets acquired during the year are shown on the Income and Expenditure statement as the capital expenditure.

Fixed assets funded by grants are expensed from restricted grant funds in the year of purchase and transferred to the capital grants fund. These are shown on the balance sheet and depreciated through the capital grants fund at rates calculated to write off the cost less residual value of each asset over expected useful life. These are expensed from revenue funds in the year of purchase and transferred to the capital fund. Fixed assets are shown on the balance sheet and depreciated through the capital grants fund at rates calculated to write off the cost less residual value of each asset over its expected useful life.[22]

Assets shown on a balance sheet can be sub-divided into intangible and tangible groups. The former category contains items such as goodwill, trademarks and expenditure on research and development. The valuation of items is subjective as their true worth can be known only, following a successful sale of either the asset separately or the business as a whole. Prudence and caution in assigning amounts to intangible assets might result in the balance sheet displaying them with conservative valuation, far removed from what they are actually worth. The assets typically attract far more objective valuations, as they usually exist as a result of a measurable transfer or exchange upon which a monetary value can be assigned.[23]

Bill Discounted

It is an accepted draft or bill of exchange sold for early payment to a bank or credit institution at less than face value after the bank deducts fees and applicable interest charges. The bank or credit institution then collects full value on the draft or bill of exchange when payment comes due.[24] A commercial bill discount is an act by which the legal holder of a commercial bill (including banker's acceptance draft and commercial acceptance draft) transfers it to BOCOM to acquire cash before its maturity date. Bill discounting is a major activity with smaller banks. The bank takes the bill drawn by borrower on his customer and pays him immediately deducting some amount as discount/commission under this type of lending. The bank then presents the bill to the borrower's customer on the due date of the bill and collects the total amount. If the bill is delayed, the borrower or his customer pays the bank a pre-determined interest depending upon the terms of transaction.[25]

A commercial bill facility is a flexible credit facility a short or long-term injection of cash to finance an individual export contract or general export growth. A commercial bill also called a bank bill or bill of exchange is a payment order directing bank to pay a sum of money to the holder of the bill at a future time.[26] It is trading or selling a bill of exchange prior to the maturity date at a value less than at par value of the bill. The amount of discount depends on the extent of time left before the bill matures, and on the perceived risk attached to the bill.[27]

A bill discounting involves effectively selling it to a bank or similar entity for an amount slightly less than at par value before the maturity date associated with the bill of exchange. The debtor tenders payment to the new owner of the discounted bill in the originally agreed upon full amount. This allows the issuer of the bill to receive cash before the actual due date associated with the bill, allowing also the buyer to make a modest profit on the cash advance extended to the bill's originator. Several factors need to be accounted for any financial institution consider before choosing to enter into a bill discounting transaction.[28]

Bills of exchange are similar to checks and promissory notes. They can be drawn by individuals or banks and are transferable generally by endorsements. The difference between a promissory note and a bill of exchange is transferable and can bind one party to pay a third party, not involved in creation. If these bills are issued by a bank, they can be referred to as bank drafts.[29] Bank interest rate is the interest rate for short-term money-market Bank interest rate is the interest rate for short-term money-market instruments like commercial paper and treasury bills. The bank discount rate is based on the instrument's par value and the amount of the discount. The bank discount rate is the required rate of return of a safe investment guaranteed by the bank.[30]

Business activities across the borders are done through letter of credit. The Letter of credit is an instrument issued in favor of the seller by the buyer bank assuring that payment will be made after certain time frame, depending upon the agreed terms and conditions, it could be either sight, 30 days from the Bill of Lading or 120 days from the date of bill of lading. Now, when the seller receives this letter of credit through bank, s[he] prepares the documents and presents them to the bank. The most important element in the process is the bill of exchange, used to negotiate a letter of credit.[31]

Invoice discounting is a form of short-term borrowing, often used to improve a company's working capital and cash flow position. Invoice discounting allows a business draw money against sales invoices before the customer has actually paid. The business borrows a percentage of the value of its sales ledger from a finance company, effectively using the unpaid sales invoices as collateral for the borrowing.[32] Business banking facility allows the traders obtain an advance from the bank pending receipt of sales proceeds, thus increasing their liquidity. The advance is based on the face value of bills drawn by the seller. The bank buys the bill before it is due and credits its value after a discount is being charged on the customer's account.[33]

Bank Liabilities

In financial accounting, a liability is defined as an *obligation* of an entity arising from past transactions or events, the settlement of which may result in the transfer or use of assets, provision of services or other economic benefits, yielding in the future. In financial accounting, it need not be legally enforceable; but can be based on equitable obligations or constructive obligations. An equitable obligation is a duty-based on ethical or moral considerations.[34]

According to IASB, the framework liability is defined as, a liability is a present obligation of the enterprise arising from past events, the settlement of which is expected to result in an outflow from the enterprise of resources embodying economic benefits. In simple words, liability is an obligation of the entity to transfer case or other resources to another party. It could be a bank loan for instance, which obligates the entity to pay loan installment over the loan duration to the bank with the associated interest cost. Alternatively, an entity's liability could be a trade payable arising from the purchase of goods from a supplier on credit. It may be classified into current and non-current liability. The current liability expects to pay off within one year from the reporting date. Non-current liability is expected to settle after an year from the reporting date.[35]

Liabilities recorded on the balance sheet (right side), liabilities include loans, accounts payable, mortgages, deferred revenues and accrued expenses.

These liabilities are the vital aspect of any company's operation, because they are used to finance operations and pay for large expansions. They can also make transactions between more efficient businesses.[36] In order for the business to have commenced, it would have had received an injection of funds from some source. This might have been from the entrepreneur's own savings or alternatively from an external body, such as a bank or the suppliers in the form of credit. At any time, it is likely that the business owes money to creditors for purchases it has made and perhaps to other financiers of operation. These amounts are depicted either current or long term liabilities.[37]

Contingent Liabilities

Contingent liabilities that may be incurred by an entity depending on the outcome of some future event such as some court case. These liabilities are not recorded in a company's accounts, but shown in the balance sheet, when both might be probable and reasonably estimable as 'contingency' or 'worst case' of financial outcome. A footnote to the balance sheet may describe the nature and extent of such contingent liabilities. The likelihood of loss is described as probable, reasonably possible, or remote. The ability to estimate any loss is described as known, reasonably [not reasonably] estimable.[38]

It is a potential obligation, depending on the outcome of some future event. A contingent liability is uncertain, which could be resolved by some future event. It is recorded in the books of accounts only, if the contingency is probable and the amount of the liability can be estimated. The outstanding lawsuits and product warrantees are common examples of contingent liabilities.[39] It is hypothetical liability dependent on some possible event or situation before becoming an actual liability. These are different for each type of business and profession, and the management makes provision by setting aside appropriate funds as reserves for them. [40]

In accounting, a contingent liability and the related contingent loss are recorded with a journal entry only, if the contingency is probable and the *amount can be estimated.* If it is only possible, or the amount cannot be estimated, a journal entry is not required. However, a disclosure is required. A product warranty is often cited as a probable and estimable contingent liability.[41]

Bills for Collection

Inter-Province Cheque Clearing System is the clearing procedure for cheque, draft, bill of exchange, and promissory note in case that any collecting branch and the paying branch are located in different clearing areas. In a documentary collection, the seller instructs his bank to forward documents related to the export of goods to the buyer's bank with a request to present them to the buyer for payment, with time and conditions of release.[42] In simple terms, export bill collection means sending of export bills to overseas buyer through his bank to collect payment under export bills. Once after completion of necessary export procedures and formalities, the exporter prepares necessary documents to overseas buyer to take delivery of the cargo. This document includes commercial invoice, packing list, certificate of origin, bill of lading or airway bill, bill of exchange, quality certificate, and other documents specifically mentioned by the buyer at the time of placing purchase order.[43]

In theory, the "Bill for collections" is the more secure trade term for an exporter than "Open Account" trading, as the exporter's documentation is sent from an exporter or supplier designated bank to the importer or buyer's bank. This invariably occurs after shipment and contains specific instructions that must be obeyed. The buyer or importer's bank will act on instructions provided by some exporter or supplier, via their own bank, and often provides a useful communication route through, which disputes are arbitrated. The Bills for Collection - process is governed by a set of rules, published by the International Chamber of Commerce (ICC) called "Uniform Rules for Collections" document number 522 (URC522). There are two types of Bill for Collection, usually determined by the payment terms agreed within a commercial global trade contract.[44]

Bills of Acceptance and Guarantee

Banker's acceptance is a short-term debt instrument from a firm guaranteed by a commercial bank. These are issued by firms as part of a commercial transaction. The instruments are similar to T-Bills, frequently used in money market funds. These acceptances are traded at a discount from face value on the secondary market, which can be an advantage because the banker's acceptance is seldom held until maturity. These are regularly used financial instruments in international trade, and vary in amount, according to the size of commercial transaction. The date of maturity typically ranges between 30 and 180 days from the date of issue. However, the banks or investors often trade with the instruments on the secondary market before the acceptances reach maturity.

Bankers acceptances are considered to be relatively safe investments, since the bank and the borrower are liable for the amount that is due when the instrument matures.[45] It is a kind of credit activity, wherein the bank acts as the payer at the application of the drawer, to effect an unconditional payment to the payee [the endorsee] against the valid commercial bills at a specified date. The main features are: (i) more creditable than the general commercial drafts; (ii) wider circulation, (iii) strong cashibility, and (iv) to ease your funds pressure and save your expenses. Clients in short of cash in commodity trade can apply for their acceptance with the bank to obtain the bank's credit support. The following documents need to be enclosed with the application: (i) The Acceptance Application Form; (ii) Business license passed annual review; (iii) Photocopy of the Code Certificate; (iv) The Certificate of Loan, or the Loan Card; (v) The audited financial statement of the previous year; (vi) The Purchase Contract signed between the buyer and the seller, and (vii) the Guarantee documents.[46]

Bill Guarantee is the Joint and several guaranty by the guarantors of a bill of exchange, taking on the liability for the undertakings(s) given by the drawer and the endorsers of the bill.[47] The guarantee is designed for banks that acquire bills of exchange for which there is an underlying export transaction. The guarantee covers non-payment of the bill of exchange. [48] The Warranty Bill of Sale is an agreement between two parties, whereas the seller wished to sell and the buyer wishes to buy the property or assets under the specified terms and conditions. This Bill of Sale Template is being used by two parties, who agree to conduct the sale with a warranty. This agreement is downloadable and customizable for specific usage.[49]

Bill of exchange[50]

Section 5 of the Indian Negotiable Instruments Act defines a bill of exchange as, "an instrument in writing, containing an unconditional order, signed by the maker directing certain person to pay certain sum of money/ the other of certain person/ the bearer of the instrument." The features of bill of exchange are: (a) It is a written document; (b) It is an unconditional order to pay a certain sum of money in future; (c) It must be signed by the maker of the bill, otherwise it will go invalid; (d) It must be dated and properly stamped; (e) The amount must be payable to a definite person or to the order or the bearer of the instrument; (f) It should contain an order made by the seller to the purchase to make payment in future; (g) The amount ordered in the bill must be certain; and (h) The payer is certain person/ the bearer or the bearer to the bill.

There are three parties to a bill of exchange, such as the *drawer*, the *drawee* and the *payer*, i.e. (a) *Drawer*: The person who draws [makes] the bill of exchange or cheque; (b) *Drawee*: The person who accepts the order/ on whom the bill of exchange is drawn; and (c) Payer: The person to whom the amount has to be paid. The Bill of exchange may be classified as *inland bill* and *foreign bill*, i.e. (a) *Inland Bill*: It is being drawn in India and made payable in/ drawn upon any person living in India; and (b) *Foreign Bill*: It is being drawn outside India, but made payable in/ drawn upon persons outside India.

Promissory Notes[51]

Negotiable Instrument Act defines a Promissory Note as "as an instrument in writing containing an unconditional undertaking signed by the maker to pay a certain sum of money/to the order of a certain person."The main characteristics of a promissory note are: (a) It must be in writing. The payment will not amount to a legal document; it is simply as oral promise; (b) It contains an unconditional order; (c) The maker must be a certain person of holding; (d) It is not payable to the bearer; (e) It must be signed by the maker; (f) The amount payable must be certain; (g) It must contain a promise by the market to make the payment in future; and (h) It should be properly stamped.

The various advantages of bill of exchange and *promissory notes* are: (a) These are helpful in increasing the size of the business, because they facilitate credit transactions; (b) A bill of exchange or a promissory note is a conclusive proof of the indebtedness of the purchaser of goods or services or credit; (c) These are legal documents, enforced in the court of law for payment in case of refusal or dishonor; (d) Foreign trade can be enhanced with the help of foreign bills of exchange; (e) These are negotiable instruments, and can be transferred easily from one person to another in settlement of debts.

Dishonor of Bills[52]

In one of the bill for payment, when the acceptor of the bill refuses to make payment of the bill on the due date or on the date of maturity, it is called the dishonor of bill. The drawer [holder of the bill] should get the bill noted with the help of an officer called *Notary public*, when it is dishonored. The latter is being appointed by the government to exercise the function of *noting the bills* within a particular area. He charges some fee for *noting such bill*, known as *noting charges*. The payment of *noting charges* is made by the holder of the bill, who gets the bill noted and can be recovered from the drawer, who in turn, recovers it from the acceptor. A bill can be dishonored in two ways, such as: (a) unaccepted by the drawee; and (b) the drawee fails to pay on due date, when presented for payment.

Renewal of Bills[53]

Sometimes, when the drawee fails to meet the bill on the date, he may request the drawer for extension of time for paying the amount of such bill. The drawee may make its part-payment in cash and accept a new bill for the remaining payable amount. The drawer by accepting his request for cancelation of old bill, draws a new bill on him for the due recovery. This is known as the renewal of bill, being charged by the drawer for the period of new bill. It may be paid in cash or can be added to the old bill amount and a new bill is accepted by the drawee.

Accommodation Bill[54]

Normally, the bills are drawn and accepted to facilitate trade. Sometimes, the bills are being drawn and accepted for the purpose of helping one or either of the parties involved without genuine business transaction in between. These bills are known as accommodation bills. The main purpose behind is to raise funds for a shorter period by discounting it with the bank. The discounting charges are being shared by either parties in the ratio of funds they have received. Journal entries are passed in the similar way as for ordinary bills. The only additional entry to be passed is for sending or receiving the amount. Accommodation bills may be of three types: (a) when the drawer is only accommodated through the bill; (b) when either of the parties are accommodated through a single bill; and (c) when either of the parties are accommodated through cross-bills.

The Difference in between:

[a] the Journal and the Ledge[55]

The difference between the *Journal* and the *Ledger* are as follows: (a) Every transaction finds recorded in the journal and later in the Ledger. The journal, as such, is known as the book of original entry. The ledger is known as the book of secondary entry; (b) The journal entry follows the chronological order i.e., and, as and when there were transactions; but the ledger remains a book for analytical record. The transactions pertaining to a particular account will appear at one place in the latter; (c) Any disputes about the accounting information upholds the journal as a book of primary entry in contrast with the latter ledger; (d) The journal is a subsidiary book, facilitating the preparation of the ledger; (e) The recording in the journal is known as journalizing, whereas the recording in the ledger is known as posting; and (f) In the journal, the unit of classification of data is the transaction, whereas in the ledger, the unit of classification of data is the amount.

[b] Book-Keeping and Accounting[56]

The difference between Book-Keeping and Accounting are:

Welsch and Anthony have distinguished between book-keeping and accountancy as "some people confuse book-keeper with an accountant and book-keeping with accounting. In fact, they confuse one of the minor parts with the whole of accounting. It is tantamount to comparing the simple administration of first aid to the injured with the prescription by the physician. Book-keeping is the routine and clerical side of accounting and requires only the minimal knowledge of the accounting model. A book-keeper records the repetitive and the uncomplicated transactions in most business. He may maintain the simple records of every small business. The accountant in contrast, is a professional, competent enough in the information design of information systems, analysis of complex economic events, interpretative and analytical processes, reporting, financial advising and consulting management."

Book-keeping is the science of recording those business transactions that result in transfer of money or its worth in books of accounts. Book-keeping is the recording of financial transactions of a business in a systematic manner so that information can be obtained any time. On the other hand, the accounting is concerned with the design of system of records, the preparation of reports based on those accounting records. The interpretation of reports based on such accounting records. Such interpretation of data and communicating results to the concerned person, interested in that information. The work of an accountant involves directing and reviewing the work of book-keepers. The accountants must posses higher knowledge in contrast with those book-keepers.

References

1. Accounting (2004),The ICFAI University Press, pp.2-4.
2. Bank accepted bills: FAQs, <http://www.banksa.com.au/corporate/ financial-markets/treasury-investments/bbfaq>

3. Hans Wagner (2012). Analyzing A Bank's Financial Statements, <http://www.investopedia.com/articles/stocks/07/bankfinancials.asp>
4. Balance Sheet, <http://www.sfu.ca/~mvolker/biz/balsheet.htm>
5. Chirantan Basu (2013). What Are the Three Most Important Metrics in the Balance Sheet? <http://smallbusiness.chron.com/three-importantmetrics-balance-sheet-36271.html>
6. Balance sheet importance, <http://www.quickbooks.co.za/ accounting-software/balance-sheet-importance/>
7. Michael Russell (2013). The Importance of the Balance Sheet as a Financial, <http://ezinearticles.com/?The-Importance-of-the-Balance-Sheetas-a-Financial&id=513212>
8. Why the balance sheet matters, <http://www.isbdc.org/why-thebalance-sheet-matters/>
9. Accounting (2004). The ICFAI University Press. p. 174
10. *Ibid.*
11. Bank assets (2013), <http://www.britannica.com/EBchecked/topic/51892/bank/273036/Assets>
12. What is the difference between a bank's liquidity and its capital? <http://www.federalreserve.gov/faqs/cat_21427.htm>
13. What are the different types of commercial bank assets? <http://www.wisegeek.com/what-are-the-different-types-of-commercial-bank-assets.htm>
14. Money at call and short notices (2013), <http://www.oxfordre ference.com/view/10.1093/oi/authority.20110803100205522>
15. Money at call (2013), <http://www.investopedia.com/terms/m/ money-at-call.asp>
16. Preparing a balance sheet, <http://www.tdbank.com/small_ business/workshops/BalanceSheet/textbalance.htm>
17. Fixed assets, <http://www.investopedia.com/terms/f/fixedasset.asp>
18. What is fixed asset? <http://www.businessdictionary.com/ definition/fixed-asset.html>
19. Accounting for fixed assets, <http://www.tutor2u.net/business/ accounts/assets_fixedassets_intro.asp>
20. Fixed assets – What are fixed assets? <http://www.e-conomic.co.uk / accountingsystem/glossary/fixed-assets>
21. Disposal of fixed assets, <http://accounting-simplified.com/ financial/fixed-assets/accounting-for-disposals.html>
22. Fixed assets accounting policies, <http://www.mango.org.uk/Guide/fixedassetspolicy>
23. Balance Sheet (2013), <http://www.completebusinessstartup.co.uk/ starting-business/balance-sheet.html>
24. What is bill discounting? <http://www.businessdictionary.com/ definition/discounted-bill.html>

25. What is bill discounting?<http://business-finance.blurtit.com/76241/what-is-bill-discounting>
26. Commercial Bill Facility (2013), <http://www.exportfinance. gov.au/Pages/Commercialbillfacility.aspx#content>
27. What is bill discounting? <http://www.investorwords.com/16211/ bill_ discounting.html>
28. What is bill discounting? <http://www.wisegeek.com/what-isbill-discounting.htm>
29. Bills of exchange (2013) <http://www.investopedia.com/terms/ b/billofexchange.asp>
30. Bank Discount Rate (2013) <http://www.investopedia.com/terms/ b/bank-discount-rate.asp>
31. What is Bill discounting? <http://www.educationobserver.com/ forum/showthread.php?tid=4381>
32. Invoice Discounting (2013) <http://en.wikipedia.org/wiki/Invoice_discounting>
33. Bills Discounting-Consolidated bank <http://www.consolidatedbank.com/index.php?option=com_content&view=article&id=57&Itemid=92>
34. Liability (Financial accounting) <http://en.wikipedia.org/wiki/Liability_%28financial_accounting%29>
35. Liabilities, <http://accounting-simplified.com/liabilities.html>
36. Liability, <http://www.investopedia.com/terms/l/liability.asp>
37. Balance Sheet (2013), <http://www.completebusinessstartup.co.uk/ starting-business/balance-sheet.html>
38. Contingent liabilities (2013) <http://en.wikipedia.org/wiki/Contingent_liability>
39. Contingent liability <http://www.investopedia.com/terms/c/ contingentliability .asp>
40. What is contingent liability? <http://www.businessdictionary.com/ definition/contingent-liability.html>
41. What is contingent liability? <http://www.accountingcoach.com/ blog/contingent-liability-contingency>
42. Documentary Collection (2013), <http://en.wikipedia.org/wiki/Documentary_ collection>
43. Difference between export bill collection and export bill discounting <http://howtoexportimport.com/Difference-between-export-bill-collectionand-expo-344.aspx>
44. Bills for Collections <http://www.amlinkint.com/English/ resources/trade-term-bill-collection.html>
45. Bankers acceptance <http://www.investopedia.com/terms/b/bankersacceptance.asp>
46. Bills Services <http://www.cib.com.cn/netbank/en/Corporate_Banking/Corporate_Financing/Bills_Services.html>
47. What is Bill Guaranty? <http://www.businessdictionary.com/ definition/bill-guaranty.html>

48. Bill of exchange guarantee <http://www.ekn.se/en/Garantier/Forbills-and-Letters-and-Credit/Bill-of-exchange-guarantee/>
49. Warranty Bill of Sale (2013) <http://www.inc.com/tools/warrantybill-of-sale.html>
50. Accounting (2004),The ICFAI University Press, pp. 74-77.
51. *Ibid.* pp. 78-79.
52. *Ibid.* p. 86.
53. *Ibid.* p. 86.
54. *Ibid.* p. 96.
55. *Ibid.* p. 35.
56. *Ibid.,* p. 6

Chapter - 14

Credit Management

"If you love those who love you, what credit is that to you? For even sinners love those who love them. And if you do good to those who do good to you, what credit is that to you? For even sinners do the same.":

— ***Jesus Christ***

Introduction

According to Shalini (2013), credit is the trust allowing one party to provide resources to another, where the latter does not immediately reimburse to the former, arranges instead either to repay or return the resource at a later date. It does not necessarily require money. The concept can be applied in barter economies as well, based on the direct exchange of goods and services. Movements of financial capital are normally dependent on either credit or equity transfers. In many countries, when a customer fills out an application for credit from a bank, store or credit card company, their information is forwarded to a credit bureau.

The risk befalls on the lender. It includes lost principal amount with interest, cash flows disruption, and increased collection costs. The loss may be complete or partial under various circumstances.[1] A good credit management system will help reduce the amount of capital tied up with debtors and minimize exposure to bad debts. Good credit management is vital to cash flow. It is profitable on paper, but lack from cash to continue business. It is best to minimize the likelihood of bad debts through good credit management practices.

Credit management calls for preparing own policies and procedures. It is sometimes possible to increase the sales by granting credit to selected clients, who may choose to do business upon convenience offered by the credit account.[2] Credit management controls and collects payments from customers. It is the function within a bank or company to control credit policies for improvement in revenues and reduce financial risks. A credit manager is a person employed by an organization, who manages with the credit department. He will decide on credit limits, acceptable levels of risk and terms of payment to customers.

Credit managers fall into one of two groups due to legal and jurisdictional expertise: (a) Commercial Credit Managers; and (b) Consumer Credit Managers. Credit managers in Australia obtain memberships from the Australian Institute of Credit Management. Those managers within the United Kingdom get accredited with the Institute of Credit Management. Construction Credit Management is an area of specialty, where it calls for some specific skill sets: [a] Strong knowledge of security measures and lien law within province, state or territory; (b) The ability to understand money dynamics through the construction pyramid; (c) Skills beyond traditional credit management where the manager may be required to deal with managerial and non-managerial staff of the white and blue collar variety; and (d) A basic knowledge of construction and the willingness to make site visits, if needed.

The trade credit insurer issues a credit limit for every buyer with whom the policyholder trades. The level of the limit is preset at the maximum amount to be owed by the buyer at any time. Limits are granted at a lower levels on justification. The credit limit granted is the maximum insured credit line for a specific buyer and the policyholders can trade on an insured basis within the approved limit throughout the policy period without any reference to the insurer.[3] The company focuses on credit management ensuring customers pay for products delivered or the services rendered. Unpaid customers are called accounts receivables (AR).[4]

Trade credit is a potential source of finance; financial managers may have to consider its position in the "pecking order" choosing between the alternative sources of funds, if they ought to minimize the cost of finance and the trade credit to finance their operations, when the price of a loan rises over the cost of trade credit. Trade credit management is part of the overall working capital. It can affect the company's profitability, liquidity and solvency. Consumers are the steam engine of any economy. They have main difficulties in borrowing if the credit dries up. They consume less because they have less entrée to credit. For this reason, the producer will sell and produce less.[5]

Principles of Bank Lending

According to a periodical's article "Sound Principles of Lending, Credit Investigation and Selection of Borrowers", lending principles have preset minimum standards of good banking practice from larger business customers while banking and doing business. The principles cover key aspects of the relationship between banks and larger business customers, from product information and credit application to ongoing communication and deal with difficulties, if things go wrong. Commercial banks follow three cardinal principles of lending viz., safety, liquidity and profitability. The concept of security has undergone radical change and profitability has been subordinated to social purpose in respect of certain types of lending.

1. *Safety*: The funds entrusted to bank by depositors, calls for the safety of funds lent. The borrower will be in a position to repay the loan, along with interest, according to loan contract terms.
2. *Liquidity*: The banks are essentially intermediaries for short-term funds. They lend funds for short-periods for working capital purpose. The loans are largely payable on demand. The banker must ensure the borrower repay the loan on demand or within a shorter period. This depends upon the nature of borrower's assets and pledge made to the banker.
3. *Profitability*: Commercial banks are profit-earning institutions; the nationalized banks are no exception. They must employ their funds profitably, to earn sufficient income, to pay interest to the depositors, salaries to the staff and to meet various overhead expenses and distribute dividends to shareholders. The rates of interest charged by banks were primarily dependent on the directives issued by the RBI.
4. *The Principle of Diversification of Risks*: A prudent banker always tries to select the borrower sagaciously and takes tangible assets as securities to safeguard his interests. Tangible assets are no doubt valuable, and the banker feels safe, while granting advances on the security of such assets, yet some risk is always involved therein.
5. *The Purpose of the Loan*: The banker enquires from the borrower About the purpose of seeking the loan. Banks do not grant loans for each and every purpose—these ensure the safety and liquidity of funds by granting loans for productive purposes only, viz., for meeting the working capital needs of any business enterprise.[6]

The banks have initial expenditure to start small trades, businesses, industries, etc., following the three-phased nationalization drive.[7]

Types of Loan[8]

According to Irby (2013), A loan ,in finance, is a debt evidenced by a note which specifies, among other things, the principal amount, interest rate, and date of repayment. It entails the reallocation of the subject asset(s) for a period of time, between the lender and the borrower. Loans can be subcategorized to ascertain, whether the debtor is an individual person (consumer) or a business. The typical loan payment type is that of fully amortizing payment, wherein each monthly rate has the same value over time.[9]

Secured Loan

According to Wellish (2013), a secured loan is obtained against some asset as collateral. A mortgage loan is a very common type of debt instrument. It is used by many individuals to buy housing from this variety, where the money is being used to purchase the property. The lender can take possession of the asset and use it to cover the loan in case of a default. Interest rates for secured loans may be lower than those for unsecured loans. The asset may need to be appraised before borrowing the secured loan.

A loan can be secured by debt. The creditor is relieved of the financial risks involved, because he can take over the property, when the debt is not properly repaid. The debtors may receive loans on more favorable terms than that available for unsecured debt, or be extended credit under circumstances, when the credit under terms of unsecured debt would not be extended the lender takes with secured loans takes possession of the asset, when there was default on loan. The same isn't true for an unsecured loan.[10]

Unsecured loans

According to Irby (2013), unsecured loans are not secured against the borrower's assets. These may be available from financial institutions under different guises or marketing packages: credit card debt, personal loans, bank overdrafts, credit facilities or lines of credit, and corporate bonds. The interest rates applicable may vary depending on the lender and the borrower. The rates on unsecured loans are always higher than for secured loans. An unsecured lender had an option for recourse against the borrower in the event of default.

Unsecured loans rely solely on credit history and income to qualify for the loan. A consumer will have a choice of fixed or floating interest rate for secured loans. An unsecured loan may be a good option for individuals without enough equity in their homes to be approved for a home equity loan. The loan may have a fixed interest rate and be due at the end of a specified term, or can exist as a revolving line of credit with variable interest rate. An unsecured loan gets faster approvals with less paperwork.[11]

Demand loans

Demand loans are short-term loans without any fixed date for repayment. These carry floating interest rate, varies according to the prime rate. They can be called for repayment by the lending institution at any time. Demand loans may be unsecured or secured, empowering to recover the balance amount at any point in time after executing the loan.

The demand loan format unlike an installment does not include a specific maturity date with specific schedule for making payments. A demand loan is often beneficial to the borrower. The repayment schedule is very open-ended. This can be important, if the purpose of the loan was to fund a new venture to become profitable.

Subsidized Loans

These are extended to needy undergraduate students. These are determined by the cost of attendance minus expected family contribution and other financial aid (such as grants or scholarships). These do not accrue any interest, while students are in school for at least half-time or during grace and deferment periods. The interest gets reduced by an explicit or hidden subsidy.

Unsubsidized Loans

Unsubsidized Loans are meant for non-needy undergraduate and graduate Students. The eligibility is determined by cost of attendance minus other financial aid (such as grants or scholarships). Interest is charged during in-school, deferment, and grace periods. The person is responsible for the interest from the time the unsubsidized loan is disbursed until fully repaid.

Concessional loans

A concessional loan [sometimes, called a soft loan] is granted on terms, substantially more generous than market loans, either through below-market interest rates or, by grace periods or a combination of both. Foreign governments may offer such loans to poor countries or to employees of lending institutions, as an employee benefit.

Conventional loans aren't insured by any government agency like the Federal Housing Administration, Rural Housing Service, or the Veterans Administration. These loans may be conforming, meaning they follow the guidelines set forth by Fannie Mae and Freddie Mac. Nonconforming loans don't meet Fannie and Freddie qualifications. Conventional loans fall under mortgages, adjustable of fixed or adjustable or balloon mortgages, or hybrid loans. Any type of loan, if not issued by a government entity will be considered as a conventional loan.

The convention loans divide between Open-Ended and Closed-Ended varieties.

1. *Open-ended loans*: A borrower can borrow over and over. Credit cards and lines of credit are the modes of open-ended loans. The borrower has a credit limit that can purchase against. Each time, he makes a purchase, it decreases the available credit.
2. *Closed-ended loans*: A borrower won't be allowed to borrow once he has repaid. The balance of the loan automatically goes down. However, he don't have any available credit on closed-ended loans.[12]

Retail Credit

Lending involves elements of risks. The element of risk, in the main bank operation leads to the necessity of credit investigation. It presupposes the right selection of borrower, calling for his credentials complete and comprehensive investigation. The lending banker will be at ease, if correct type of borrowers find selected. The banker often needs to collect chain of information about the borrower.

Usual loan application forms filled in by the applicant provide the banker with the required particulars, payable advance amount. It is a fundamental precept of banking everywhere that advances are being made to customers in reliance on his promise to repay, rather than the security held by the banker. Although, lending involves some degree of risks, it is necessary for any bank to develop sound and safe lending policies. New lending techniques keep such risk to a minimum. The banks ought to follow certain principles of sound lending, i.e. Safety, Liquidity, Profitability, Purpose, Security, Spread/ Diversity.[13]

Business Credit

The government of India has ratified the Credit Information Companies Act [2005]. The Credit Bureau formally is being established as the first credit bureau. Credit rationing refers to the situation, where the lenders limit the supply of additional credit to borrowers, even if the latter are willing to pay higher interest rates. *Credit Sesame* is a free web-based tool enabling consumers manage credit and save money on their loans. It provides consumers with a free credit score.

Credit reports are considered an insightful, accurate, historical and enlightened information source for companies and individuals, seeking to initiate a business credit relationship with other businesses. Many credit management companies specialize in business credit reports. Business credit monitoring is the monitoring of a business' credit history, detecting any suspicious activity or changes. People are familiar with consumer credit reports. Many are unaware that a similar reporting system exists alarming to changes in any business' credit activities.

The activities are the filing of latest accounts, board appointments and resignations, share capital amendments, and changes to the credit rating. The use of these reports are varied and may include protecting against suspected fraud to assess the performance of such business.

Credit Process

Any process a business or an individual must go through to become eligible for a loan or pay for goods and services over an extended period. It refers to the business processes or lenders undertaking, when evaluating request for credit. Granting credit approval depends on the willingness of creditor to lend money. The lender's assessment of the ability and willingness of the borrower to return the money or pay for goods obtained with interest in a timely fashion will be on priority. In general, the granting of credit depends on the confidence the lender has in the borrower's credit worthiness.

Credit worthiness encompasses the borrower's ability and willingness to pay as one of key factors defining a lender's credit policies. Creditors and lenders utilize a number of financial tools to evaluate the credit worthiness of any potential borrower. Some of the factors lenders consider evaluating such individual or business, seeking credit: *credit worthiness, size of debt burden, loan size, frequency of borrowing, length of commitment, besides social and community consideration*. The decision to grant credit to certain customer must be evaluated on a case-by-case basis. Each small business grappling with this issue ought to gather and evaluate financial information, decide whether to grant credit and if so, how much, and communicate the decision to the customer in a timely manner.[14]

Many avenues available to small businesses for gathering information about credit applicants. A small business's sales force can often collect trade references and financial statements from potential customers. It can also contact local attorneys to find out about liens, claims, or actions pending against the applicant, and can hire independent accountants verify financial information.[15] According to an article in some periodical 'The documentary credit process (2013)', processes of a documentary credit are:

1. The contract is being made between the importer and the exporter
2. The importer asks its bank to issue a documentary credit to the exporter.
3. The importer's bank sends the documentary credit to the exporter's bank (advising bank).
4. The exporter's bank advises the exporter over the issue of the documentary credit.
5. After dispatch of goods, the exporter delivers the required documents to its bank. The documents are examined against the terms and conditions stipulated in the documentary credit. If the requirements have been complied with, the exporter will be able to obtain payment.
6. The exporter's bank sends the documents to the importer's bank and receives payment either at sight or term.
7. The importer's bank delivers the documents to the importer upon reimbursement, after which the goods may be handed over.[16]

Recovery and NPA Management

According to Khanna (2012), a strong banking sector is important for flourishing economy. The industry has undergone a sea change after the 1991-first phase- economic liberalization, thereby credit management. The banks became very cautious in extending loans, though they lend funds to agriculture, industry, personal and housing loans. Nonperforming assets (NPAs) become the major concern reflecting on their poor performance. A higher level of NPAs suggests higher probability of credit defaults affecting the profitability and net-worth eroding the asset value. of banks and also erodes the value of the asset. The NPA growth involves the necessity of provisions, which reduces the overall profits and shareholders' value.[17]

According to Kumar and Singh (2012), the issue of NPAs shook the entire banking sector from the target-oriented approach. It deteriorates the qualitative aspect of lending. Willful defaults, ineffective supervision of loan accounts and lack of technical and managerial expertise on the part of borrowers, are the causes. NPAs put detrimental impact on the profitability, capital adequacy ratio and credibility of banks.[18] According to Chatterjee (2012), the Indian banking system has gone through significant transformation following financial sector reforms. Several prudential, payment, integrating and provisioning norms were introduced to improve efficiency and pruning of the NPAs to improve financial health of the banking sector. NPA involves the necessity of provisions, any increase could bring down the overall profitability of banks and so its health.[19]

According to Singh (2013), commercial banks are the major player to develop the economy. A major threat to banking sector is the prevalence of Non-Performing Assets. NPAs or their overall performance suggests higher probability of a large number of credit defaults affecting the profitability and net worth of banks eroding the value of assets thereby. The NPA growth involves the necessity of provisions, which reduces the overall profits and share-holders value.[20]

The Indian banking sector has emerged as one of the strongest drivers of India's economy. The industry has made outstanding advancement in last few years, even during the times when the rest of the world struggled with financial meltdown. India's economic development and financial sector liberalization led to a transformation of the sector over the past two decades. Today, it is at the crossroads of an invisible revolution, following significant developments and recent investments.

Most of the banks provide various services such as mobile banking, SMS Banking, Net banking and ATMs to clients. Indian banks, the dominant financial intermediaries in India, have made high quality progress over the last five years, as is evident from several factors, including annual credit growth, profitability, and the trend in gross non-performing assets. The annual rate of credit growth clocked 23 per cent during the last five years. The profitability (average return on net worth) stood at around 15 per cent during the same period, while gross NPAs fell from 3.3 per cent [As on March 31, 2006] to 2.3 per cent [As on March 31, 2011].[21] However, banks are facing tougher challenge with slowdown in global and domestic economy.[22]

The NPA is defined as the credit facility in respect of which the interest and/or installment of principal has remained 'past due' for a specified period of time. It is a classification used by financial institutions that refer to loans in jeopardy of default. Once the borrower has failed to make interest or principle payments for 90 days the loan is considered to be a non-performing asset. Non-performing assets are problematic for financial institutions, since they depend on interest payments for income. Troublesome pressure from the economy can lead to a sharp increase in non-performing loans and often results in massive write-downs.[23/24]

Net NPAs are those types where the bank has deducted the provision. It shows the actual burden of banks. Bank balance sheets contain a huge amount of NPAs. The process of recovery and loan write off of loans isvery time consuming. The banks have to make provision against the NPAs, according to the central bank guidelines. The difference between gross and net NPA is quite high. It can be calculated by Net NPA = Gross NPA – (Balance in Interest Suspense account + DICGC/ECGC claims received and held pending adjustment + Part payment received and kept in suspense account + Total provisions held).[25]

According to Balasubramaniam (2012), Gross NPAs are the sum total of loan assets classified as NPAs as per RBI guidelines as on the date of Balance Sheet date. It reflects the quality of the loans made by Banks, comprising the nonstandard assets like as sub-standard, doubtful, and loss assets. It is arrived at through, Gross NPAs Ratio = Gross NPAs/Gross Advances.[26] According to article "Non-Performing Assets: Meaning, types and assets", NPA have been divided or classified into four types: (a) *Standard Assets*: A standard asset is a performing asset. These generate continuous income and repayment, as and when they fall due. These had a normal risk and are not NPA in the real sense, don't need any special provision; (b) *Sub-Standard Assets*: These assets (loans and advances) are NPAs for a period of 12 months; (c) *Doubtful Assets*: Assets hanging for period beyond twelve months. and (d) Loss Assets: Assets cannot be recovered at all.

NPA arises due to a number of factors or causes like: (a) *Speculation*: Investing in high risk assets to earn high income; (b) *Default*: Willful default by the borrowers; (c) *Fraudulent practices*: Fraudulent Practices like advancing loans to ineligible persons, advances without security or references, etc.; (d) *Diversion of funds*: Most of the funds are being diverted for unnecessary expansion and diversion of business; (e) Internal reasons: Many internal reasons like inefficient management, inappropriate technology, labour problems, marketing failure, etc. resulting in poor performance of the companies; and (f) External reasons: *External reasons:* like a recession in the economy, infrastructural problems, price rise, delay in release of sanctioned limits by banks, delays in settlements of payments by government, natural calamities, etc.[27]

There are several reasons for an account becoming NPA. They are internal factors and external factors. Internal Factors are (a) Funds borrowed for a particular purpose, but not use for the said purpose; (b) Project are not completed on time; (c) Poor recovery of receivables; (d) Excess capacities created on non-economic costs; (e) Inability of the corporate to raise the capital through the issue of equity or other debt instrument from capital markets; (f) Business failures; (g) Diversion of funds for expansion/ modernization/setting up of new projects/helping or promoting sister concerns; (h) Willful defaults, siphoning of funds, fraud, disputes, management disputes, misappropriation etc., and (i) Deficiencies on the part of the banks viz. in credit appraisal, monitoring and follow-ups, delay in settlement of payments/subsidiaries by government bodies etc. External factors are: (a) Sluggish legal system; (b) Scarcity of raw material, power and other resources; (c) Industrial recession; (d) Shortage of raw material, raw material/input price escalation, power shortage, industrial recession, excess capacity, natural calamities like floods, accidents; (e) Failures, nonpayment/ over dues in other countries, recession in other countries, externalization problems, adverse exchange rates etc, and (f) Government policies like excise duty changes, Import duty changes etc. (Source: Article of Chaitanya, 2013).[28]

According to the RBI, India's central bank, the factors causing deterioration of asset quality had been both external and internal. The economic slowdown has resulted in borrowers under stress causing defaults and rise in NPA, the inadequate appraisal and monitoring of credit proposals also contributed to the crisis in no small manner. According to RBI, the gross NPA of the scheduled commercial banks in India increased from 2.5 per cent of the gross advances [2010-11] to 3.1 per cent in [2011-12]. The total gross NPA of scheduled commercial banks in India stood at Rs 97,900 crore (Rs 979 billion) [At the end of 2010-11]. This increased to Rs 142,300 crore (Rs 1,423 billion) [At the end of 2011-12].

The scenario did not show any improvement [2012-13], despite there being increased attention on loan recovery and higher provisioning by the banks being paid. Gross NPAs of 40 listed banks went up by 43.1 per cent during the year. The restructured assets book of banks showed showed an upward bias with recast assets under CDR around 50per cent more than the whole of the previous year.[29]

Non-performing asset is a loan or an advance where; (a) Interest and/ or installment of principal remain overdue for a period of more than 90 days in respect of a term loan; (b) The account remains 'out of order' in respect of an Overdraft/Cash Credit; (c) The bill remains overdue for a period of more than 90 days in the case of bills purchased and discounted; (d) The installment of principal or interest, there on remains overdue for two crop seasons for short duration crops; (e) The installment of principal or interest there on remains overdue for one crop season for long duration crops; (f) The amount of liquidity facility remains outstanding for more than 90 days, in respect of a securitization transaction undertaken in terms of guidelines on securitization [Dated February 1, 2006; (g) In respect of derivative transactions, the overdue receivables representing positive mark-to-market value of a derivative contract, if these remain unpaid for a period of 90 days from the specified due date for payment.[30]

According to Deolalka (2012), with the increasing focus internationally on NPAs during the 1990s affected the risk-taking behavior of banks, governments and central banks have typically reacted to the problem differently depending on the politico-economic system under which the banks operate. In some countries such as Japan, banks have been encouraged to write off bad loans with retained earnings or new capital or both. This ensures that the cost of resolving the NPA problem is borne by the banks themselves. However, this policy is unsuitable for countries such as India, where the banks have neither adequate reserves nor the ability to raise new capital. In some countries, the banks are State owned so the final responsibility of resolving the problem lies with the respective national government.[31]

According to Rajeev and Mahesh (2010), though the issue of NPA was given more importance when the Narasimham Committee Report (1991) highlighted its impact on the financial health of the commercial banks and subsequently various asset classification norms were introduced, the concept of classifying bank assets based on its quality began [1985- 86]. The RBI advised commercial banks [November 7, 1985], to introduce the Health Code System, indicating the quality of individual advances under the following eight categories, i.e., Satisfactory, Irregular, Sick, viable, Advances recalled, Suit filed accounts, Decreed debts, Bad and Doubtful debts.[32]

According to Reddy (2012), the Narasimhan Committee has recommended the prudential norms on income recognition, asset classification and provisioning. Income recognition, in a change from the past is now not on an accrual basis, but when it is actually received. Past problems faced by banks were to a great extent attributable to this. There have been noticeable improvements in the financial health of banks, in terms of asset quality. NPA levels pre- and post- are not strictly comparable, as there has been a significant tightening of accounting norms.[33] According to Krishnan (2013), the deterioration in asset quality is the highest for the industries segment, and within it large and medium enterprises, a segment which accounts for nearly half of the bank credit. Sectors such as aviation and textiles are the worst offenders. Needless to say, public sector banks are at the receiving end with their impaired assets ratio at 12.1per cent, more than double that of the larger private banks.[34]

According to 'The Hindu' (May 30, 2013), worried over rising nonperforming assets, the Reserve Bank of India has tightened rules for restructuring of most types of loans in line with global practices. As per the latest RBI notification, provisioning on the newly restructured account has been raised to five per cent from June 1 from two per cent now. However, for the old restructured account, it will be done in a phased manner. The RBI also said that existing "regulatory forbearance"would no longer be available from April 1, 2015. As per existing guidelines, an account after restructuring is not classified as NPA.[35]

According to the 'Business Standard' (May 31, 2013), the RBI has said that loans recast after April 1, 2015 should be classified as non-performing asset and provisioning norms for fresh standard restructured advances would be increased to five per cent from 2.75 per cent, for the interim period from June 1, 2013. From the promoter's point of view, RBI's recent requirements for restructuring are too stringent. Promoters will not only have to bring in more funds as part of their contribution, but will also have to give personal guarantees.[36]

According to 'The Economic Times' (June 28, 2013), the government will reconsider a clause that requires all state-run banks to treat a borrower's account as non-performing if a loan to the company by any bank has become a bad asset in the books of that bank. PSBs, which had a net NPA of 2.12 per cent in December 2012, have already in a representation to the finance ministry, sought to delete this clause citing increase in the provisioning amount that has to be made towards such accounts. Bankers have argued that adhering to a common NPA norm will further weaken the banks given that RBI has already come up with stringent guidelines in June 2013, increasing the provisioning on the newly restructured account by 300 bps to five per cent from June. There are cases where a company has taken a loan for a particular project from one bank, which has not taken off and hence the account has turned poor but the same company is keeping other account standard with most banks.[37]

According to Krishnan (2013), perhaps the RBI's intention is not to just allow restructuring of loans, but the restructuring of companies, since it is advocating leveraged buyouts. However, even that is not easy for listed companies, because of a whole lot of norms put in place by the capital markets regulator. A buyout will not only mean buying the promoter stake, but also that of the public, in which case de-listing norms will kick in bringing a new set of headaches, said a corporate law expert.[38]

According to 'The Hindu' (December 2, 2013). Although recently a very large number of bank accounts have been opened, the actual number of transactions per account is still small, suggesting inadequacies on both demand and supply sides. Financial literacy will create awareness of bank schemes and enhance the access to the financial system thereby. Increased use of technology should help in achieving the goal of financial inclusion.[39]

According to 'The Hindu' (Sep 30, 2013), earlier highlighted reflecting deterioration in economic activities, net non-performing assets of banks to have increased to 1.68 per cent of the total loan [At the end of 2012-13]. The net NPA of banks was 1.28 per cent [At the end of 2011-12]. Net NPA of the 26 public sector banks, including the State Bank of India, rose to 2.02 during the year as compared to 1.53 in the previous fiscal. The SBI and its five associates recorded a net NPA of 2.04 per cent against 1.76 per cent in the comparable period. Net NPA of new private sector bank rose marginally to 0.45 per cent as compared to 0.42 per cent. Tight liquidity situation resulted in the increase in cost of funds of all commercial banks to 6.12 per cent as against 5.90 per cent [2011-12]. As far as the state-owned banks were concerned, the cost of funds rose to 6.27 per cent from 6.06 per cent [2011-12].[40]

Net non-performing assets or bad loans of 40 listed banks have jumped by 38 per cent or around Rs. 35,424 crore in the first six months of current financial year ended September 30, 2013. Net NPAs of 40 listed banks [As on March 31,2013were Rs.93,109 crore, which rose to Rs.1,28,533 crore, [As on September 30, 2013]. Top public sector banks like State Bank of India, Bank of Baroda, Punjab National Bank, Central Bank, IDBI Bank and Union Bank have all reported more than 30percentrise in net NPAs during this period. Out of the total forty listed banks, fourteen banks have reported more than 50percentjump in net NPAs during these six months.[41]

According to 'The Times of India' (Oct 23, 2013), State Bank of India, the country's largest lender, may have the highest proportion of bad debt, but it is the smaller public sector players that suffer from concentration risk with the top 30 non-performing assets accounting for over half the sticky assets. In case of SBI, the share of the top 30 NPA accounts was a little over 15 per cent, a buffer provided by the large asset pool that the state-run bank enjoys. SBI's gross NPAs were estimated at 6.3 per centof its gross loans, compared to 5.3 per cent for Punjab & Sind Bank. At the end of June, 2013, the gross NPAs of public sector banks, which include the principal and the interest dues, were estimated at around Rs. 1.83 lakh crore, with the value of top 30 accounts estimated at close to Rs. 64,000 crore, or 35 per cent of the total bad debt. A loan is classified as an NPA if the borrower does not pay the installment for 90 days. The pressure on smaller banks is the fact that several of them, such as Bank of Maharashtra and Corporation

Bank, witnessed restructured accounts turn into NPAs. While the average for public sector banks was 27percentduring the June quarter (2013), in case of Bank of Maharashtra, nearly half the restructured accounts, which were under financial strain, turned NPA. State Bank of Travancore (48 per cent) was at second position, followed by Syndicate Bank (45per cent) and CanaraBank (43per cent).[42]

According to the 'Business Standard' (November 14, 2013), reflecting the economic slowdown, banks, especially public sector lenders, saw a substantial rise in non-performing assets. State Bank of India saw the highest growth in NPAs, at Rs. 3,314 crore, followed by Rs. 2,284 crore for United Bank of India. Punjab National Bank (PNB)'s NPAs rose by Rs. 1,436 crore. According to India Ratings and Research, the situation has deteriorated rapidly for weaker banks. Quarterly losses in Central Bank of India and United Bank of India during the quarter were equivalent to about a tenth of their equity. Central Bank posted a net loss of a little over Rs. 1,500 crore, as it had to make high provisions for bad loans.[43]

According to NDTV Profit t.v.(Oct 30, 2013), the aim of the RBI, when it comes to non-performing assets is to make them productive. RBI Deputy Governor K C Chakrabarty said that banks were free to bring about structural changes in companies where promoters have defaulted. Attributing rising bad loans in the banking sector mainly to large borrowers,

Finance Minister P Chidambaram said that the government would monitor 30 NPA accounts of each PSU bank. Although rising nonperforming assets are a function of economic slowdown, Chidambaram said they are "unacceptable" and the banks should beef up efforts by setting up a separate vertical to recover dues from written-off accounts. The RBI raising the repo rate to fight inflation and the government forcing banks to cut the interest rates for certain segments to boost growth does give an impression that the government and the RBI are pursuing different goals.[44]

Around the world, finance is an important common thread, which brings many sectors together and acts as catalyst for economic development of the country. The role of banking sector in economic transformation is significant as banks play vital role in providing the desired financial resources to the needy sectors. Banks lubricate the wheels of the real economy and remain the conduits of monetary policy transmission and constitute the economy's payment and settlement system. The growth of the banking industry is closely linked with the growth of the overall economy. India is one of the fastest growing economies in the world and is set to remain on that path for many years to come.

The problem of NPAs in the Indian banking system is one of the foremost and the most formidable problems that the impact had the entire banking system. Higher NPA ratio trembles the confidence of investors, depositors, lenders etc. It also causes poor recycling of funds, which in turn will have deleterious effect on the deployment of credit. The non-recovery of loans effects not only further availability of credit, but also financial soundness of the banks. Some of them are: profitability, asset contraction, liability management, capital adequacy, shareholders confidence, public confidence.[45]

According to 'The Hindu' (November, 21, 2016), As of June 2016, the total amount of Gross Non-Performing Assets (NPAs) for public and private sector banks is around Rs. 6 lakh crore. The figures along with total debt for each of the 49 public and private sector banks were shared by the Union Ministry of Finance in response to a Parliament question. The amount of top twenty Non Performing Assets (NPA) accounts of Public Sector Banks stood at Rs. 1.54 lakh crore. The advances given by banks are called assets, which generate income via interests and installments. If the installment is not paid until the due date, it is called a bad loan. If it extends beyond 90 days, it is termed NPA. The ratio of NPAs to total advances given by a bank is a commonly used indicator reflecting the health of the banking system.

Table 1: Gross NPAs OF Public/ Private Sector Banks [June 30, 2016]

Sl. No.	Bank	Total Advances Rs. In Crore)	Gross NPA (Rs. In crore)	NPA Ratio (%)
1.	Allahabad Bank	145,328	18,769	12.92
2.	Andhra Bank	137,228	14,137	10.3
3.	Bank of Baroda	269,115	35,604	13.23
4.	Bank of India	274,391	43,935	16.01
5.	Bank of Maharashtra	103,148	13,040	12.64
6.	Bharatiya Mahila Bank Ltd	627	3	0.4
7.	Canara Bank	311,615	30,480	9.78
8.	Central Bank of India	185,719	25,107	13.52
9.	Corporation Bank	142,787	15,726	11.01
10.	Dena Bank	81,114	9,636	11.88
11.	IDBI Bank Limited	202,304	21,724	10.74
12.	Indian Bank	122,173	8,690	7.11
13.	Indian Overseas Bank	149,217	30,239	20.26
14.	Oriental Bank of Commerce	150,301	17,209	11.45
15.	Punjab & Sind Bank	63,134	4,566	7.23
16.	Punjab National Bank	356,958	55,003	15.41
17.	Syndicate Bank	167,759	13,475	8.03
18.	UCO Bank	115,166	21,495	18.66
19.	Union Bank of India	242,935	25,560	10.52
20.	United Bank of India	70,781	10,104	14.28
21.	Vijaya Bank	90,199	6,589	7.31
22.	State Bank of Bikaner & Jaipur	74,033	4,593	6.2
23.	State Bank of Hyderabad	112,420	9,436	8.39
24.	State Bank of India	1,193,325	93,1317	7.80
25.	State Bank of Mysore	55,228	4,323	7.83
26.	State Bank of Patiala	85,239	11,365	13.33
27.	State Bank of Travancore	68,276	6,401	9.38
28.	Catholic Syrian Bank Ltd.	7,859	455	5.79
29.	City Union Bank Ltd	21,216	555	2.62
30.	Dhanlaxmi Bank Limited	6,771	475	7.02
31.	Federal Bank Ltd	59,408	1,747	2.94
32.	ING Vysya Bank Ltd	-	-	-
33.	Jammu & Kashmir Bank Ltd	50,640	4,715	9.31
34.	Karnataka Bank Ltd.	35,412	1,389	3.92
35.	Karur Vysya Bank Ltd.	39,382	702	1.78
36.	Lakshmi Vilas Bank Ltd.	20,183	432	2.14
37.	Nainital Bank Ltd.	2,776	145	5.21
38.	Ratnakar Bank Ltd.	22,373	253	1.13
39.	South Indian Bank Ltd.	41,705	1,652	3.96
40.	Tamilnad Mercantile Bank Ltd.	22,329	489	2.19
41.	Axis Bank Ltd.	300,173	7,909	2.63
42.	Bandhan Bank Ltd.	13,358	29	0.22

(Contd...)

43.	DCB Bank Ltd	13,464	231	1.72
44.	HDFC Bank Ltd	440,955	4,724	1.07
45.	ICICI Bank Ltd.	364,429	17,208	4.72
46.	IndusInd Bank Ltd.	93,667	861	0.92
47.	Kotak Mahindra Bank Ltd.	122,384	3,059	2.5
48.	Yes Bank Ltd	203.411	845	0.82
49.	IDFC Bank Ltd	49,714	3,030	6.09

Source: The Hindu (November 21. 2016), <http://www.thehindu.com/data/Details-of-NPA-figuresof-public-private-sector-banks/article16670548.ece>

A stable and sound banking system is required for a healthy growth of an economy. The gross NPA of Indian Overseas Bank (IOB) has risen to Rs.35,098.25 crore, which is 22.39 per cent of its total lending. IOB registered a loss of Rs.646.66 crore in the March, 2017 quarter compared with a net loss of Rs 936.19 crore in the corresponding quarter March, 2016. The gross NPA of IDBI Bank has risen to 21.25 per cent or Rs.44,752.59 crore of its total lending. The Bank reported a loss of Rs. 3,199.76 crore for the quarter ended March 31, 2017, almost twice the net loss of Rs. 1,735.81 crore it posted in the corresponding quarter last year. The gross NPA of Central Bank has risen to 17.81 per cent or Rs. 27251.33 crore of its total lending. The Bank reported a loss of Rs 591.77 crore for the quarter ended March 31, 2017 compared with a net loss of Rs 898.04 of the corresponding quarter a year ago.

The gross NPA of Bank of India has risen up to 13.22 per cent or Rs 52044.52 crore of its total lending in March, 2017. The bank reported a net loss of 10.46 billion rupees for March quarter. Net loss for the quarter ended March 31 narrowed from a loss of 35.87 billion rupees a year earlier. The gross NPA of PNB is 12.53 per cent, Rs 55,370.45 crore of its total lending in March, 2017. At the end of March quarter, the bank's fresh slippages stood at Rs 22,415 crore as against Rs 42,252 crore in the same period last year. The gross NPA of Oriental Bank is 13.73 per cent, Rs 22,859.27 crore of its total lending in March, 2017. The bank reported a net loss of Rs 1,218.01 crore for March quarter, whereas it had made a net profit of Rs 21.62 crore during the similar quarter of preceding fiscal year.

The gross NPA of Dena Bank is 16.27 per cent, Rs 12618.73 crore of its total lending in March, 2017. The bank's loss widened to Rs 575 crore in March 2017 from Rs 326 crore in March 2016. The gross NPA of Canara Bank is 9.63 per cent, Rs 34202.04 crore of its total lending in March,

2017. The bank posted a profit of Rs 2.14 billion in the quarter ended March 31 compared with a loss of 39.05 billion rupees a year earlier.

Strategies for Overcoming NPAs

According to Prasad and Veena (2011), "various steps have been taken by the government and RBI to recover and reduce NPAs. These strategies are necessary to control NPAs: (a) Preventive management and (b) Curative management.

Preventive Management

Preventive measures are to prevent the asset from becoming a non-performing asset. Banks has to concentrate on the following to minimize the level of NPAs.

1. *Early Warning Signals*: The origin of flourishing NPAs lies in the quality of managing credit assessment, risk management by the banks concerned. Banks should have adequate preventive measures, fixing pre-sanctioning appraisal responsibility and having an effective post-disbursement supervision.
2. *Management related warning signals*: Lack of co-operation from key personnel, change in management, ownership, or key personnel, desire to take undue risks, family disputes, poor financial controls, Poor financial controls, diversion of funds.
3. *Banking related signals*: Opening of account with other bank, return of outward bills/dishonored cheques, sales transactions not routed through the account.
4. *Watch-list/Special Mention Category*: The grading of the bank's risk assets is an important internal control tool. It serves the need of the management to identify and monitor the potential risks of a loan asset.
5. *Willful Defaulters*: RBI has issued revised guidelines in respect of detection of willful default and diversion and siphoning of funds. As per these guidelines, a willful default occurs when a borrower defaults in meeting obligations to the lender, when it has the capacity to honor the obligations or when funds have been utilized for purposes other than those for which finance was granted.

Curative Management

The curative measures to maximize recoveries so that banks funds locked up in NPAs were released for recycling. The Central government and the RBI have taken steps for controlling the incidence of fresh NPAs and creating legal and regulatory environment to facilitate the recovery of existing NPAs of banks. They are

1. One Time Settlement Schemes: This scheme covers all sectors sub– standard assets, doubtful or loss assets [As on 31st March 2000]. The cases on which the banks have initiated action under the SRFAESI Act and also cases pending before Courts/DRTs/ BIFR, subject to consent decree being obtained from the Courts/ DRTs/BIFR are covered.
2. Lok Adalats: Lok Adalat institutions help banks to settle disputes involving account in "doubtful" and "loss" category, with outstanding balance of Rs. 5 lakh for compromise settlement under Lok Adalat. Debt recovery tribunals have been empowered to organize Lok Adalat to decide on cases of NPAs of Rs. 10 lakh and above.
3. Debt Recovery Tribunals (DRTs): The Debt Recovery Tribunals have been established by the Government of India under an Act of Parliament (Act 51 of 1993) for expeditious adjudication and recovery of debts due to banks and financial institutions.
4. Securitization and SARFAESI Act: Securitization is a relatively new concept that is taking roots in India of late. It is still in its infancy with only a few market players. Securitization is considered an effective tool for improvement of capital adequacy. The SARFAESI Act intends to promote Securitization, pool together NPAs of banks to realize them and make enforcement of Security Interest Transfer."[46]

Credit Monitoring

According to the book of ICFAI University Press, after the funds pass from the bank into the hands of the borrower, the banker ought to begin from the very next moment the process of monitoring the asset. There are various ways wherein an asset can and should be monitored. In this regard, the three methods of supervision are: (i) financial, (ii) physical and (iii) legal and follow-up. Good lending depends on sound appraisal and assessment of creditworthiness. This can be more appreciated from the fact that the basic features that constitute a good lending decision. Further credit assessment is done and a lending decision is being taken, based on promises and assurances by the borrower about future performance. It may be possible that a loan given, based on a sound appraisal may still go bad due to failure on the part of the borrower to fulfill the given promises regarding performance. For ensuring safety of the advance and for supervision of credit, the bankers looked in a limited way to the following: (a) availability of tangible security and (b) borrowers compliance to the various stipulated terms and conditions.

Working capital requirements and the fixation of credit limits are assessed based on 'carrying' or 'holding' of current assets, other current liabilities and the working capital gap. Periodical monitoring of the working capital facilities would give the bank an idea about the current assets and current liabilities of the borrower from time to time for an assessment of the working capital gap. The field officer must ensure adequate coverage of advances. For this purpose, the loan should be under his constant attention.[47]

Security against Bank Loan

Advances can be extended against the security of government of India Relief Bonds issued in different series with 15per cent margin on the face value. ICICI Bank loans against securities comes to customer at attractive interest rates, based on the trends prevailing in the market at the time of the loan. Customer will pay only when he use the money for the required number of days the money. The rates vary according to the product-variant. In the overdraft account, interest will be charged only on the amount draw and for the period that draw. Interest will be charged on a daily basis, but will be debited to account only once a month. The various stages involved were as follows: (a) Signing of the loan agreement, (b) Pledging of the securities in our favour, (c) Opening the Current account, and (d) Once the Current account is opened, customer can avail of the credit limit.[48] AXIS Bank also gives loans against (a) mutual fund, (b) debt mutual fund and [c] life insurance policy.[49]

With HDFC Bank's Loan against Securities, one can get an overdraft against your securities like Equity Shares, Mutual Fund Units while still retaining ownership. It is possible to get an overdraft against customers NRE / NRO / FCNR while still retaining ownership.[50] Kotak Mahindra Bank also gives loans between 10 lakh to 3 crore against income documents and bank statements.[51] Let us take a look at the different loan options available in the event of an emergency:

- Secured Loan: This type of loan has a security/collateral that needs to be kept with the bank in order to obtain a loan. Loan options in this category can be classified into three categories: Gold loans, Loan against securities, and Loan against property.

- Unsecured Loan: This type of loan doesn't require pledging any security/collateral through personal loans and credit card options.[52]

The interest rates and terms on both secured and unsecured loans vary widely, so it is vital to shop around for the best deal. For larger sums, meanwhile, it may be worth considering remortgaging to free up some cash. Mortgage rates are being generally lower than secured loan rates. The downsides to this include potentially high fees and the fact could end up paying the interest on the whole amount owed for a 25-year mortgage term. Secured loans are made available for much larger amounts than personal loans. The repayment periods on secured loans can also be longer, while the fixed monthly payments should make it easy to manage repayment plan. Some loans even offer the option of a payment holiday of, say two or three months at the start of the agreement.[53]

References

1. Shalini H. S (2013). A study on causes and remedies for non performing assets in Indian public sector banks with special reference to agricultural development branch, State Bank of Mysore, <http://www.ijbmi.org/papers/Vol%282%291/Version_1/D212638.pdf>
2. Credit management (2013),< http://www.smallbusiness.wa.gov.au/ credit-management/>
3. Category: credit management, <http://en.wikipedia.org/wiki/Category: Credit_management>
4. The importance of credit management, <http://johngreijmans.com/ blog/2013/01/07/the-importance-of-credit-management/>
5. The Importance of trade Credit Management, <http:// mohammadwahid-abdullahkhan.blogspot.in/2011/10/importance-of-trade-creditmanagement.html>
6. Principles of sound lending, <http://www.updatedindianbanking. com/td.asp?id=138>
7. Sound Principles of Lending, Credit Investigation and Selection of Borrowers, <http://bankerguide.wordpress.com/2013/05/30/sound-principlesof-lending-credit-investigation-and-selection-of-borrowers/>
8. Loan (2013),< http://en.wikipedia.org/wiki/Loan>
9. LaToya Irby (2013). Types of Loan, <http://credit.about.com/od/ avoidingdebt/a/types-of-loans.htm>
10. Susan Wellish (2013). Secured Loans Compared to Unsecured Loans, <http://www.realtor.com/home-finance/homebuyer-information/securedloans-compared-to-unsecured-loans.aspx?source=web>

11. LaToya Irby (2013). How Secured Loans Are Different From Unsecured Loans Should You Take Out a Secured Loan? <http://credit.about.com/ od/avoidingdebt/ a/secured-loans-vs-unsecured-loans.htm>
12. Secured and Unsecured Loans (2013), < http://www.moneysense. gov.sg/ understanding-financial-products/credit-and-loans/types-of-loans/ secured-and-unsecured-loan.aspx>
13. Sound Principles of Lending, Credit Investigation and Selection of Borrowers, <http://bankerguide.wordpress.com/2013/05/30/sound-principlesof-lending-credit-investigation-and-selection-of-borrowers/>
14. Credit Evolution and approval (2013). <http://www.inc.com/ encyclopedia/credit-evaluation-and-approval.html>
15. The documentary credit process (2013). <https:// www.danskebank.com/en-gb/ Corporate-Banking/Trade-and-Export-Finance/Documentary-Credits/Pages/The-Documentary-Credit-process.aspx>
16. The documentary credit process (2013). <https://www.dansk ebank.com/en-gb/ Corporate-Banking/Trade-and-Export-Finance/DocumentaryCredits/Pages/The-Documentary-Credit-process.aspx>
17. Parul Khanna (2012). Managing Non-Performing Assets in Commercial Banks, Non-performing asset. <http://www.gjimt.ac.in/wp-content/ uploads/2012/12/ pdf13.pdf>
18. Dr. Mohan Kumar and Govind Singh (2012), Mounting NPAs in Indian Commercial Banks, <http://www.ijtbm.com/webmaster/upload/May_2012_ Govind%20Singh.pdf>
19. Chandan Chatterjee, Jeet Mukharjee and Dr. Ratan Das (2012). Management of Non-performing assets: A current scenario. <http:// www.indianresearchjournals.com/pdf/IJSSIR/2012/November/22.pdf>
20. Asha Singh (2013). Performance of NPAs in Indian Commercial Banks, <http:/ /indianresearchjournals.com/pdf/IJMFSMR/2013/September/9.pdf>
21. Indian Banking Industry (2012).<http://www.isesec.com/Admin/Research/ 1659808644_Indian%20Banking%20Industry.pdf>
22. Banking sector-Outlooks & top picks, <http:// www.moneycontrol.com/ news_html_files/broker_report/2013/Aug-310813-07310813.pdf>
23. Non-performing asset (2013).<http://en.wikipedia.org/wiki/Nonperforming_ asset>
24. Non-performing asset-NPA, <http://www.investopedia.com/terms/ n/non-performing-assets.asp>
25. <http://currentaffairs.gktoday.in/what-is-npa-what-are-the-loan-classificationnorms-what-is-provisioning-coverage-ratio-pcr-1120123120.html>
26. C.S.Balasubramaniam, Non-Performing assets and profitability of commercial banks in India: Assessment and emergent trends, <http:// www.abhinavjournal.com/images/Commerce_%26_Management/Jul12/5.pdf>
27. Non-Performing Assets: Meaning, types and assets, <http:// kalyancity.blogspot.com/2011/07/non-performing-assets-npa-meaning-types.html>

28. Krishna Chaitanya V (2013). Causes of Non-Performing assets in public sector banks, <http://www.indianmba.com/Faculty_Column/FC56/ fc56.htm>

29. Indian Banking Sector-Distressed Times Ahead?, <http://www.dtaconsulting.com/cms/Uploads/Knowledge/162a7de6-d1b5-429a-a73f-9034b47e4fb5-A.pdf>

30. <http://currentaffairs.gktoday.in/what-is-npa-what-are-the-loan-classificationnorms-what-is-provisioning-coverage-ratio-pcr-1120123120.html>

31. G. H. Deolalka, The Indian Banking Sector: On the Road to Progress, <http://aric.adb.org/pdf/aem/external/financial_market/India/india_bnk.pdf>

32. Meenakshi Rajeev and H.P.Mahesh (2010). Banking Sector Reforms and NPA: A study of Indian Commercial Banks, <http://www.isec.ac.in/WP%20252%20-%20Meenakshi%20Rajeev%20and%20H% 20P%20Mahesh. Pdf>

33. Prashanth K Reddy, A comparative study of Non Performing Assets in India in the Globa context - similarities and dissimilarities, remedial measures, <http://crisil.com/youngthoughtleader/winners/topic3-Prashanth-ReddyIIM-AHM.PDF>

34. Ravi Krishnan (2013), Kinks in the non-performing assets of public sector banks, <http://www.livemint.com/Money/7mbFYLLH9SNy Bam VGNpqIK/The-kinks-in-the-NPAs-of-banks.html>

35. The Hindu (May 30, 2013).RBI tightens loan restructuring norms, <http://www.thehindu.com/business/Industry/rbi-tightens-loan-restructuringnorms/article4766632.ece>

36. Business Standard (May 31, 2013).Analysis: RBI's new provisioning norms are badly timed.

37. The Economic Times (June 28, 2013).NPA clause of public sector banks likely to be changed, <http://articles.economictimes.indiatimes.com/2013-06-28/news/40256033_1_indian-banks-provisioning-state-run-banks>

38. Ravi Krishnan (2013). RBI's new NPA norms: the spirit is willing, but flesh is weak, <http://www.livemint.com/Money/HUVqx7 AVIAJHbNHn 7CxtVL/RBIs-new-NPA-norms-The-spirit-is-willing-but-flesh-is-wea.html>

39. The Hindu (December 2, 2013).NPA reduction, a key issue, <http://www.business-standard.com/article/finance/analysis-rbi-s-newprovision in g- norms- are- badly-timed -11 3 0 5 3 1 0 0 62 1 _ 1 .h tmlhttp :// www.thehindu.com/opinion/columns/C_R_L__Narasimhan/npa-reduction-akey-issue/article5408776.ece>

40. The Hindu (Sep 30, 2013).Net NPA rises to 1.68% in 2012-13: RBI, <http://www.thehindu.com/business/Economy/nest-npa-rises-to-168-in-201213-rbi/article5186516.ece>

41. Non-performing assets of 40 Indian banks soar 38% in 1H FY 14: Report, <http://www.commodityonline.com/news/non-performing-assetsof-40-indian-banks-soar-38-in-1h-fy-14-report-57017-3-57018.html>

42. The Times of India (Oct 23, 2013).Smaller banks face higher NPA risk, <http://timesofindia.indiatimes.com/business/india-business/Smaller-banksface-higher-NPA-risk/articleshow/24563304.cms

43. Business Standard (November 14, 2013).State-run banks see NPA slippage in Q2, <http://www.business-standard.com/article/finance/state-runbanks-see-npa-slippage-in-q2-113111400024_1.htmld>

44. NDTV Profit (OCT 30, 2013). Aim to make non-performing assets productive, says Raghuram Rajan, <http://profit.ndtv.com/news/industries/ article-aim-to-make-non-performing-assets-productive-says-raghuram-rajan-370834>

45. Non Performing Assets Impact on Bank Balance Sheet,<http://www.allbankingsolutions.com/Articles/NPA-impact-on-Balance-Sheet.htm>

46. G.V.Bhavani Prasad and D.Veena (2011). NPAs Reduction Strategies for Commercial Banks in India, <http://www.ijmbs.com/13/ bhawani.pdf>

47. Credit Management (2004),ICFAI University Press, pp.226-240.

48. Loan against security, ICICI BANK, <://www.icicibank.com/Personal-Banking/loans/loan-against-securities/faqs.html>

49. Loan against security, Axis bank, <http://www.axisbank.com/ personal/loans/loan-against-security/loan-against-security-eligibility.aspx>

50. Loan against fixed deposit, HDFC Bank, <http:// www.hdfcbank.com/nri_banking/loans/loan_fixed_deposit.htm>

51. Loan against property, Kodak Mahindra Bank, <http:// www.kotak.com/personal-banking/loans/loan-against-property.html# product_features>

52. Need to take an emergency loan? Here are your obtains, <http:// profit.ndtv.com/news/your-money/article-need-to-take-an-emergency-loan-hereare-your-options-372979>

53. Guide to unsecure vs. secure loan, <http://www.moneysuper market.com/shop/loans/unsecured-secured-loans-guide/>

54. http://economictimes.indiatimes.com/markets/stocks/news/indias-big-bad-loanproblem-banks-with-highest-npas/indias-big-bad-loan-problem-banks-withhighest-npas-/slideshow/58928031.cms

Chapter - 15

Customers

"There is only one boss, the customer. And he can fire everybody in the company from the chairman on down, simply by spending his money somewhere else."

— ***Sam Walton***

Introduction

Business is an important component in the modern economy. A customer is the recipient of a goods, service, product, or idea, obtained from a seller, vendor, or supplier for a monetary or other valuable consideration. Customers are generally categorized into two types: An intermediate customer or trade customer who is a dealer that purchases goods for resale, and an ultimate customer who does not in turn re-sell the things bought but either passes them to the consumer or actually is the consumer.[1]

Customer satisfaction is more important for any businessman to sustain in by market. It is a term frequently used in marketing. It is a measure of how products and services supplied by a company meet or surpass customer expectation. Its importance of customer satisfaction diminishes when a firm has increased bargaining power.[2] Customers are the most important people for any organization. They are the resource upon which the success of the business depends.[3]

The customer is the foundation of any business' success. One of the primary goals of any marketing strategy should be to identify and meet the needs of the consumer. Considering customer importance at all stages of the marketing process helps company to ensure greater customer satisfaction and increase its long-term goal of repeat business.[4] The marketing objectives of a small business typically are being aimed at raising brand awareness and attracting and retaining customers. All marketing initiatives to be effective, should take the customer's point of view into consideration.[5]

"The customer is always right" is a famous business slogan. Excellent customer service begins at the initial greeting, whether that's in person, on the phone, or via email.[6] Good customer service is an integral part of any successful business. One of customers' biggest complaints is a lack of personal connection when they try to reach a company by phone. This is business's first line of contact, so make sure phones are being answered by a real person.[7] Customers are extremely important to a company because a customer is the one and only individual that can tell how well business is going.[8]

For businesses, the current trend to attract customers now in consumer market is participating in group buying sites by selling their products and services at deeply discounted prices. Consider another channel of increasing sales- through customer retention and loyalty activities. Loyal customers are familiar with their favourite brands and willing more to try out and explore recommendations and new products.[9]

The consumers are now more likely to choose a company that offers a superior and personalized customer experience. Personalization is becoming a mandatory component of the customer experience. Moving forward, marketers will need to understand, leverage and harness customer data to collect and create unique behavioural patterns and distribute targeted messaging[10] Satisfied customers are looking for a memorable experience and an energetic service, where it matters the most. Any business needs to keep customers and clients happy, but in the hospitality industry it is important to keep the guests engaged in order for repeating business and for referral purposes.[11] Internet has opened up a world of possibility for a newly empowered consumer. They have the freedom to buy what they want, from whom they want, at any time they want.[12]Keeping customers makes good business sense, but it's not always easy.[13] Strong customer service is perhaps the most important form of marketing process.[14]

Types of Customer

Mark Hunter in his paper The five types of customers mentions them as: (a) Loyal Customers, (b) Discount Customers, (c) Impulse Customers,

(d) Need-Based ones and (e) Wandering Customers. Loyal Customer can [should] influence buying and merchandising decisions. Discount Customer category helps ensure inventory is turning over and, as a result, it is a key contributor to cash flow. Impulse Customer will purchase what seems good at the time. Need Based Customer has a specific intention to buy a particular type of item. It is important to remember that Need-Based Customers can easily be lost to Internet sales or a different retailer. Wandering Customer has no specific need or desire in mind when they come into the store. Rather, they want a sense of experience and/or community.[15]

Organizations will often set up different structures to deal with different sets of customers. This is because they will often give some groups more time and attention than others. The advantages of organizing in a pattern based on having different sets of customers are: (a) Different types of customers can be dealt with by separate departments, (b) Customers will be more inclined to deal with a business with departments concentrating on their particular needs, and (c) It is easier to check on the performance of individual products.[16]

According to Davis (2013), the customer segmentation refers to the division of the customer base into specific types according to purchasing behavior patterns. Understanding about the various types of customers that may encounter while attempting to sell products or services is an important part of the marketing process. On the basis of customer segmentation, customer can be divides as: (a) Ready-to-Buy Customers, (b) Potential Customers, (c) Repeat Customer, (d) Sale or Discount Customers, and (e) Impulse Buying Customers.

Ready-to-buy customers often have a sense of urgency. They have done some preliminary research or at least have an idea of something that they need. The issue for a salesperson or service provider becomes finding out what the requirement is and filling it. Potential customers are simply gathering information or browsing. This kind of customer is usually in no hurry to make a purchase, given that there is no urgent need to do so. The most loyal customer is a repeat customer, or one who regularly uses a company's services and purchases its products. This type of customer is the lifeblood of the business and should be respected as such. Sale or discount customers always shop for the best deals available on the items they want to purchase. Impulse buying customers are those, who make purchasing decisions based upon a whim or a great sales presentation usually are not in a position of needing anything in particular.[17]

Types of Account Holders

According to Muraleedharan (2009), "bank is a financial institution and a financial intermediary that accepts deposits and channels those deposits into lending activities, either directly by loaning or indirectly through capital markets. A bank links together customers that have capital deficits and customers with capital surpluses. Bank account is a financial account between a bank customer and a financial institution. It can be a deposit account, a credit card, or any other type of account offered by a financial institution. Bank accounts may have a positive, or credit balance, where the bank owes money to the customer; or a negative, or debit balance, where the customer owes the bank money. A deposit account is a savings account, current account, or other type of bank account, at a banking institution that allows money to be deposited and withdrawn by the account holder. Saving accounts are accounts maintained by retail financial institutions that pay interest but cannot be used directly as money in the narrow sense of a medium of exchange. These accounts let customers set aside a portion of liquid assets, while earning a monetary return.

Individuals

An individual account is an account for use by an individual for personal needs. It is a relative term to differentiate that from those accounts for corporate or business use. An individual account in most of the banks, can be opened in the resident or non-resident category, depending on the resident status of the applicant. The customer's income, assets credit history, whether the customer is married or single and whether he/she alone is responsible for paying off the debt are considered by the creditor. The account will appear on his/her credit report, and sometimes on that of any authorized user."[18]

Joint Account

Joint account is a bank account shared by two or more individuals. Any individual who is a member of the joint account can withdraw from the account and deposit to it. Usually, joint accounts are shared between close relatives or business partners.[19]

Joint accounts can be established on a permanent basis, such as an account between a couple where their salaries are deposited, or may be temporary, such as an account between two parties, who contribute funds for a short-term purpose. In the event of a death of one of the account holders, the remaining account holders will have sole access to the funds, as well as any debts associated with the account.[20]

It can also be useful to ensure that funds are only paid from the account provided both or all account holders have signed the instructions to the bank. Signing arrangements are at the choice of the account holders. Options range from any of the holders besides all joint holders to sign every instruction to the bank. Any joint account holder can cancel the joint account mandate. This will mean that the bank will need the signatures of all the account holders before it can pay any further items from the account.[21] There are many advantages to sharing an account with partner. If married, living with partner or in a relationship with someone really trust, opening a joint account could be a much more convenient approach to managing money together.[22]

Joint bank accounts are easy to use because either spouse can access the money to make payments at any time. A single joint account eliminates the possibility of having too much money in one account and not enough in the other when needed it, reducing the chance of an overdraft.[23]

Illiterates

According to Muraleedharan (2009), bank generally is open deposit account to illiterate persons. The account of such a person may be opened provided s[he] calls on the bank personally with a witness, known to the depositor and the bank. At the time of withdrawal/repayment of deposit amount and/or interest, the account holder should affix his/her thumb impression or mark in the presence of the authorized officer, who should verify the identity of the person. An illiterate account holder may lodge in person a passport size recent photograph with the bank subject to provision of rules regarding withdrawals [24] The bank will record identification marks in account opening form and in the remarks column provided in the concerned ledger folio/account opening screen of computer.[25]

Blind Person

Accounts in the name of blind persons can be opened/operatable singly or jointly with other. The blind person(s) may operate the account singly (i.e., through a power of attorney) or jointly with any other person. The power of attorney obtained thus should be duly notarized or attested by a magistrate. In all cases where a withdrawal order form or pay-in-slip is presented by the blind customer, a supervising official will ensure, after making enquiry with the blind person, that the correct amount has been entered therein in the case of withdrawals, the chief cashier/head cashier (or in his absence any other supervising official) should satisfy himself that the correct amount is paid. An official making verification of this nature will record on the relative voucher the fact of having made the necessary enquiries.

Minors

The date of birth of the minor had to be furnished while opening a minor's account. The bank had to record the date of attaining majority and on attaining majority, allow minor to operate account after getting the specimen signature in the account opening form. The account can be opened in any of the following modes: (a) by a natural guardian, i.e., father or mother in circumstances approved by the bank, on behalf of the minor; (b) by a natural guardian, i.e., father or mother in circumstances approved by the bank, in the joint names of himself/herself and the minor, payable to either or survivor; (c) by a person in the name of any minor of whom s[he] is the guardian appointed by a competent Court under any enactment for the time being in force; and (d) by a minor of age 10 and above in his/her single name, in circumstances approved by the Bank, to be operated upon by himself/herself, provided s[he] can put uniform signatures.

Accounts under Rules 10 (a) and 10 (b) will be opened, where the funds to be lodged comprise of the guardian's own money and the guardian's intention is in the case of Rule 10 (a) to utilize the money for the benefit of the minor and make the money, eventually lying to the credit of the account available to minor or his/her attaining majority and in the case of Rule 10 (b) to provide that with effect from the date of the minor attains majority, the account be also be operated upon by the minor. The guardian must make a declaration of the date of the minor's birth. The date upon which the minor will attain majority shall be recorded at the Bank and in the passbook. In the case of accounts under Rule 10 (a) and 10 (c), upon the minor attaining majority, the right of the guardian to operate the account will automatically come to an end, whereafter the guardian shall not operate on the account.[26]

Accounts of Partnership Firm and Companies

A limited liability partnership (LLP) is a partnership wherein some or all partners(depending on the jurisdiction) have limited liabilities. It therefore exhibits elements of partnerships and corporations. Limited liability partnerships are distinct from limited partnerships in some countries, which may allow all LLP partners to have limited liability, while a limited partnership may require at least one unlimited partner and allow others to assume the role of a passive and limited liability investor.[27] Partnership is a relation of mutual trust and faith. Partnership accounts should present a true and fair picture of the partnership business. It is a relationship between persons who have agreed to share the profit of a business.

The documents needs to open an account of partnership firm are: A certified true copy of the partnership deed; Registration Certificate; Copy of last Income Tax Returns filed; Proof of Bank Account: Any of the following may be submitted: (a) Copy of Bank Statement (should be in the name of the firm) & Copy of first page of the Bank Pass Book; A cancelled cheque (only if the account holder's name is printed on it); PAN of the firm; Authorization from all the partners to open a demat/Trading account with Geojit; List of personnel authorized to operate and maintain, duly authorized by the partners; Proof of identity of partners; and DP should be opened in the name of the authorised partner.[28]

General Precautions [Opening/ Operating Accounts]

Banking was in existence in India during the Vedic times(2000 BC to *1400 BC). According to the Banking Companies Act, 1970, the aim of nationalization of banks in India is "to control the heights of economy and to progressively meet and serve better the needs of development of the economy in conformity with national policy and objectives."* Many banks are established for carrying out non banking financial services. Banks play a very significant role in the economic development of the country. The relationship between a banker and a customer is of great significance. It depends upon the services rendered by the banker to the customer. The general relationship between the banker and a customer will be that of a debtor and *a creditor i.e. borrower and lender.*[29]

Online banking is safe and convenient as long as customer takes a number of simple precautions. Please make sure the customer follow the advice given: (a) Visit Internet banking site directly; (b) Avoid accessing the site through a link from another site or an e-mail and verify the domain name displayed to avoid spoof websites; (c) ignore any e-mail asking for password or PIN; (d) not to use cyber cafés/shared PCs to access our Internet banking site; (e) Update PC with latest anti-virus and spy ware software regularly; (f) Disable the 'File and Printing Sharing' feature on operating system; (g) Log off PC when not in use; (h) Do not store ID/PIN in the Internet Explorer Browser; and (i) Check account and transaction history regularly.[30]

For the purpose of calculation of interest, the lowest clear balance at credit in an account between the tenth day and the last day of each month is computed as required products by the system. A supervising official should check in the interest calculations by the computer system random. At the time of closure of account, interest should be applied by debit to Interest Accrued Account and the ultimate balance paid to the depositor against his cheque or withdrawal form in the usual manner.[31]

The Basel Committee on Banking Supervision in its paper on Customer Due Diligence for Banks [published in October 2001] referred to the intention of the working group on cross-border banking develop guidance on customer identification. Customer identification is an essential element of an effective customer due diligence programme, which the banks need to put in place to guard against reputational, operational, legal and concentration risks. These guidelines represent a starting point for supervisors and banks in the area of customer identification.[32]

References

1. Customer (2013),<http://en.wikipedia.org/wiki/Customer>
2. Customer satisfaction (2013), <http://en.wikipedia.org/wiki/Customer_centricity>
3. Why customers are important?, <http://businesscasestudies.co.uk/ business-theory/marketing/why-customers-are-important.html#axzz2qdn82onH>
4. Customer importance in market (2013), <http:// smallbusiness.chron.com/customer-importance-marketing-22741.html>
5. Customer importance in marketing (2013), <http:// yourbusiness.azcentral.com/customer-importance-marketing-3684.html>
6. The Importance of Good Customer Service (2013), <http:// www.hdkeys.com/The_Importance_of_Good_Customer_Service>
7. The Importance of Great Customer Service, <http:// www.is4profit.com/business-advice/business-strategy/the-importance-of-greatcustomer-service.html>
8. The importance of customer service, <http://businesscasestudies. c o .u k /b u s iness-theory/operations /th e- importance - of - customer - service. html# axzz2qdn82onH>
9. <http://www.nextupasia.com/5-reasons-why-customer-loyalty-is-so-important-inour-digitized-marketplace/>
10. The importance of customer experience, <http:// www.technicallymarketing.com/index.php/2013/05/10/the-importance-of-thecustomer-experience-10-important-stats-for-2013/>
11. The importance of customer service in the hospitality industry, <http:// www.northwestbusinesslife.co.uk/news-item/the-importance-of-customerservice-in-the-hospitality-industry/>

12. <http://www.simplybusiness.co.uk/knowledge/articles/2012/08/2012-08-07-importance-of-custo>
13. Keeping customers — the importance of loyalty, <http:// www.marketing-donut.co.uk/marketing/customer-care/selling-more-to-existingcustomers/keeping-customers-the-importance-of-loyalty>
14. The Importance of Strong Customer Service for any Business, <http://blog.localaxis.com/2013/07/the-importance-of-strong-customer.html>
15. Mark Hunter (2013). The 5 Types of Customers, <http:// sbinfocanada.about.com/od/customerservice/a/customertypesmh.htm>
16. Types of customer (2013), <http://businesscasestudies.co.uk/ business-theory/marketing/types-of-customer.html#axzz2qdn82onH>
17. Susan S. Davis (2013). What are the five types of customer segmentation?, <http://smallbusiness.chron.com/five-types-customersegmentation-10566.html>
18. D. Muraleedharan (2009). Modern Banking: Theory and Practice,PHI Learning Private Limited, p.278.
19. Joint Account (2013), <http://en.wikipedia.org/wiki/Joint_account>
20. Definition of Joint account (2013), <http://www.investopedia.com/ terms/j/jointaccount.asp>
21. Understanding Joint Accounts (2013), <http://www.bba.org.uk/ customer/article/understanding-joint-accounts/savings>
22. Advantage and disadvantage of joint bank account (2013).<http://www.thinkmoney.co.uk/news-advice/advantages-and-disadvantages-of-a-jointbank-account-0-3789-0.htm>
23. <http://budgeting.thenest.com/advantages-disadvantages-joint-bank-accountspouse-21449.htm>
24. D. Muraleedharan (2009). Modern Banking: Theory and Practice, PHI Learning Private Limited, p.280.
25. *Ibid.*
26. Saving Bank Accounts (2013), <http://www.kollamdcb.com/index.php?option=com_content&view=article&id=60&Itemid=66>
27. Limited liability partnership (2013), <http://en.wikipedia.org/wiki/Limited_liability_partnership>
28. Account Opening Documents (Partnership Firm), <http://www.geojitbnpparibas.com/about-us/documents-required-partnershipfirm>
29. Banking Law (2013), <http://hanumant.com/Banking%20law%20-%20Meenakshi%20Natesan.html>
30. South Indian Bank, Instructions for safe banking and precautions while operating internet banking, <http://www.southindianbank.com/News/newsdetails.aspx?news_id=135>
31. Savings bank account, <http://www.iob.in/uploads/Saving%20Bank%20Rules.pdf>
32. General Guide to Account Opening and Customer Identification (2003), <http://www.bis.org/publ/bcbs85annex.htm>

Chapter - 16

Non-Banking Financial Intermediaries [NBFI]

"Gold and silver, like other commodities, have an intrinsic value, which is not arbitrary, but is dependent on their scarcity, the quantity of labour bestowed in procuring them, and the value of the capital employed in the mines which produce them." — ***David Ricardo***

Introduction

The financial system facilitates transfer of funds, through financial institutions, financial markets, financial instruments and services. Financial institutions act as mobilisers and depositories of savings, and as purveyors of credit or finance. They provide various financial services to the community. They act as intermediaries between savers and investors. All banks and many non-banking institutions also act as intermediaries, and are called as non-banking financial intermediaries. Financial institutions are divided into the banking and non-banking ones.[1] The Indian Financial

System was transpired from the traditional Barter system to the money lenders, the Nidhis and Chit Funds. In the later stages, the concept of cooperatives was started and the same was introduced in India during 1904 by way of "Cooperative Society Act" and it paves the way in introduction of cooperative banking institutions in India.

A financial intermediary is a financial institution that connects surplus and deficit agents. A financial intermediary is typically an institution that facilitates the channeling of funds between lenders and borrowers indirectly.

In the context of climate finance and development, financial intermediaries generally refer to private sector intermediaries, such as banks, private equity, venture capital funds, leasing companies, insurance and pension funds, and micro-credit providers. Increasingly, international financial institutions provide funding via companies in the financial sector, rather than directly financing projects.[2] Non-Banking Financial Companies have rapidly emerged as an important segment of the Indian financial system. Moreover, it assume significance in the small business segment, as they primarily cater to the credit requirements of the unorganized sector such as wholesale and retail traders, small-scale industries and small borrowers at the local level. It is a heterogeneous group of financial institutions, performing a wide range of activities like hire-purchase finance, vehicle financing, equipment lease finance, personal loans, working capital loans, consumer loans, housing loans, loans against shares and investment, etc.[3]

Non-banking financial companies are primarily responsible for receiving deposits under any scheme or arrangement or any other manner, or lending, similar to banks, but they don't have a banking license. These focus on business related to loans and advances, acquisition of shares, stock, bonds, debentures, securities issued by the government or local authority or other securities of like marketable nature, leasing, hire-purchase, insurance business, chit business.[4] The working and operations of NBFCs are regulated by the RBI within the framework of the RBI Act, 1934 (Chapter III B) and the directions issued by it under the Act. As per the RBI Act, a 'non-banking financial company is defined as:-(i) a financial institution which is a company; (ii) a non banking institution, which is a company with principal business of receiving deposits, under any scheme or arrangement or in any other manner, or lending in any manner; (iii) such other non-banking institution or class of such institutions, as the bank may, with the previous approval of the Central Government and by notification in the Official Gazette, specify.[5]

What is NBFI?

Non-bank financial intermediary is a collection of institutions. These range from leasing, factoring and venture companies as well as those who conduct contractual savings and institutional investors. They compete with banks and force them be more efficient in delivery of services. They are also actively involved in the securities markets and allocation of long-term financial resources.[6]

Non-banking Financial Institutions carry out financing activities, but their resources were not directly obtained from the savers as debt. Instead, these Institutions mobilize the public savings for rendering other financial services including investment. Such institutions are financial intermediaries and when they lend, they are known as Non-Banking Financial Intermediaries or Investment Institutions.[7]

Their Importance

NBFIs play an important dual role in the financial system. They complement with the role of commercial banks by filling gaps in the range of services. They also compete with commercial banks and force them be more efficient and responsive to the needs of customers. Most of the NBFIs are actively involved in the securities markets and in the mobilization and allocation of long-term financial resources.[8] NBFIs are an important part of the Indian financial system. The NBFIs at present consist of a heterogeneous group of institutions that cater to a wide range of financial requirements. The major intermediaries include financial institutions (FIs), non-banking financial companies and primary dealers.[9] The NBFIs also play important role in macroeconomic stability particularly with respect to price stability.[10]

The NBFIs in India

The intermediaries complement and compete with commercial banks, forcing them be more efficient and responsive to customers' needs. Especially, it will be so with pension funds and other institutional investors that mobilize large long-term financial resources. These could act as countervailing forces to uphold the dominant position of commercial banks. The intermediaries comprise a mixed bag of institutions, ranging from leasing, factoring, and venture capital companies to various types of contractual savings and institutional investors (pension funds, insurance companies, and mutual funds).[11]

Insurance Regulatory & Development Authority is regulatory and development authority under the government of India in order to protect the interests of the policyholders and to regulate, promote and ensure orderly growth of the insurance industry. It is basically a ten members' team comprising chairman, five full -time members and four part-time members; all appointed by the government of India. This organization came into being in 1999 after the bill of IRDA was passed in the Indian parliament.[12]

Various non-banking financial institutions are Provident and Pension Funds, Small Savings Organizations, Life Insurance Corporation, General Insurance Corporation, Unit Trust of India, Mutual Funds, Investment Trusts, Investment Companies, Finance Corporations, Nidhis, Chit Funds, Hire-Purchase Finance Companies, Lease Finance Companies, National Housing Bank, Housing and Urban Development Corporation, Housing Development Finance Corporation, and other housing finance companies, Manufacturing companies accepting public deposits, Venture Capital Funds and National Cooperative Bank of India. Let discuss some of the above subsidiaries.[13]

Life Insurance Corporation of India

Life Insurance Corporation of India (LIC) is an Indian state-owned insurance group and company, headquartered at Mumbai. It was founded in 1956, when the parliament of India passed the Life Insurance of India Act that nationalised the private insurance industry in India. LIC's slogan *yogakshemam vahamyaha* [Sanskrit], which translated into means "Your welfare is our responsibility". From its creation, the LIC commanded a monopoly of soliciting and selling insurance products in India. It offers a variety of products to its customers such as insurance plans, pension plans, unit-linked plans, special plans and group schemes. Today, the company has eight zonal offices, around 109 divisional offices, 2,048 branches and 992 satellite offices and corporate offices.[14]

The company has tie-ups with certain banks and service providers to offer on-line premium collection facility in select cities. Besides, ECS and ATM premium payment facility to its customers, the company has also commissioned IVRS and information centres at Mumbai, Ahmadabad, Bangalore, Chennai, Hyderabad, Kolkata, New Delhi, Pune, amongst other cities. It has also launched Satellite Sampark offices in order to provide easy access to its policy holders. It offers a wide array of insurance products to its customers such as insurance plans, pension plans, unit-linked plans, special plans and group scheme.[15] LIC has crossed many milestones and has set unprecedented performance records in various aspect of life insurance business.[16]

The General Insurance Corporation of India

GIC is the sole reinsurance company in the Indian insurance market with over four decades of experience. The entire general insurance business in India was nationalised by the government through the General Insurance Business (Nationalisation) Act ~1972. 55 Indian insurance companies and

52 other general Insurance operations of other companies were nationalized through the act. GIC and its subsidiaries had a monopoly on the general insurance business in India until the landmark Insurance Regulatory and Development Authority Act (IRDA Act) of 1999 came into effect on April 19, 2000. This act also amended the GIBNA Act and Insurance Act of 1938.[17]

The General Insurance Corporation of India Limited, a government company registered under the Insurance Act, 1938 as well as the Companies Act, 1956 having been notified as "Indian Reinsurer" has ceased to carry on direct insurance business [w.e.f. March 21, 2003]. The following companies, which were its erstwhile subsidiaries, conduct business in all areas of insurance, i.e. (a) National Insurance Company Limited, Kolkata; (b) The New India Assurance Company Limited, Mumbai. (c) The Oriental Insurance Company Limited, New Delhi; (d) United India Insurance Company Limited, Chennai.[18]

Mutual Funds

A mutual fund is a type of professionally managed collective investment scheme pooling money from many investors to purchase securities. Sometimes they are referred to as "investment companies" or "registered investment companies". Mutual funds are not taxed on their income and profits, as long as they comply with the requirements established in the U.S. Internal Revenue Code. Mutual funds pass the taxable income on to their investors by paying out the dividends and capital gains at least annually. These may invest in many kinds of securities.

The types of securities that a particular fund may invest in are set forth in the fund's prospectus, which describes the fund's investment objective, investment approach and permitted investments. The first mutual funds were established in Europe. Mutual funds were introduced into the United States in the 1890s. The first open-end mutual fund with redeemable shares was established on March 21, 1924.[19]

Another attractive feature of mutual funds is the variety of funds available, each offering a different investment objective and level of risk. Generally, the higher the risk, the greater the potential return on investment. Most mutual funds fall into one of the following categories: Stock Funds, Bond Funds, and Money Market Funds. Mutual funds offer an alternative for investors who lack the time or expertise to make regular and complex investment decisions.[20]

Mutual funds have had organizational structure as per their Security Exchange Board of India guidelines; SEBI is the specified authority and holds the responsibility of Trustee and AEEST Management Companies. The objectives are to control, to promote, to regulate, to protect the investor's right and efficient trading of units. Operation of Mutual fund starts with investors saving their money on it , than MF manager handling those funds and strategic investment on scrip.[21]

Investment Trusts

It is a form of collective investment found mostly in the UK. These are closed-end funds, constituted as public limited companies. The first investment trust was the Foreign & Colonial Investment Trust, started in 1868 "to give the investor of moderate means the same advantages as the large capitalists in diminishing the risk of spreading the investment over a number of stocks". Unit investment trusts are one of the three types of investment companies; the other two are the mutual funds and the closed-end funds. Unit investment trust is an investment company that offers a fixed, unmanaged portfolio, generally of stocks and bonds, as redeemable units to investors for a specific period of time. It is designed to provide capital appreciation and/or dividend income.[22]

Investment Company

It is a corporation or trust engaged in the business of investing the pooled capital of investors in financial securities. This is most often done either through a closed-end fund or an open-end fund (also referred to as a mutual fund).[23] The investment company invests money on behalf of its shareholders, who in turn share in the profits and losses. It is a company, whose main business is holding securities of other companies purely for investment purposes.[24]

Nidhi

Nidhi in the Indian context/language means "treasure". The companies doing Nidhi business, viz., borrowing from members and lending to members only, are known under different names such as *Nidhi, Permanent Fund, Benefit Funds, Mutual Benefit Funds* and *Mutual Benefit Company*. Nidhis are more popular in south India and are highly localized single office institutions. They are mutual benefit societies, because their dealings are restricted only to the members; and membership is limited to individuals. The principal source of funds is the contribution from the members. Since Nidhis come under one class of NBFCs, RBI is empowered to issue directions to them in matters relating to their deposit acceptance activities.[25]

Pension Fund

A pension fund is any plan, fund, or scheme facilitating retirement income. It is a common asset pool meant to generate stable growth over the long term, and provide pensions for employees when they reach the end of their working years and commence retirement.[26] A type of retirement plan, usually tax exempt, wherein an employer makes contributions toward a pool of funds set aside for an employee's future benefit. The pool of funds is then invested on the employee's behalf, allowing the employee to receive benefits upon retirement. [27]

Housing Development Finance Corporation [Hudco]

It is an Indian financial conglomerate based in Mumbai. It was founded in 1977 as the first specialised mortgage company in India. It was promoted by the ICICI. It extends housing finance to individuals and corporate for purchase/ construction of residential houses. It is one of the largest providers of housing loans in India. HDFC provides mutual fund services through its subsidiary HDFC Asset Management Company Limited. The company has been providing life insurance since the year 2000, through its subsidiary HDFC Standard Life Insurance Company Limited.[28]

Chit Fund

A totally Indian concept, the chit fund system has now been globally operated and won universal acclaim. It is a typical indigenous financial institution peculiar to South India, particularly Andhra Pradesh, Tamil Nadu and Kerala. Chit funds grew at a time when banking and credit facilities were inadequate and people had to rely in general with a large measure on indigenous sources for many productive and consumption needs.

Chit funds have been meeting a part of the genuine credit needs of the people, both in urban and rural areas. They have served as a medium of saving for many people. Chit funds organized professionally by individuals or institutions, like a firm or company are in the nature of financial intermediaries. A chit fund is primarily a mutual benefit society wherein some people join to save and others to borrow. Unlike the other financial intermediaries, chit fund connects the borrowing class directly with the lending class and the pooled saving is lent out to the same group of savers.[29]

National Housing Bank

A state-owned bank and regulation authority in India, created on July 8, 1988 under the section 6 of the National Housing Bank Act (1987).The RBI-owned institution, was established to promote private real estate acquisition. It is an apex level financial institution catering to the housing sector in the country. It was established on July 9, 1988. It works as a facilitator in promoting housing finance institutions or providing assistance to other institutions of such type. It is headquartered at Delhi with offices in all the major cities of India.

The institution had been set up when regional and local level housing finance institution were nearly absent and the banking sector was not willing to do housing finance on any significant level. NHB has come up with guidelines for recognising HFCs for its financial assistance, guidelines for financial assistance. Besides it has also issued guidelines for prudential norms for income recognition, asset classification etc.[30]

Housing & Urban Development Corporation Ltd [Hudco]

As a premier techno-financial body, it was set up in 1970 by the government of India to facilitate housing and infrastructure development in the country with a social motto of serving the 'unserved' and thus bridging the 'housing divide' in the country. Today, it stands tall as a *Mini-Ratna* PSU and also remains the savior of the housing needs of the poor. Its financial assistance for housing projects is made available to the states and their agencies, which include Housing Boards, Rural Housing Boards, Slum Clearance Boards, Development Authorities, Improvement Trusts, Municipal Corporations, State/City parastatals, Apex Cooperative Housing Federations, etc.; Primary Cooperative Societies Public and Private Sector Agencies; NGOs/ CBOs, Private Developers, Joint Sector and Individuals.[31]

Hire-purchase Companies

Hire-purchase is a mode of financing the price of goods to be sold on a future date. In a hire purchase transaction, the goods are let on hire, the purchase price is to be paid in installments and hirer is allowed an option to purchase the goods by paying all the installments. Hire-purchase is a method of selling goods. In such a transaction, the goods are let out on hire by a finance company (creditor) to the hire-purchase customer (hirer). The buyer is required to pay an agreed amount in periodical installments during a given period. The ownership of the property remains with creditor and passes on to hirer on the payment of the last installment.[32] Hire-purchase companies are those providing such type of facilities.

Conclusion

NBFIs comprise a mixed bag of institutions. Traditionally, they included financial institutions excluding commercial banks. It has come to include mainly the leasing, factoring and venture capital companies as well as various types of contractual savings and institutional investors, with the assimilation of building societies and other thrift deposit institutions with commercial banks accepting deposits and making loans.

It plays an important dual role in the financial system. They complement with the role of commercial banks, filling gaps in the range of services, but compete with the commercial banks and force them to be more efficient and responsive to the needs of customers. Rapid expansion of NBFIs can affect employment growth, particularly through expanding small and medium sized enterprises. The latter have limited access to bank credit due to strict collateral requirements against loans. They also face constraints in accessing the capital market. NBFIs, on one hand could ease the financial constraints of those enterprises; on the other, they could also help in expanding business opportunities, which have spill-over effects on creating employment opportunities.

References

1. Financial system and Non-Banking Financial Companies – The Structure and status profile., Chapter III, <http://shodhganga.inflibnet.ac.in/ bitstream/10603/8650/11/11_chapter%203.pdf>
2. Financial intermediary, <http://en.wikipedia.org/wiki/Financial_intermediary>
3. Non-Banking Financial Companies (2014), <https:// www.dnb.co.in/BFSISectorInIndia/NonBankC2.asp>
4. Non Banking Financial Company- Boosting economic growth, <http://www.mbaskool.com/business-articles/finance/312-non-banking-financialcompany-boosting-economic-growth.html>
5. Non-banking financial companies, <http://business.gov.in/ business_financing/non_banking.php>
6. <http://www.ask.com/question/what-is-a-non-bank-financial-intermediary>
7. Non-Banking Financial Institutions, <http://www.banknetindia. com/finance/fbanking.htm>
8. The Role of Non-Bank Financial Intermediaries (with particular reference to Egypt), <http://elibrary.worldbank.org/doi/book/10.1596/1813-9450-1892>
9. <http://rbi.org.in/Scripts/PublicationsView.aspx?Id=14631>
10. Mohd Aminul Islam and Jamil bin Osman, Development Impact of Non-Bank Financial Intermediaries on Economic Growth in Malaysia: An Empirical Investigation, <http://ijbssnet.com/journals/Vol._2_No._14;_July_2011/21.pdf>

11. The Role of Non-Bank Financial Intermediaries (with Particular Reference to Egypt), <http://elibrary.worldbank.org/doi/book/10.1596/1813-9450-1892>
12. Chapter III - Overview of General Insurance Business in India (Problems, Challenges, Prospects etc.) <http://shodhganga.inflibnet.ac.in/ bitstream/10603/5899/9/09_chapter%203.pdf>
13. Financial system and Non-Banking Financial Companies – The Structure and status profile, Chapter III, <http://shodhganga.inflibnet.ac.in/ bitstream/10603/8650/11/11_chapter%203.pdf>
14. Life Insurance Corporation of India (2014), <http:// en.wikipedia.org/wiki/Life_Insurance_Corporation_of_India>
15. Life Insurance Corporation of India, <http://www.dnb.co.in/BFSI/Adv%5CLife%20Insurance%20Corporation%20of%20India.pdf>
16. Life Insurance corporation of India, company and area profile, <http://shodhganga.inflibnet.ac.in/bitstream/10603/4848/13/13_chapter%204.pdf>
17. General Insurance Corporation of India, <http://en.wikipedia.org/ wiki/General_Insurance_Corporation_of_India>
18. General Insurance Corporation of India, <http://cag.nic.in/html/ reports/commercial/2006_10/chapter_5.pdf>
19. Mutual funds (2014), <http://en.wikipedia.org/wiki/Mutual_fund>
20. Mutual funds (2014), <http://www6.ingretirementplans.com/SponsorExtranet/WhatIsAMutualFund.pdf>
21. Overview of mutual fund industries in India, <http:// shodhganga.inflibnet.ac.in/bitstream/10603/2160/8/08_chapter%201.pdf>
22. Investment trusts, <http://www.investopedia.com/terms/u/uit.asp>
23. Investment company (2014), <http://www.investopedia.com/terms/ i/investmentcompany.asp>
24. Investment company (2014), <http://en.wikipedia.org/wiki/Investment_company>
25. Nidhi (2014), <http://www.arthapedia.in/index.php?title=Nidhi(Mutual_Benefit_Society)>
26. Pension Fund (2014), <http://www.investopedia.com/terms/p/ pensionfund.asp>
27. Pension plan (2014), <http://www.investopedia.com/terms/p/ pensionplan.asp>
28. Housing Development Finance Corporation (2014), <http://en.wikipedia.org/wiki/Housing_Development_Finance_Corporation>
29. Chit Funds -The Evolution, Operational scenario, Role and Regulatory Framework, Chapter IV, <http://shodhganga.inflibnet.ac.in/ bitstream/10603/8650/12/12_chapter%204.pdf>
30. Role of National Housing Bank in Housing Finance Business, <http://www.mbaskool.com/business-articles/finance/109-role-of-nationalhousing-bank-in-housing-finance-business-in-india.html>
31. Housing & Urban Development Corporation, <http:// en.wikipedia.org/wiki/Housing_and_Urban_Development_Corporation_Limited>
32. http://www.psnacet.edu.in/courses/MBA/Financial%20services/3.p

Bibliography

1. Bakhtiar K Dadabhoy (2013), Barons of Banking: Glimpses of Indian Banking History, Random House.
2. Brajesh Kumar Tiwari (2011), Changing Scenario of Indian Banking Industry,Lambert Academic Publishing.
3. Cheryl Payer (2008), The World Bank: A Critical Analysis, Monthly Press Review.
4. D. Muraleedharan (2009), Modern Banking: Theory and Practice, PHI Learning Pvt. Ltd.
5. Devesh Kapur, John Prior Lewis, Richard Charles Webb (1987), The World Bank: Its First Half Century, Volume 1, Brookings Institution Press.
6. H.R. Gupta (2011), Practical Banking in India, Gyan Publishing House.
7. Hong Kong Institute of Bankers (2012), Bank Lending, John Wiley & Sons.
8. Ibrahim F. I. Shihata (2000), The World Bank Legal Papers, Martinus Nijhoff Publishers
9. Jagdish Narayan Saxena (1977), The Changing Profile of Indian Banking, A. D. Shroff Memorial Trust.
10. John Maynard Keynes (2006), Indian Currency and Finance, Cosimo, Inc.
11. John R. Brick (1980), Bank management: concepts and issues, R.F. Dame.
12. K. C. Shekhar (2009), A Handbook on Indian Currency and Banking Theory and Practice,Volume 1, Kerala.
13. Kumar (2008), A New Beginning: The Turnaround Story of Indian Bank, Tata McGraw-Hill Education.

14. Linny Stovall (1995), Pursuit of Happiness: A Left Bank Book, Blue Heron Pub.
15. M. R. Das (2004), WTO: Opportunities and Challenges for Indian Banking, Himalaya Publishing House.
16. R. K. Uppal (2006), Indian Banking Industry and Information Technology, New Century Publications.
17. R. Uppal (2010), Indian Banking in the Globalised World, New Century Publications.
18. Raymond De Roover, Henrietta M. Larson (1999), The Rise and Decline of the Medici Bank: 1397-1494, Beard Books.
19. René Smits (1997), The European Central Bank: Institutional Aspects. Kluwer Law International.
20. S. P. Suneja (1997), Indian Banking Today & Tomorrow, Volume 22, the University of California.
21. Sampat Singh P (2004), Leadership In Indian Banking, ICFAI Books.
22. Sushil J. Lalwani (1992), Changing Profile of Indian Banking, Books Treasure.
23. Timothy Koch, and S. McDonald (2009), Bank Management, Cengage Learning.
24. Vasant C Joshi and Vinay V Joshi (2009), Managing Indian Banks: The Challenges Ahead, SAGE Publications.
25. Yakov Amihud, Geoffrey Miller (1998), Bank Mergers & Acquisitions, Springer.

Index